Project Management Institute

Increasing Project Flexibility: The Response Capacity of Complex Projects

Serghei Floricel, PhD
Sorin Piperca, PhD Candidate
Marc Banik, PhD

Library of Congress Cataloging-in-Publication Data

Practice standard for earned value management / Project Management
Institute. -- 2nd ed.
    p. cm.
  Includes bibliographical references and index.
  ISBN 978-1-935589-35-8 (pbk. : alk. paper) 1. Project
management--Standards. I. Project Management Institute.
  HD69.P75P65155 2011
  658.4'04--dc23
                            2011035062
ISBN: 978-1-935589-37-2

Published by: Project Management Institute, Inc.
                       14 Campus Boulevard
                       Newtown Square, Pennsylvania 19073-3299 USA
                       Phone: +610-356-4600
                       Fax: +610-356-4647
                       Email: customercare@pmi.org
                       Internet: www.PMI.org

"PMI", the PMI logo, "PMP", the PMP logo, "PMBOK", "PgMP", "Project Management
Journal", "PM Network", and the PMI Today logo are registered marks of Project
Management Institute, Inc. The Quarter Globe Design is a trademark of the Project
Management Institute, Inc. For a comprehensive list of PMI marks, contact the PMI Legal
Department.

PMI Publications welcomes corrections and comments on its books. Please feel free to
send comments on typographical, formatting, or other errors. Simply make a copy of the
relevant page of the book, mark the error, and send it to: Book Editor, PMI Publications,
14 Campus Boulevard, Newtown Square, PA 19073-3299 USA.

To inquire about discounts for resale or educational purposes, please contact the PMI Book
Service Center.
                       PMI Book Service Center
                       P.O. Box 932683, Atlanta, GA 31193-2683 USA
                       Phone: 1-866-276-4764 (within the U.S. or Canada)
                       or +1-770-280-4129 (globally)
                       Fax: +1-770-280-4113
                       Email: info@bookorders.pmi.org

10 9 8 7 6 5 4 3 2 1

Dedication

To Roger Miller, "who taught all of us that complex projects will have to be steered through many unexpected circumstances"

Executive Summary

A significant portion of project management literature and practice highlights the importance of the unexpected events that occur during project execution and the managers' ability to address them. This research program investigated the role of project organizations in responding to unexpected events. We assumed that a social structure, with characteristics that cannot always be cultivated and controlled in a deliberate manner, emerges in project organizations. Moreover, some properties of this structure, which constitute what we call its response capacity, have a key influence on the project response to unexpected events. To enhance our understanding of the response capacity and its influence on the success of a complex project, we proceeded in three stages: theoretical development, qualitative investigation, and quantitative exploration.

In the theoretical development stage, presented in Chapters 1 and 2 of this report, we drew upon three fundamental sociological theories to understand the nature of the social structure of complex projects and the process of its emergence. We also built on prior research in project management to propose three properties of the project structure that make up its response capacity. We termed these properties, respectively, cohesion, flexibility, and resourcefulness, and further suggested two dimensions for each property. Although we deemed that these properties cannot be fully planned or programmed, we argued that their nature and effectiveness may be influenced by the nature of project planning activities. Our main hypothesis then proposes that planning influences the success of a complex project not only directly but also through the impact it has on the emergence of response capacity properties, which, in turn, impinge on the efficacy of project response to unexpected events and, eventually, on project performance. To expand this hypothesis, we relied on project management literature to propose four properties of planning activities—the knowledge used in planning, the degree of centralization, the nature of the arguments included in the plan documents, and the way the plan proposes to allocate risks—as well as four properties of project performance—completion, technical, operation, and value creation. Based on these concepts, we elaborated a series of specific hypotheses on what we call "influence trajectories" that connect project planning, response capacity, and performance.

In the qualitative investigation stage, which is detailed in Chapter 3 of this report, we relied on 17 field case studies of complex projects that were recently completed in three kind of sectors: "infrastructural" (energy, airports, etc.), "digital" (telecom, information systems), and "discovery" (biotechnology, pharmaceuticals). These studies allowed us to refine the concepts of planning and response capacity by enabling the identification of concrete activities and relations that correspond to the dimensions we developed theoretically. They also enabled us to assess the relations between these variables within each case, as well as compare these relations across cases to detect patterns of influence. Results largely supported the patterns of influence that we predicted between the dimensions of planning and performance. For example, using what we call "experimental" knowledge in planning increases the operational and value creation performance in projects. Producing plan documents that provide detailed and impartial information rather than documents that try to "promote" the project to resource providers increases the chances of full, timely, and inexpensive completion of the project. Adopting a risk approach that emphasizes the integration and cooperation between various participants rather than the strict allocation of responsibilities to them also seems to increase the chances of high operational and value creation performance. However, contrary to our expectations, a centralized, rather than pluralist, approach to planning appears to increase the chances of technical and operational performance. Results concerning the impact of response capacity also revealed important affects on performance, except for what we call the configurational dimension of the flexibility of project structure, which did not have a discernible impact on any performance dimension. Examples of such positive influence include the role of organizational cohesion based on participant voluntary adherence to project goals via the growth of personal ties to other participants. As we predicted, this kind of participant "embedding" in the project organization, rather than offering incentives, appears to increase the chances of achieving high completion, technical, and operational performance. Another possibility of maintaining organizational cohesion, namely by coercing participants also had an impact on performance. However, contrary to our expectations, it was a formal attitude, deeming contracts and agreements as clear and nonnegotiable, which appeared to increase the chances of project completion. Likewise, for what we term sequential flexibility, namely the ability to change decisions later on, it was a proactive attitude, rather than increasing the agility of the project organization, which appeared to favor the value creation performance. Finally, the two dimensions of resourcefulness each had a positive impact on some dimensions and a negative one on other dimensions of performance. In addition, the pattern detection effort revealed many possible influence trajectories that would connect planning variables to performance via the impact the former have on the response capacity properties of the project organization. In particular, the positive effect of centralized planning on technical and operational performance could occur via the fact that it increases the resourcefulness of the project organization, mainly its ability to explore with external partners, to find ideas and solutions to the problems that the project experiences. Moreover, we discovered that a number of weak or mixed impacts of planning variables occur because of the fact that the latter affect different response capacity properties, some with beneficial consequences and others with detrimental consequences.

In the quantitative exploration part, we relied on the concrete examples gathered in the qualitative part to create a survey that would measure the concepts developed theoretically. Results reported in Chapter 4 of this report are based on 71 answers to this survey, referring to projects in a variety of "infrastructural" and "digital" sectors. Results confirm the key influence of the response capacity properties, which appears to explain more than 20 percent of performance variation in complex projects. However, some specific results differ from those obtained in the qualitative stage, which can be explained by the fact that these results are based on the independent assessment by project participants rather than on the researchers' rating of project properties. Concretely, embedding participants through personal relations does not seem to have the same clear positive impact suggested by the case studies; the impact is positive on operational performance, but negative on the technical performance and possibly on the value creation performance. However, the positive impact of maintaining cohesion through a formal attitude vis-à-vis the means of coercion such as contracts is corroborated with respect to the operational performance. Yet, quantitative results did not corroborate the qualitative finding of a positive impact of taking proactive steps to cultivate sequential flexibility in the project organization. In fact, we obtained a clear indication that the opposite—creating an agile structure that can rapidly respond to any event as it arrives—has a strong, positive relation with all dimensions of performance. For the dimension of resourcefulness that concerns the ability to obtain resources for the additional activities needed to respond to unexpected events, we obtained, like in the qualitative part, a positive impact on some dimensions of performance and a negative one on other dimensions. However, for the other dimension of resourcefulness—the ability to generate ideas and solutions that can address the unexpected events—we found no significant relation to any performance dimension. Instead, in contrast to the qualitative study, we found an impact of what we term the configurational dimension of flexibility, namely the ability to effect changes in one part of the project without affecting others. As we expected theoretically, when this ability is based on the development of a sophisticated understanding of the interactions between project parts, configurational flexibility has a positive impact on technical performance. We also found that planning variables also have a strong impact on performance, explaining more than 12 percent of the variation in overall performance. Results confirmed the findings from case studies that a centralized planning process, and having plan documents that present impartially all the information needed by decision makers are both positively related to some dimensions of performance. However, contrary to what we saw in the case studies, a plan that allocates risk between participants, rather than attempting to foster integration, appears more often related to high performance. Also, the type of knowledge used in planning did not appear to be related to any dimension of performance. In terms of influence trajectories, we found a strong indication for one such trajectory. Specifically, planning centralization does not seem to affect the overall performance of projects directly, but rather via the positive impact, it has on the emergence of an agile mode of achieving sequential flexibility. In other words, a centralized approach during planning sows the seeds for the development of interaction routines between participants, which expedite and make more effective the decision making in response to the unexpected events that occur during execution. We deepened the study of the relation between planning and response capacity and found that the properties of response capacity can be further grouped in a "mechanistic" dimension and an "organic" dimension. The elements that form the mechanistic dimension appear to be more easily amenable to deliberate cultivation and are more likely to be influenced by the properties of planning. On the other hand, the elements of the organic dimension appear more likely to emerge in a less controllable fashion and without relation to the planning approach. At best, some conditions, such as collocation and frequent meetings, may help steer this emergence in the right direction. Put simply, this suggests that project performance is influenced by the planning approach directly, and indirectly, via its impact on the mechanistic properties of response capacity, as well as, in an autonomous manner, by the organic properties of response capacity. In addition, the quantitative stage confirmed some insights obtained from the case studies, namely that the nature of the complexity that a project faces initially has a direct influence on project performance as well as an impact on the planning approach that will be adopted by participants.

In summary, results confirm the important role that response capacity plays in the success of complex projects, both directly, and as part of an influence trajectory that spans from initial complexity conditions, via planning to the various dimensions of performance. The results that support this conclusion, as well as many other interesting findings, including edifying examples from the case studies, are found in the following report. We kindly invite you to read the entire report, and we look forward to receiving your feedback and suggestions.

Contents

Foreword

Prescriptions for the front-end structuring of complex projects focus on the identification of major uncertainties and on the measures that could mitigate the ensuing risks. However, many events and circumstances that affect a project over its life cycle cannot be anticipated. A frequent source of failure is that projects cannot adapt to changing circumstances (Floricel & Miller, 2001; Verganti, 1999). Results reported in this paper aim to enhance our understanding of how the planning stage of a project can be used to increase the chances that a project will achieve its goals in spite of unexpected occurrences. What we term the response capacity of complex projects first came to the attention of project management scholars in the 1980s, with the surge of an economics-inspired practice of allocating risk between project participants via long-term contracts in a way that would protect owners and ensure success. Turnkey contracts, build-operate-transfer (BOT) arrangements, and more recently, public-private partnerships (PPPs) were promoted as a panacea to cost overruns, financial shortages, and inefficient exploitation. But many such projects failed, mainly because the contractual structure put in place for dealing with anticipated uncertainties and risks constrained participants' response to unexpected events.

Inspired by a Scandinavian view of projects as temporary organizations (Lundin & Söderholm, 1995), we addressed this issue by taking a closer look at projects as organizations. We believe that, despite their temporary nature, the organizations put in place for complex projects can acquire enough influence to shape the subsequent decisions and actions of project participants. Therefore, we wanted to understand the processes that instill such powerful properties in organizations and how organizations are influenced by the decisions made during planning. In addition, we wanted to know what specific properties of such organizations enable or constrain the responses to unforeseen circumstances, and how they condition the success of a project. Our decision to move away from decision-theoretical frameworks and toward organizational processes parallels the evolution of the field of business strategy, which turned its attention from providing outwardly oriented decision frameworks, such as Porter's five forces or the BCG matrix, and recently gave more attention to understanding the organizational processes that occur in firms. In particular, strategy is now conceptualized primarily as nurturing organizational capabilities, such as operational routines and competencies, and, more recently, innovative and dynamic capabilities, which give firms a competitive advantage and enable them to sustain this advantage by adapting to changes in their competitive environment (Wernerfelt, 1984; Barney, 1991; Teece, Pisano, & Shuen, 1997). We were convinced that a similar move would enrich our understanding of projects and of their success or failure. Because of the special nature of complex projects, we could, in turn, provide useful insights for the understanding of strategizing in ongoing organizations.

Based on these assumptions, we embarked on a research journey that consisted of three main stages. The first stage consisted of the development of a theoretical framework for addressing these issues and the elaboration of a series of preliminary hypotheses. In the second stage, we performed field case studies of 17 complex projects, aiming to refine the theoretical framework and to provide a first corroboration of the preliminary hypotheses. The third stage consisted of a survey of 71 complex projects recently completed around the world. This report presents these empirical and theoretical results. It will proceed as follows.

Chapter 1 presents the foundations of our theoretical framework. It begins with a theoretical introduction that underscores the importance of the response capacity and places this concept in the context of project management research. In line with the prior research in this field as well as in other fields, such as strategy, the concept of response capacity stresses an organizational structure that emerges during project execution. In order to theorize this process, we briefly review three fundamental schools of thought that depict social structures as emerging from interactions between social actors. Using insights derived from these schools, we develop a process model that includes three project stages—planning; execution, when most unexpected events occur; and exploitation—and two connecting processes, organizational structuring and reaction to unexpected events, respectively. These processes are depicted as deviating from planners' intent. The structuring process deviates because it includes some aspects that planners overlook, others that are more intricate than expected, and some aspects of which participants have only marginal awareness. Because of these emerging and concealed aspects, the resulting structure shapes the reaction to unexpected events in ways that are also unintended, and sometimes incomprehensible. Therefore, reaction processes affect the likelihood and success of project exploitation.

Based on the process model outlined in the first chapter, Chapter 2 presents a series of dimensions that characterize the planning of the project, its emergent structure, its success, as well as the structuring and reaction processes. The assumption that planning only plants the seeds for future structuring processes prompted us to seek its relevant aspects not in planners' substantive decisions but rather in more fundamental characteristics of planning activities. We reviewed the debates in project management literature to identify four key dimensions of planning that are most likely to influence the emerging structure: (1) the nature of knowledge used in the planning process; (2) the number and importance of participants in the planning process; (3) the nature of the arguments advanced in the plan documents; and (4) the basic approach for addressing risk adopted in the plan. We characterize the extremes of each dimension and suggest how they are likely to influence the subsequent structuring processes. Then, we use prior research on complex projects to identify three properties of the emergent project structure that compose the response capacity of the project, namely cohesion, flexibility, and resourcefulness. For each of these properties we propose two dimensions and, like in the case of planning, theorize their extremes and the way they condition the reaction to unexpected events. Also, we briefly discuss the structuring and reaction processes and propose dimensions to be used when describing the influences between variables. Based on the constructs for planning and response capacity, as well as on the usual dimensions of project performance, the subsequent section of Chapter 2 proposes a number of hypotheses about trajectories that start with a planning aspect, influence a response capacity property, and, eventually affect a dimension of project performance.

Chapter 3 presents the results of our qualitative empirical research, which is based on 17 retrospective field studies of complex projects recently completed in North America and Europe. The chapter begins with a description and justification of the methods that we used for this phase of our research. It also describes the projects we studied, purposefully selected from three types of sectors, which we call discovery, digital and infrastructural. The following section presents the results of a semi-grounded comparative analysis related to the planning, response capacity, and performance variables as well as to the two processes included in our theoretical framework. This section explains how this qualitative research led to a better understanding of the mechanisms at work in complex projects, as well as to refined definitions of our variables and a better evaluation of their range of variation and possible impact on other variables. In the subsequent section, we discuss the results of a comparative analysis of the influence trajectories between planning, response capacity, and performance. This analysis is based on an intra-case assessment of all variables, using specially developed tables that summarize all available evidence with respect to each variable, followed by a cross-case comparison and identification of patterns. This stage of the research enabled us to provide a preliminary corroboration to our hypotheses and to refine them for the subsequent quantitative research. The variance on each dimension and the influence trajectories that we detected are amply illustrated with examples from the case studies. A discussion and conclusion section closes Chapter 3.

Chapter 4 presents the results of a quantitative empirical research involving 71 complex projects recently completed worldwide. The chapter begins with a description of the research methods and sample. The main research instrument is a psychometric-type survey, which includes items that capture each of the variables included in the theoretical framework. The survey was administered to project leaders and managers closely involved in complex projects. The subsequent section presents results referring to each variable, and concerns their reliability and the relation between survey items and the composite measures, as well as the relations between variables referring to the same construct. This enables us to assess, for example, whether the various dimensions of the response capacity of the project are complementary. The subsequent section presents two types of analyses used to detect the role of response capacity in the influence trajectories from planning to project performance. The first type of analysis is regression analysis, which enables us to sort out the influence of multiple context, planning, and response capacity variables on each other and on several indicators of project performance. Among others, it enabled us to detect the mediation effect of distinct response capacity variables. A second type of statistical method was discriminant analysis, which allowed us to assess the respective role of planning and response capacity as multidimensional constructs in accounting for inter-case differences in project performance, which is also seen as a multidimensional construct. A discussion and conclusion section clarifies the implications of these findings and qualifies them in light of the methods that were used.

Chapter 5 revisits our theoretical and empirical results to underscore the most important conclusions for the project management research. In addition, we suggest that the nature of our setting, complex projects, enabled us to draw interesting conclusions about the interplay between deliberate and routine aspects in strategizing and organization structuring. We also suggest that the limitations of our study, particularly those resulting from the methods we used, would warrant further research and we propose some possible directions.

This research was a collaborative effort. In addition to the three authors, a number of doctoral candidates and a number who have master's degrees were involved in drafting the case reports that served as a basis for the qualitative research (which will remain confidential and hence are not included in the report). Concretely, the case writing activity involved these doctoral candidates: Sorin Piperca (who is also a co-author of this report and wrote six cases) and Kerstin Kuyken (two cases). The master's degree students included the following: Emmanuel Vincent (who also played a key role in participant recruiting for the qualitative stage and wrote five cases), Marie-Eve Charland (three cases) and Chemseddine Belhadia (one case). The authors also thank Adrien Sicard and Nicolas Dziasko, who, in addition to Sorin Piperca, Kerstin Kuyken, and Chemseddine Belhadia, helped the first author with the data collection procedure. In addition, the authors would like to acknowledge the feedback received on the theoretical chapter from participants at an internal seminar of the project management group at the Umeå University School of Business and Economics (Umeå, Sweden, May 2009), and from anonymous reviewers and participants at the annual meeting of the Academy of Management in Chicago, IL, USA, in 2009. Feedback was received on the empirical research during an internal seminar of the research Chair in Project Management at the University of Quebec in Montreal, Canada, in April 2010, and from anonymous reviewers and participants at the Academy of Management annual meeting in Montreal, in August 2010. The authors would also like to acknowledge the generous financial support received from the Social Sciences and Humanities Research Council of Canada (http://www.sshrc.ca), project title "Increasing the Response Capacity of Complex Projects," and from Project Management Institute (http://www.pmi.org/Knowledge-Center/Research-Current-Research.aspx), project title "Increasing Project Flexibility: Preparing for the Unknown in the Concept Stage." This study is part of the activities of the Research Chair in Project Management at the University of Quebec in Montreal (UQAM) (http://www.chairegp.uqam.ca/en/research/axes/8-les-modes-de-gouvernance-en-gestion-de-projet.html).

1

Understanding the Response Capacity of Complex Projects

1. Introduction

Since it was realized that the survival and performance of organizations depend on their capacity to adapt to changes in their market, technological, social and regulatory environment, researchers sought to understand what enables adaptation, and why some organizations adapt more successfully than others do. The answers to this question have been set apart by their implicit position on what sociologists call the problem of action and structure (Giddens, 1984; Emirbayer & Mische 1998). On the one hand, answers emphasized the deliberate action of individuals with singular qualities such as foresight and leadership (Cockburn & Henderson, 2000) or the purposeful, ad hoc self-organizing by groups of individuals (Jarzabkowski & Seidl, 2008). On the other hand, successful adaptation is attributed to enduring structural properties in the organization (Teece et al., 1997; Rindova & Kotha, 1998), in the form of centralized routines (Zollo & Winter, 2002) or distributed processes (Eisenhardt & Martin, 2000). However, these theorizing efforts have often turned into fruitless debates, not in the least because in ongoing organizations it is difficult to disentangle deliberate, creative action from structurally conditioned reaction.

However, a class of organizations enables researchers to observe, distinguish, and understand the interaction of deliberate forethought and structural conditioning. This class consists of complex projects, such as those designing and building major airport terminals, high-capacity extraction or energy-production facilities and land transportation infrastructures, as well as those developing information systems, pharmaceutical drugs, and highly innovative products. These projects are sizable enough and different enough from other projects and from the normal activities of sponsor organizations to require a special planning effort, which involves the design of dedicated organizational and contractual structures. Because of the unique nature of projects, planners aim to start with a clean slate and break with past routines when designing such structures. Despite taking a fresh start, the duration and number of participants in such projects are high enough to sustain endogenous processes that lead to emergence of new, project-specific routines and other unintended structural elements. Unlike in ongoing organizations, where routines can be lost in the fog of history, the complex structures of projects can be traced to decisions made in planning as well as to other occurrences. In addition, most complex projects have to respond at some time during their execution or early exploitation phases to major unexpected events. Such events force participants to react in ways that are neither planned initially nor considered "business as usual." However, the urgency of the situation increases the likelihood that, in spite of a desire to be unencumbered by the past, the response to such events will be influenced obviously or subtly by emergent project structures. Together, project planning, the emergence of specific structures, and the need to respond to unexpected events provide a "quasi-experimental" setting for disentangling the role of deliberate foresight from that of structural conditioning in the response of organizations to changes in their environment and to other issues with which they are confronted.

Project management research started paying attention to responding to unexpected events after the 1980s and the early 1990s, a period during which practitioners experimented with innovative institutional and contractual arrangements for the development of infrastructure projects, such as project finance, build-operate-transfer (BOT), public private partnerships (PPPs) and turnkey contracts (Miller & Lessard, 2001; Miller, 2000). These approaches shared a belief that long-term contracts could "freeze" the future for the life of the project and limit the owners' and financial backers' exposure to uncertain events that could affect their net revenues. Planning became the design of contractual structures that pass most risks to other participants via different forms of fixed price contracts. While this approach enabled even small entrepreneurial entities to sponsor large infrastructure projects, such structures not only proved difficult to design and negotiate but also revealed that attempting to freeze the future reduces the subsequent ability to respond to unexpected events. The result were many project failures, which were caused not as much by the market or technical issues raised by the unexpected events as by the ensuing conflicts between participants, by the disintegration of project organizations, etc. (Floricel & Miller, 2001).[1]

Practitioners responded to this unexpected outcome of anticipatory planning by resorting to the opposite approach. For example, owners agreed to bear most, if not all, risks, and started to emphasize the creation of a collaborative environment rather than the reduction of project costs (Hobbs & Andersen, 2001, Davies, Gann, & Douglas, 2009). However, these approaches, which go back to some extent to more traditional contractual arrangements, raise the possibility of a return to the cost overruns that had plagued complex projects in the past (see e.g., Merrow, 1988) and had stimulated contractual innovation rooted in the tenets of economic sciences. Faced with this dilemma, researchers undertook a concerted effort to lift the veil of the instrumental and prescriptive rationality that project management and economics had cast on these issues and to study the raw reality of the social processes that occur in projects (Lundin & Söderholm, 1995). Researchers attempted to grasp the nature of unexpected events (Hälgren & Wilson, 2008) and the organizational response to them (Söderholm, 2008) to understand how planning for anticipated activities and risks combine with cultivating an organizational

---

[1]For example a study by a United Kingdom company "on global megaprojects found that poor performance (such as the Channel Tunnel and London's Jubilee Line Extension) was associated with fixed-price or Private Finance Initiative (PFI) contracts, which transfer risk and responsibility to a prime contractor, with penalties incurred for delays, mistakes, and scope changes. Twenty-one such projects are delayed, over budget, or poorly integrated because of disputes, adversarial practices, and protracted legal battles between clients and contractors" (Davies, Gann, & Douglas, 2009, p. 108).

flexibility to respond to unexpected events (Verganti, 1999; Floricel & Miller, 2001; MacCormack et al., 2001), as well as to uncover how all these aspects influence the success of complex projects.

These contributions produced numerous insights about the social processes that shape complex projects and their reaction to unexpected events, but their disparate nature precludes them from providing practical guidance to project planners. This chapter attempts to integrate some of these insights in a comprehensive theoretical framework, built around the concept of response capacity, which captures structurally conditioned ability of complex projects to respond to unexpected events. The focus of our theoretical effort, social processes in organizations, was inspired by the evolution of the strategy field, which used to be dominated by instrumental and prescriptive rationality views (Ansoff, 1965; Boston Consulting Group, 1968), but more recently moved toward views that give a much larger place to understanding the organizational processes that occur in firms. In particular, business strategy is now conceptualized primarily as nurturing organizational capabilities, such as routines and competencies, and, more recently, innovative and dynamic capabilities, that give firms a competitive advantage and enable them to sustain this advantage by adapting to changes in their competitive environment (Wernerfelt, 1984; Barney, 1991; Teece et al., 1997). We were inspired above all by the view of dynamic capabilities as embedded across many ordinary organizational processes (Eisenhardt & Martin, 2000) and by a related stream of the innovation management literature (Henderson & Clark, 1990; Dougherty, 2001), which highlights the rigidities induced by such processes. However, because of the particular nature of the organizations that we studied and of our research question, we went beyond the strategy literature and sought to ground our theoretical development in more fundamental sociological theories about the emergence and nature of social structures and their relation to social action (Giddens, 1984; Callon, 1986; Luhmann, 1995).

The response capacity concept and the theoretical framework built upon these premises enable us to argue that organizational structures and unexpected events make planning more subtle than what current instrumental and normative models imply. Simply put, the latter imply that planning consists of programming project activities with as much precision and detail as possible and then creating structures that control the implementation of these activities. The project organization, if considered explicitly, is reduced to the role of a tool for project leaders, and its structure is seen as an "iron cage" that restricts the participants' freedom and punishes deviations from the plan. We argue that the project planning and the processes that lead to the emergence of organizational structures, in short, structuring processes, interact in many other ways beside the rigidity of an iron cage in case of unexpected events. In planning, project participants try to jointly build a set of stable frameworks, which enables them to obtain resources, gain legitimacy, and initiate action. In doing so, planners gather or produce knowledge, but also take into account some preexisting rules and principles, as well as various internal and external interests. They also need to present an acceptable "front" to resource investors and to stakeholders (Goffman, 1958; Flyvbjerg, Holm, & Buhl, 2006) as well as ensure that responsibilities and risks are shared in ways that would ensure project success. However, as the project advances toward execution, new participants who were not involved in the initial planning enter the project organization and unforeseen circumstances occur as well. Participants try to sort out other participants and start to develop working relationships and, eventually, stable interaction patterns, as well as a language with specific meanings, which enables them to understand each other and coordinate their actions (Weick, 1979; Barley, 1986). The result of this process is an evolving social structure, which includes many aspects ignored by planners and others that are more complex than expected (Emirbayer & Mische, 1998). These structures not only supplement but also deviate from the planners' intent. This means that project organizations become social systems with a significant autonomy from the planners' will. We argue that the deviation, which takes place during the structuring process, means that the planners' intent has the unforeseen consequence of channeling project organizations in certain trajectories, often undesirable. In line with Giddens' (1984) idea that structuring processes are fraught with unintended consequences, we also argue that emerging structures shape the response to unexpected events in ways that deviate from, or even totally contradict, the anticipations included in the plan (Floricel & Miller, 2001). Overall, instead of a planning that impacts outcomes as a rational blueprint, pulling action through a sort of teleological engine (Van de Ven & Poole, 1995), we postulate a trajectory that influences the project success via two deviating processes, which together amount to the "structuring detour" (Figure 1-1).

Another crucial assumption we make is that project outcomes can be, at least in part, traced back to the emergent organizational structure, and, eventually, to elements in planning. In other words, although largely unintended, the outcome of the structure formation process is not entirely indeterminate (see e.g., Barley, 1986). This traceability holds out the perspective that measures can be taken as early as the planning stage, as well as during project execution, to improve the response to unexpected events and the chances of project success. However, the key for this is understanding the characteristics of the planning process and of the resulting plans that influence the nature of the subsequent structuring processes, as well as the characteristics of the emergent structure, most notably its response capacity properties. These properties shape the reaction to unexpected events in ways that affect the project performance.

By means of this theoretical development, we hope to make two contributions. The first is to provide a framework that moves beyond description and aims to enable prediction and hence the elaboration of practical recommendations for project planners. Among others, we show that some aspects of planning, which are rarely considered directly, may have a significant influence on emergent project structures and on subsequent performance. Second, we hope to contribute more broadly to the fields of strategy and organization theory, by clarifying how certain mechanisms contribute to the emergence of social structures and the role of the actors' deliberate intent in these processes. The chapter proceeds as follows. In section 2, we explain the theoretical bases by presenting three kinds of mechanisms that contribute to the creation of social structures and by explaining in more detail the overall process described in Figure 1-1. In section 3, we detail the variables that capture two important aspects of this process, planning and response capacity, as well as the project performance. In section 4, we present a series of testable hypotheses about influence trajectories that originate in a certain aspect of planning, pass through aspects of the response capacity, and influence project performance. In section 5, we discuss the main implications of this theoretical development.

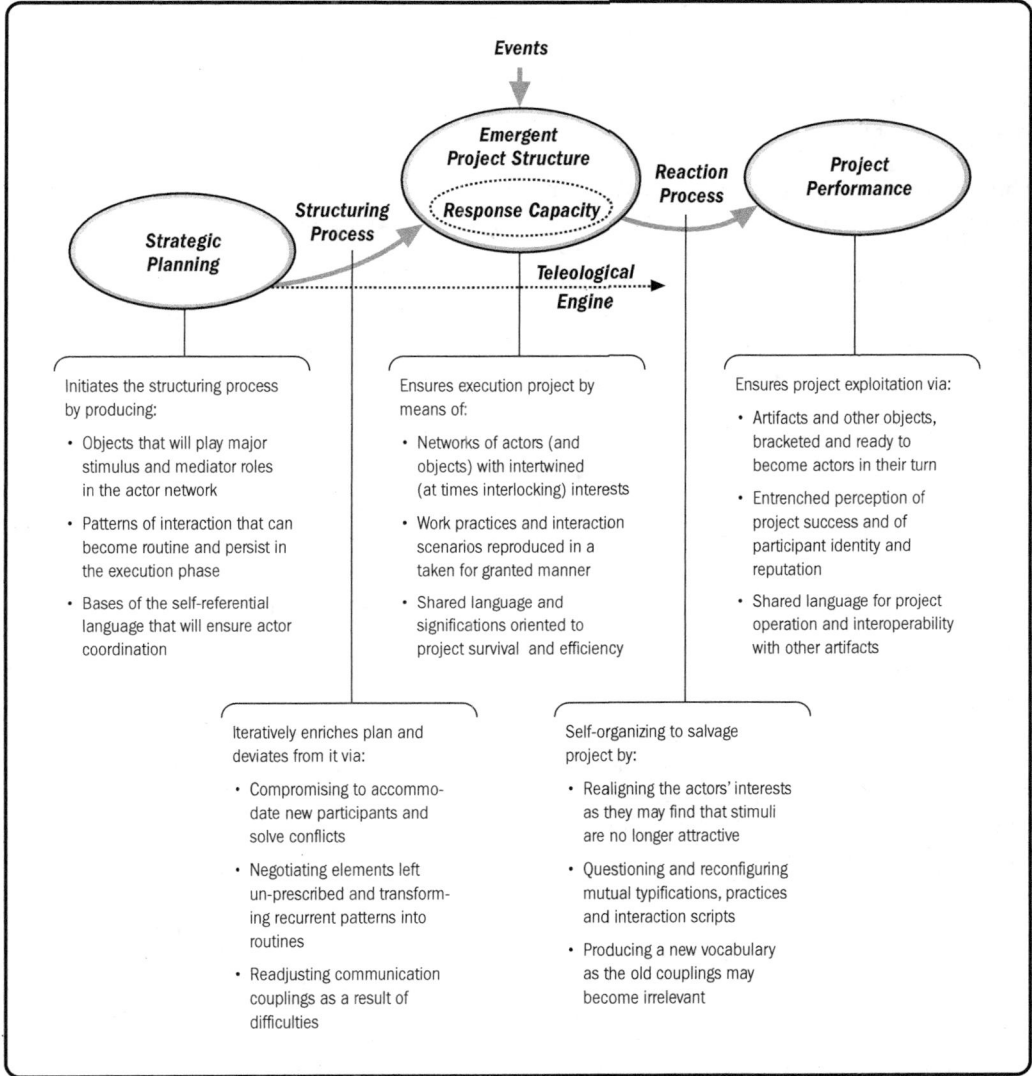

Figure 1-1   An overview of relevant processes in complex projects (the structuring detour)

2. Theoretical Background

The implicit paradigm that informs the conceptualization of organizational structure in the project management literature could be called "instrumental functionalism" (Hodgson, 2004; Winter, Smith, Morris, & Cicmil, 2006). Like other functionalist views, it assumes that organizational differentiation—the grouping and subordination of actors, and the breakdown and scheduling of their tasks—together with the means for coordinating their activities, follow hierarchically (top-down) from the imperative of achieving project goals (Packendorff, 1995). Contrary to ecological functionalist authors (see e.g., Nelson & Winter, 1982; Stinchcombe, 1990), who argued that such structural properties emerge from actors' random trials and nonpurposeful selection by the organizational system, instrumental functionalism assumes that structure is a matter of deliberate rational design informed by normative rules (Kerzner, 2009). A corollary of this view is an emphasis on control, which is rooted in a belief that this design will only achieve project goals if participants' actions are kept within tight bounds, and random deviations banished. These beliefs led project management research along two routes. One route took up refining the normative rules by accounting for the limited rationality of planners and actors (Simon, 1978; March & Shapira, 1992), and for the uncertainty affecting their activities (Krishnan, Eppinger, & Whitney, 1997; Winch, 2004; Chapman & Ward, 1994). The other, inspired by incomplete contracts (Williamson, 1981; Hart, 1988) and principal-agent (Holmstrom, 1979) theories, focused on improving the control over actors' behavior, by considering, beside limited rationality and uncertainty, their opportunism and limited ability to assess the skills and monitor the behavior of other actors, as well as the ambiguity of contracts and other ties between them. Practice-oriented contributions, the bulk of this literature, focus on developing normative methodologies rooted in the belief that naming, mapping and arranging project activities in specific ways creates better tools for controlling actors' behavior (Packendorff, 1995). At least 70 such tools are widely used in project practice (Besner & Hobbs, 2008).

So far, few design rules and tools have been linked systematically to project performance. As the introduction suggests, some novelties may have even harmed performance. Their persistent use and development may be due to self-interested promotion by a strong professional field (Hodgson, 2004) or to symbolic manipulation by project participants (Sapolsky, 1972). As a result, many researchers decided to take a fresh look at projects as organizations (Ludin & Soderholm, 1995). Using a descriptive (non-normative) approach, they produced interesting insights about project processes (Denis, Lamothe, & Langley, 2001), their embeddedness in broader social contexts (Miller & Floricel, 2001; Engwall, 2003), and even about the underlying rationalities (Lawrence & Phillips, 2004). However, in the quest for realism, the early interest in projects as unitary entities was replaced by a focus on two kinds of micro-level processes. One direction, drawing upon the "practice turn" in organization theory and strategy (Whittington, 1996), describes ad hoc project practices and contrast them with normative models (Soderholm, 2008; Hälgren, 2007). The other process, inspired by the actor-network theory, focuses on the real role of "objects," such as the tools mentioned previously as well as documents, drawings, databases, etc. (Carlile, 2002; Sapsed & Salter, 2004; Papadimitriou & Pellegrin, 2007; Sergi, 2009). While further eroding the hold of instrumental functionalism, this micro focus provides little insight about project organizations seen as a whole, leaving normative tools as the only practical guideline. Yet, this growing body of empirical results could become a catalyst for new conceptualizations of projects as social entities, accounting for their spatiotemporal unity without reification,[2] and rethinking their structures in ways that accommodate social construction, objects, routine interactions, and situated practice.

---

[2]This term means seeing things that are not out there (in the reality of social relations), attempting to make objects out of mere ideas. For example, an organizational chart is an idea that does not have an equivalent social entity. A particular way of reifying is attributing human-like properties to social entities, including functional differentiation.

To develop such a conceptualization, we combined insights from three socio-logical views, namely actor-network theory (Callon, 1986), structuration theory (Giddens, 1984) and the communication systems view (Luhmann, 1995), integrating them by way of a metatheoretical perspective that emphasizes social mechanisms (Swedberg & Hedstrom, 1996). All three schools of thought see social systems as "flat" networks, which, unlike the reified edifices of instrumental functionalism, are compatible with the recent project management literature. However, each of them highlights a specific mechanism by which aggregate social entities such as projects, which we will call, for conciseness, systems, emerge from the interactions of component entities, which we will call actors. The following paragraphs offer a brief and necessarily partial outline of these perspectives, starting with the views emphasizing actors and ending with those giving prominence to systems. For each view, we describe the nature of what constitutes a social structure; the process by which the structure extends "spatially," tying together larger aggregates; as well as the process by which it persists in time. Moreover, we describe how resulting aggregates condition subsequent actions and instill a particular pattern of evolution in systems such as projects.

The first perspective, grouped liberally under the term "actor-network theory" (Latour, 1987; Callon, 1986; Hughes, 1983; Pinch & Bijker, 1984; Law, 2004), gives actors' intentionality a predominant role in shaping social systems. However, intentionality itself is seen as a socially neutral urge instilled in actors by the forces that rule them, say, as biological and physical entities. This led some actor-network theorists to argue that, seen from an equally neutral viewpoint, nonhuman beings and inanimate objects are actors on a par with humans (Latour, 1991). Networks emerge when an actor engages other actors to join some initiative by "translating" the latter in ways that resonate with these actors' urges (Callon, 1986). Worded differently, network links hinge on a deliberate effort to create stimuli that make the initiative a required passage point for other actors. Efforts to trigger an adequate response can range from creating the necessary physical conditions for nonhuman actors to manipulating cultural symbols to put up a "front" (Goffman, 1958) that attracts human actors. Further extension is achieved when actors construct "convergence places" between different networks (Callon, 1991). However, actors' heterogeneity and autarchic urges make it likely that some of them will drift away in pursuit of other stimuli. Thus, a social system is a fragile interweaving of networks, whose ramifications attract heterogeneous actors—human and nonhuman. What puts a certain structure in these actors' behavior and creates stability in systems is the transformation of some stimuli into "facts" and "artifacts" (Pinch & Bijker, 1984). Namely, through a process of "blackboxing" (Latour, 1987), which means de-emphasizing and eventually bracketing the network of actors that constructed them and the history of manipulations and compromises that gave them a specific shape, networks become point-like objects and stimuli that trigger standard responses. This way, artifacts, such as looming technical systems (Hughes, 1983), as well as facts, such as legitimated knowledge (Fleck, 1979) or plans, contracts, and drawings in the case of projects (Ewenstein & Whyte, 2009), start to look quite immutable. They exert an ordering and even inertial influence on action, in their role of interaction mediators, namely as focal points, mirrors and prisms of communication (Star & Griesemer, 1989; Knorr Cetina, 1995; Carlile, 2002), but also as participating actors, infusing new initiatives with apparent urges (Winner, 1977). In light of these mechanisms, the evolution of systems such as complex projects is an open-ended but path-dependent unfolding, in which newly black-boxed objects anchor the networks that construct further objects, and so on.

The second perspective that inspired us, structuration theory, stresses the recurrent reproduction of social structures by means of actions that follow a similar pattern repeatedly (Giddens, 1984). In this perspective, actors also actively construct network links, by negotiating roles and interaction norms (Barley, 1986). However, they are knowledgeable and capable of monitoring and justifying their own actions, which relegates nonhuman entities to more passive roles, subject to interpretation by human actors (Orlikowski, 1992). Cognition, as a mediator between stimuli and responses, has an even more critical role by assuming that social action is more effective if, rather than reopening the social construction process every time, actors would rely on past mutual categorizations, like those attributing formal or informal authority over resource allocation, and on preexisting interaction scripts. By relying on them repeatedly, categorizations become habitual frames, and interaction scripts turn into routine trajectories and practices. With time, actors become only marginally aware of the origin or influence of these routines, and, by relying on them, inadvertently contribute to their reproduction. In this recurrent reproduction process, they acquire a compelling, objective nature and become social structures, which shape subsequent actions in subtle ways (Berger & Luckmann, 1966; Garfinkel, 1967; Weick, 1979). Networks coagulate from recursive interactions and extend as distinct trajectories intersect, and actors make sense of and reconcile their junctures, to form a continuous field of shared frames and practices that they can skillfully navigate (Bourdieu, 1977). By emphasizing local-to-global emergence and unintentional reproduction, this perspective suggests that social structures can easily deviate from instrumental organizational charts and activity schedules, and that social systems such as complex projects are historic and accidental assemblages (Barley, 1986), rather than consistent functional edifices. The taken-for-granted structures exert a subtle influence on actors, increasing the chances of reproducing the same patterns, which makes such structures self-sustaining. Hence, structural inertia is the dominant effect of this mechanism. But structures exist only via reproduction in social action, which enables three forms of change, all of them unmanageable: gradual drift, as a result of forgetting and slight deviations by actors; moderate renegotiation to accommodate new actors and circumstances, and radical meltdown as a result of clashes with other systems or to major events (Emirbayer & Mische, 1998).

The third perspective, communication ecosystems (Luhmann, 1995), is a branch of functionalism, which assumes that social systems set boundaries and differentiate internally in ways that refer to and support their own reproduction. Assuming self-reference gives priority to systems and leaves actors in a secondary role. This top-down assumption contrasts with the bottom-up view of the actor-network theory, in which actors drive system coalescence, and with the balanced perspective of structuration theory, in which actors and structures condition each other recursively (Kontopoulos, 1993). The top-down nature of the communication ecosystem view is further expressed in the fact communication is seen as the essential social property of social systems, which can be detached from the perceptions and interests of particular actors. Contrary to other functionalist approaches that superimpose systemic schemes in a top-down manner on actors, this view sees a social system as a "flat" network and highlights distributed communications, especially the couplings expressed as shared language and meaning that actors negotiate locally, as the building blocks of internal differentiation. Besides, unlike in the instrumental functionalist view discussed earlier, differentiation does not result from applying exogenous schemes but from the evolutionary self-organization of this ecology of communication couplings. In this process, "blind" variation is triggered by problems and occurs in episodes, such as crisis meetings in projects, in which actors suspend past couplings and try new language and meaning possibilities (Hendry & Seidl, 2003). Even if this supposes that actors are capable of conceptualizing their actions, actors cannot grasp the entire complexity of the system. Thus, it is the "invisible hand" of the system that selects "winners" among the new coupling possibilities, in light of its self-preservation urge. Concretely, the system continues to throw problems at actors until they stumble upon a viable communication coupling among themselves (Stinchcombe, 1990). The resulting set of routine communication couplings creates, as long as actors stay in the normal "operating" mode, a referential framework that restricts their freedom in attributing meaning to external events and to each others' actions, and helps them detect and interpret problems (Luhmann, 1993). While these couplings can change because of the variations that take place in episodes, the system restructuring is always partial, because, without preserving at least some past couplings, the possibility of self-referentiality, and the very existence of the system, ceases. Although more flexible than the routines of structuration theory, the path dependency in this case is more directional than the one discussed for actor network theory, yet still unintended.

In spite of their different scientific and even ontological assumptions, these three mechanisms can be seen as complementary, because they build on assumptions about actors and interactions that are compatible and postulate processes that may occur in parallel. For example, actors can be calculative strategists driven by autarchic urges, such as survival instincts, as supposed by the actor-network theory, while also evolving in a socially constructed "world" that tacitly distorts their perceptions and colors them with significations, as structuration theory assumes, as well as attempting to develop an explicit task-specific language to coordinate locally with other actors in light of an imperfect conceptualization of the overall system (Emirbayer & Mische, 1998). A school of thought that advances such eclectic explanations is the "social mechanisms" perspective (Davis & Marquis, 2005; Hedström & Swedberg, 1996). Hedström and Swedberg (1996) define mechanisms as generic causal sequences that may or may not be involved in producing a specific social pattern. From this perspective, the schools discussed above can be seen as proposing three distinct mechanisms for the formation and structuring of social systems (see Table 1-1). This view also suggests that, although complementary, depending on the prevalent conditions, some mechanisms have more chances to be expressed in a given system or at a given time than others do. For example, in more stable conditions, the routinizing mechanism of structuration theory may prevail over the variation episodes of the communication systems perspective.

Table 1-1:   A comparison of the three mechanisms

	Mechanism		
	Actor-network translation	Recurrent structuration	Communication ecosystem
Anchor	Actors' urges (bottom-up)	Field of practice (heterachical)	System survival (top-down)
Social links	Co-optation via stimuli	Interaction scripts	Language coupling
System formation	Manipulation and interweaving of stimuli	Unintended routinization of paths and interaction	Variation episodes and systemic selection
Peculiarity	Objects as actors on a par with human actors	Recursive determination of structure and action	Communication as essence of the social
Inertial factors	Punctualization of facts and artifacts	Taken for granted categories and practices	Self-reference requires historic elements
Influence on actors	Mediate and anchor interactions	Provides rules and resources for action	Sets expectations and reference for interaction
System evolution	Fragile path dependent unfolding	Structural inertia and external clashes	Functional auto-organization

3. Outline of the Project Structuring Process

With the three views discussed previously, and the mechanismic perspective as a basis for integrating them, we now have all of the ingredients needed for explaining the archetypical process that informs our theorization of complex projects (see Figure 1-1). In this process, we focus on three "moments" in the life of a project, namely planning activities, which produce the initial blueprint for the project; execution activities, during which an organizational system with an emergent structure works to implement the plan; and exploitation activities, which take over the resulting artifacts and bring to light the success of the project. We also pay special attention to two processes that connect these "moments:" the structuring process, which we see as enriching, as well as deviating from, initial plans; and the reaction process, which reorganizes the system in the wake of unexpected events, in an attempt to complete the project. These three stages and two processes often overlap and iterate in practice, but disentangling them and establishing a conceptual precedence in the prototypical process enables the conceptualization of the social mechanisms at work.

The first stage, planning, is a translation activity, during which project sponsors create stimuli that connect to their initiative a number of key participants and stakeholders that bring support and resources. Through negotiations, this process eventually establishes and brackets to some extent a series of facts about the project as well as a number of objects, such as the plan itself, which details technical concepts, schedules, financial flows, and organizational charts, as well as contracts and agreements between participants. Planning has three kinds of impact on subsequent activities, but this influence is akin to sowing the seeds of subsequent structuration rather than to creating a teleological straitjacket, like traditional planning literature supposes. One impact is through the objects it produces, which subsequently focalize and mediate actors' interactions, and become themselves central players in the project network. For example, new actors read in these objects some cues regarding the likely authority and resource distribution in the network. Second, planning activities are themselves social interactions. Even if they concern only a small number of participants, they can set the tone for subsequent social interactions, by establishing some routines. Eventually, these may start being taken for granted, carried over by the planners who stay with the project, and tacitly adopted by those who enter the project later on. These routines send a powerful signal of what interactions between actors are likely to be (even in spite of planners' rhetoric). Finally, through the plan and other legal and regulatory documents, planning activities also create a core of self-referential language and meaning that participants can use to coordinate their activities. Some early participants may also develop specific bilateral couplings that would persist in the execution activities.

Planning provides planners and those who carry on their intent with important symbolic resources that can be used for manipulating other actors, both internal and external. However, the structuring of the project system is likely to deviate from this initial intent as well as complete it in many unforeseen aspects. This deviation and enrichment is related to the entry of concrete actors, as opposed to generic carriers of functional roles, such as "contractors," as well as to the difficulties that participants encounter when attempting to implement this vision in practice. Projects in general are characterized by the successive entry of actors with different competencies, for example engineers then constructors, which replace planners, who often simply leave the project organization. It is not unusual for the organization to grow from tens of planners to thousands of experts and workers at the peak of execution. The signs of structuring deviation are conflicts and adjustments of explicit rules and procedures as well as of interaction patterns. Such structuring processes occur in three ways. First, new actors bring with them specific agendas, strategies, and assumptions. Existing members of the network adjust project stimuli (incentives, penalties) in order to accommodate these entrants, for example, by compromising between opposite interests. The second process involves negotiating concrete roles and interaction scripts, clarifying the aspects left unprescribed in the plan, and reconciling the contradictory stimuli and prescriptions that the plan and subsequent decisions may include. In the process, actors develop new tacit assumptions, practices, and routines, which may become taken for granted in their turn. Finally, difficulties prompt actors to adjust the communication couplings between them.

The result of the structuring process is an organization with an emergent structure, which in normal conditions operates smoothly to transform blueprints into artifacts. This structure is characterized by a network of actors with intertwined, less often interlocking, interests and propensities. Among these actors, the artifact, as its degree of completion increases, becomes a stimulus that is more and more difficult to question. The structure also consists of a rather smooth field of practices, trajectories, and interaction scripts, which, to varying degrees, are reproduced in a taken for granted manner. Finally, it also includes a language and specific significations shared by pairs of actors or more broadly across the organization. Given the diminishing number of problems that actors have to deal with, these seem increasingly aligned with project survival and efficiency. The response capacity of the project is related to this emergent structure, an assumption inspired by the dynamic capabilities literature and its focus on the past, for example, on routines and asset positions (Teece et al., 1997). However, contrary to some currents in this literature (see e.g., Zollo & Winter, 2002, p. 340), we deemphasize the role of meta-routines that change routines, even though steering committees and other extraordinary structural elements can play a role in response capacity. Instead, in line with our three sources of theoretical inspiration and their view of social structure as "flat" network: with innovation research and its emphasis on the perverse effect of taken for granted structures (Henderson & Clark, 1990; Christensen, 1997; Dougherty, 2001) and with a view of dynamic capabilities as embedded in the ordinary practices and routines of organizations (Eisenhardt & Martin, 2000, p. 1106), we see response capacity as a series of properties distributed in the entire project network. Their nature and influence are clarified below in the discussion of the response process and in the next section.

In light of the project management literature discussed in the Introduction, our process model highlights the key role of unexpected events in complex projects. Most unexpected events are a frequent or even normal occurrence in complex projects (Halgrén, 2007), resulting from external developments and internal cumulative processes (Hwang & Lichtenthal, 2000). However, such events can usually be addressed with the normal stimuli, routines, and communication couplings. Thus, our focus is on major unexpected events, which also affect almost every complex project. They typically result from environmental jolts or turbulence (Emery & Trist, 1967; Meyer, 1982) or a highly unusual convergence or amplification of internal factors (Davies, Dodgson, & Gann, 2009). Such events create a perceptual and interpretive discontinuity for participating actors (Luhmann, 1993). The proximate outcome is an increase in participants' uncertainty about project prospects (Emery & Trist, 1965), and hence in their anxiety (Lopes, 1987). This emotional reaction renders explicitly visible ("opaque") aspects of the plan and of the project organization that used to be taken for granted ("transparent") before the event (Davies et al., 2009). Hence, many punctualized stimuli (plan, contract, blueprints or even artifacts), routines (interaction scripts and behavior norms), and communication couplings (language and meanings) among actors are likely to be reconsidered. Actors will manipulate project stimuli strategically in an attempt to realign actors' interests with the project, perhaps in an interlocking manner again, renegotiate practices and choreograph new interaction scripts for the remaining activities, and seek new terms and significations that advance project survival in the new circumstances.

However, in the same way that planning influences the structuring process in subtle ways, the emergent structure will subtly carry over in the response to unexpected events in spite of the emotional reaction that will unfreeze many punctualized, routinized, or operating elements. The three theories that inspired us suggest that some stimuli, routines, and significations embedded in the emergent structure are likely to persist and to condition actors' interpretation and reaction to events. First, some "actors," "facts," and "artifacts" will remain punctualized in the network. To begin with, this concerns the project itself, although a possible reaction is to shut the project down. Some already built artifacts will also be preserved, although major changes are possible. Then it concerns some actors, although everyone, even the sponsors, can be replaced. Some agreements, although major renegotiations can also take place, as well as some knowledge and assumptions, will also be preserved. The response to unexpected events will rely on these elements rather than question them. A second aspect is the fact that some typifications, scripts, and trajectories will continue to be reproduced routinely. If a preexisting field of socially constructed practices is needed in order to be efficient, it is likely that some practices that actors have jointly developed for the project will be preserved. In fact, some scholars argue that in crises, the participants' tendency to reproduce preexisting practices may even be reinforced by the startling effect and anxiety that follow major events (Billings, Milburn, & Schaalman, 1980). Actors will fall back on their social "reflexes," meaning on reactions that are routine as opposed to deliberate, because of the urgency of the situation and the realization that complete conscious mastery is not possible by any means (Beck, Bonns, & Lau, 2003, p. 3). In other words, actors draw heavily on the most entrenched typifications, relations, and scenarios rather than reconsider them all. Finally, the self-referentiality of the communication systems cannot be preserved if all couplings are suspended at the same time. The episodes that generate new language and meaning will likely suspend only some operational couplings at a time, while preserving the others.

Project reaction is determined largely by the elements that resist the structural unfreezing and provide stimuli, footsteps, and constraints to which actors will refer reflexively. Considering this, a key theoretical issue regarding the response capacity of complex projects is to understand, given the particular properties of an emergent structure, what structural elements are likely to be preserved and how these will influence the response to unexpected events. In turn, according to the project management literature this response is likely to influence the success of the project. As detailed in Chapter 2, success is multidimensional and the reaction is likely to have a differentiated impact on different dimensions.

2

The Properties of Planning and Response Capacity

I. Introduction

This chapter details the variables related to three theoretical categories: strategic planning, the response capacity of emergent project structure, and project performance. Figure 2-1 summarizes the key variables in a cross-sectional model. Horizontal arrows suggest that the model mirrors the relations of (causal) precedence between the stages depicted in the process model of Figure 1-1, while vertical dotted arrows suggest relations of conditional priority between the groups of variables referring to each of the three stages. The following sections explain these variables and the reasons for which they were selected.

2. Planning Dilemmas and Properties

If planning is likely to condition the emergent structure, and the latter is likely to carry over the influence into the reaction of the project system to unexpected events, and, through this reaction, impact project performance, the key issue becomes the identification of planning aspects that affect the emergent structure and, through its structural properties, differentiate the reaction to events. Given the multiplicity of structuring mechanisms discussed in the previous section, this amounts to identifying a comparable number of planning aspects that would activate different mechanisms. However, if planning is only to sow the seeds of structuring, but not determine it as an iron cage, the relevant aspects are likely to be more basic approaches rather than some substantive decisions made by planners. The adoption of such basic approaches is likely to be rooted in the planners' beliefs about the possibilities, constraints, and rationality of their activities.

A rich source of insights for understanding the anticipative and intentional stance of human actors that characterizes planning (Emirbayer & Mische, 1998) are the philosophical and sociological reflections on rationality (Weber, 1968), which are strongly echoed in organization theory and strategy research (Simon, 1978; Mintzberg, 1994; Langley, 1989). These reflections guided our quest to understand the planning aspects that the project management literature singles out as making a difference. In order to increase the practical relevance of the theory, we also sought distinctions that pose a dilemma for managers, and also leave degrees of freedom, rather than impose a choice.

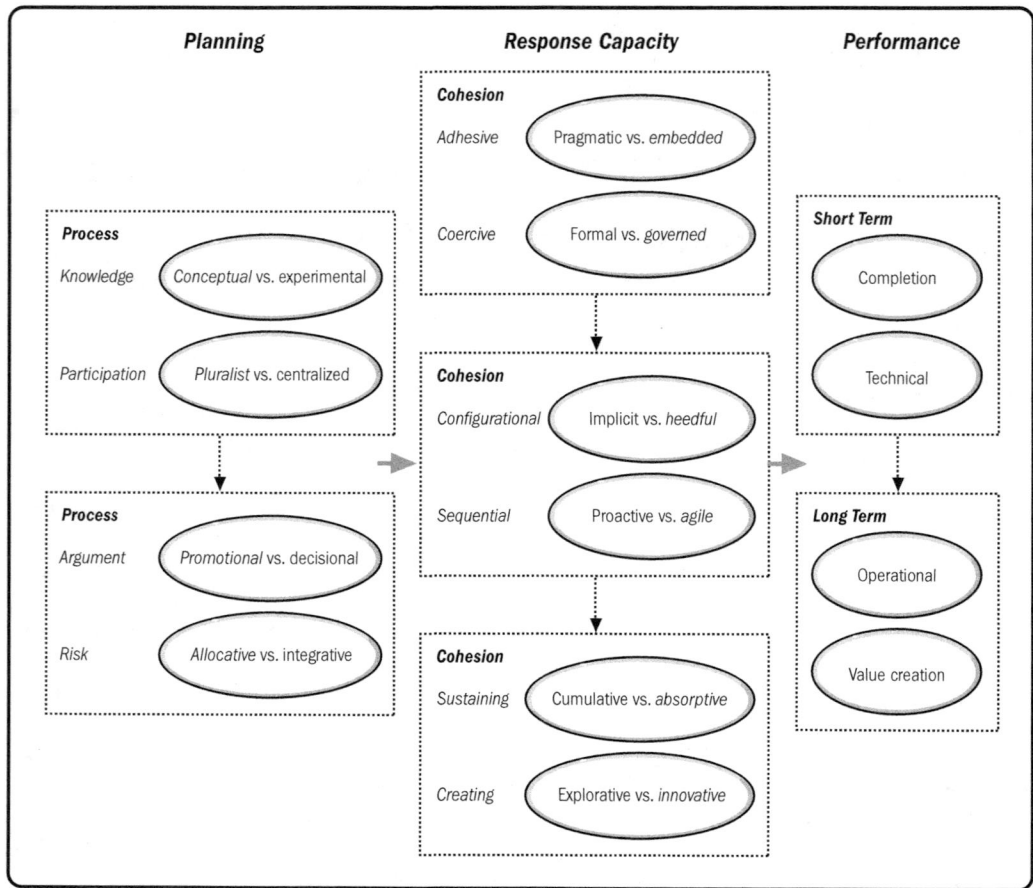

Figure 2-1   The variables included in the theoretical framework

A first distinction was suggested by the idea advanced in the previous chapter that planning sows structuring seeds both through the objects it creates and through the early routines and language bases it develops. The latter aspects suggest that important properties may concern planning as a *process* rather than as an outcome. The planning process is a sequence of activities that, for many complex projects, lasts several years (Miller & Lessard, 2001). It gradually converts a vague idea, into a well-defined concept, and, eventually, into operational plans with detailed schedules of activities, allocation of people and resources, organizational charts, and artifact blueprints. The first variable about the process is inspired by the distinction decision theory makes between substantive and procedural rationality (Simon, 1978; Einhorn & Hogarth, 1981). This distinction echoes the concern of the project management literature with the uncertainty that precludes straightforward planning, and the ensuing advice to use more iterative or evolutionary processes (Boehm, 1988). Recent contributions in the field of innovation and strategic planning have linked the dynamics of planning processed to the knowledge available and used by planners (Gavetti & Levinthal, 2000; Krishnan et al., 1997). Hence, our first variable about the process captures its cognitive rationality, namely the way it uses and produces *knowledge*. At one extreme, a *conceptual* process takes advantage of preexisting generic models and data, including rules derived from experience with previous projects and develops the plan in a linear, deductive manner. At the other end, an *experimental* process produces specific knowledge as it goes, in a more inductive and iterative way, by observing other projects, trying various approaches, seeking feedback from concerned actors, and building and testing mockups and prototypes. A first effect on subsequent structuring comes from the fact that knowledge objects involved in these alternatives will have a different status. Conceptual processes activate knowledge and procedures that have already been bracketed as "facts" (Latour, 1987), with origins unavailable for scrutiny, and represented in normative rule-like forms, at times even imposed by regulation. Such objects are likely to play an inertial role in the actor-network. Moreover, if incorporated in the language base, because of its more generic but also more partial nature, such "theoretical" knowledge creates communicational couplings that cover more possibilities, but with less precise meaning and less clear systemic implications (Simondon, 1988; Nightingale, 1998; Fleming & Sorenson, 2004). Also, because it echoes the specialization of preexisting knowledge and assumes a more linear development, a conceptual process is more easily broken down into subproblems that are treated separately, and hence is less likely to create a kernel of taken for granted routines that connect a broad cross-section of project actors. By contrast, an experimental process is less likely to use punctualized knowledge and therefore it creates networks with fewer inertial "facts." Because it concerns the project in more specific and holistic ways, iterating between problem grasping and solving, it yields communication couplings that cover fewer possibilities but are more precise and signal, albeit not necessarily explain, more systemic interactions and ramifications. Its longer iteration, more holistic approach, and concrete feedback favor the development of encompassing routines and strong links between actors.

A second dimension of the planning process echoes old philosophical doubts about the existence of one single truth and rationality, or of many incommensurable belief systems and rationalities (Clegg, 1990; Law, 2004). In administrative sciences, this dilemma pervades many issues, from the relative effectiveness of institutions that centralize knowledge versus those that exploit distributed knowledge (Hayek, 1945) to resource and legitimacy dependence on external actors (Pfeffer & Salancik, 1978; Donaldson & Preston, 1995), and to recent concerns with pluralism and social responsibility (Eisenhardt, 2000; Campbell, 2007). The project management literature echoes these issues in its concern for stakeholder analysis (Cleland, 1986) and for the impact of institutional arrangements on project planning (Miller & Floricel, 2001). Therefore, our second variable reflects the social rationality of the planning process as expressed in the number and contribution of *participants*. On the one hand, *pluralist* processes involve, on equal footing, a large number of participants and stakeholders with distinct interests and viewpoints. On the other hand, in *centralized* planning, one actor clearly dominates the others. The influence of this variable on subsequent structuring begins with the fact that pluralist planning creates networks that are more ramified, because of the sheer number of players involved. Also they are more fragile, because all the compromises needed to accommodate their diverse interests give actors more chances to later find that project stimuli are, in fact, not attractive. Yet, the more protracted negotiations that occur in this kind of process (Denis et al., 2001) are also likely to create a kernel of interaction routines, which will be reproduced during structuring, because the stimuli put in place for various players require mutual adjustments and clarification. In addition, with so many perspectives scrutinizing the project, a pluralist planning process will likely produce richer language and meanings, and will make more effort to ensure that key portions of this language are shared by most participants (Dougherty, 1992). On the other hand, centralized planning, driven by an actor that already occupies a "compulsory passage point" (Callon, 1986), will more likely aim to anchor the other actors around the project in ways that mirror a functional hierarchy. Instead of a language shared by all participants, the communication ecosystem will evolve bilateral couplings between the dominant actor and the actors responsible for each function.

However, planning also influences structuring via the objects it creates—namely the plan and related documents such as charts and contracts. As these outcomes become actors in the project network, their *contents* stimulate actors, suggest interaction scripts, and set the bases of project language. A first distinction about these objects echoes another philosophical conundrum about the nature of goals. At least since Hume (1748), thinkers have argued that goals cannot be deduced from knowledge about the reality, and called attention to the primacy of subjectivity and volition (Polanyi, 1966). Administrative sciences echoed these calls in Weber's (1968) view of bureaucracy as perfecting the rationality of means with little regard to goals, and in the tradeoff that decision theory and strategy see between perfecting goals and optimizing decision procedures (Keeney, 1994). These issues are also central in the project management literature; for example, the focus on the "fuzzy front end" of projects (Williams & Samset, 2010), particularly for radical innovation, in which both probabilities and goals are difficult to ascertain (Reid & de Brentani, 2004); the role of leadership (Turner & Müller, 2005); the ability to "sell" projects (Lampel, 2001); and risk management (Chapman & Ward, 1996). Furthermore, these issues appear in studies that found systematic benefit overestimation and cost underestimation in complex projects and suggest that plans are used as symbolic tools to gain support for such projects (Merrow, 1988; Boehm & Pappacio, 1988; Flyvbjerg, Holm, & Buhl, 2002; Flyvbjerg et al., 2006). Even a recent surge of interest in "project offices," which develop and enforce standard project management procedures in organizations, can be seen as a shift in emphasis from defining goals to rationalizing means (Aubry, Hobbs, & Thuillier, 2007). Thus, a first dimension captures the cognitive rationality of the *argument* that a plan provides for subsequent decisions and actions. On the one hand, *promotional* plans stress project goals by appealing to emotions and values, while providing partial, selective, and fuzzy arguments to back them. On the other hand, *decisional* plans emphasize the means by rationalizing project prospects and risks based on available knowledge about the relevant reality and its relation to the achievement of project goals and by presenting arguments in as clear, objective, and complete manner as possible (Langley, 1989). The use of promotional plans is likely to entail more important deviations during the structuring process, as initial, more appealing, stimuli are corrected by downgrading benefits, adding overlooked costs and risks, and redistributing them between participants. Schemas, trajectories, and interaction scripts are renegotiated as well to integrate unforeseen participants and perform unanticipated activities. The language and meaning of communications are also likely to shift from a moral and emotional discourse to more neutral technical terms. The likelihood that these elements will become punctualized, taken for granted, or routine, and therefore inertial, is lower because of their constant upheaval. On the other hand, a decisional plan is likely to set projects on less deviant trajectories, but to concurrently create emergent structures with higher inertia ("iron cages").

Finally, a second, more social dimension of plan contents reflects an equally old conundrum about human nature, whether it is fundamentally good (trustworthy, hardworking, farsighted) or not. Economics, whose answers are rather negative, responded with the belief that consequences can be prevented or mitigated by designing appropriate contract forms (Holmstrom, 1979; Williamson, 1981). Similarly, administrative sciences emphasized dominative structures that clearly define tasks and allocate responsibilities and rely on close supervision to ensure performance and coordination (Burns & Stalker, 1961). However, more recently, organization and strategy scholars with a more positive view of the conundrum argued that shared responsibilities and collaborative processes activate the distributed knowledge needed for innovation and enable adaptation in dynamic environments (Prahalad & Hamel, 1990; Dougherty, 2001). In the project management literature, the negative answer translated in an emphasis on operational planning and on the new contractual frameworks described in the introduction. The positive answer led to practices such as partnering (Naoum, 2003) that stimulate collaboration between participants. Hence, this dimension deals with the social rationality of the measures that the plan proposes for addressing project *risk*. At one extreme, *allocative* plans purport to minimize the residual risk for project owners and financial partners by strictly delimiting responsibility areas and "pushing" the respective risks to other participants via fixed-price and sole-responsibility contracts. At the other extreme, *integrative* plans propose to minimize risk by ensuring that participants trust each other, exchange knowledge and information, and collaborate fully. In such plans, owners support all risks or share the burden with other participants via cost-plus contracts or relational agreements, such as joint ventures or long-term framework agreements (Davies, Gann, & Douglas, 2009; Macneil, 1978; Williamson, 1981; Hobbs & Andersen, 2001). Allocative plans propose a network of punctualized stimuli and interlocked interests and aim to create a surrogate of stability for the project duration. While subsequent structuration may show that this goal is unrealistic, these stimuli instill inertia in the actor-network. In addition, they induce adversarial typifications between contractual parties and interaction routines that weaken the links between them (Floricel & Miller, 2001). Communication couplings tend to be restricted to prescribed information and presented in a format that is meaningful from a contractual perspective. Integrative plans, on the other hand, create stimuli that need constant negotiation, for example by letting parties work together to define contractual specifications, technical solutions and costs, and therefore increase the chances that they will develop stronger links and richer communication couplings.

Of course, the choice between the alternatives provided by each of the four dimensions is to some extent contingent on the initial project context. For example, project novelty or technological and institutional innovativeness favor an experimental process because the needed knowledge is not available (Shenhar, 2001).

In contrast, a stable context, such as that of regulated monopolies, preserves the relevance of past knowledge and favors a conceptual process (Hirsh, 1989). Likewise, projects that touch on many interests and raise sensitive issues, are likely to trigger social, regulatory, or political scrutiny, as well as those that depend on rare external resources favor pluralistic planning. Also, urgent needs and narrow opportunity windows favor promotional plans, while strict procedures, criteria and oversight imposed by external regulation or internal rules will favor decisional plans. Similarly, the obligation to deal with less well-known or less reputable partners will favor allocative plans, while a history of collaboration may favor integrative plans. Despite these tendencies, planners still have a leeway in the choice between alternative approaches (Verganti, 1999). For example, they can strategize to buffer the project from institutional interference (Oliver, 1991), acquire or develop internally the required resources (Floricel & Miller, 2001), build symbolic fronts, for example by emphasizing the leaders' foresight, or follow procedures only ceremonially (Goffman, 1958; Meyer & Rowan, 1977).

3. Properties of Emergent Structure and Response Capacity

As argued in Chapter 1, response capacity refers to the embedded characteristics of the emergent project structure that influence the reaction to unexpected events and subsequent success. These properties were deduced by a logical analysis of conditions for an efficient response and inspired by the project management literature (Floricel & Miller, 2001). First, if unexpected events produce a discontinuity between "before" and "after" (Luhmann, 1993) in actors' perceptions of project stimuli, it is normal that many early reactions are centrifugal (Hirschmann, 1970). At best, participants simulate support to the project, but reallocate efforts and resources elsewhere; in the worst case, they attempt to exit, blame others, and minimize losses at their expense. Others can imitate or counter such reactions, triggering conflicts and paralyzing the reaction at the project level. Hence, the first condition for an effective response is the *cohesion* of the project organization. Second, if this condition is satisfied, the response often requires the re-opening or revising of project elements (Söderholm, 2008). The ability to change them depends on the *flexibility* of the project system, another response capacity property that we deem important (Bettis & Hitt, 1995). Finally, participants require ideas, skilled personnel, funds, and other resources in order to develop and implement new viable courses of action. Thus, a third response capacity property is the *resourcefulness* (Thomas, 1996) of the project organization. The variables corresponding to these properties are detailed in the following. They were built by assuming that projects face only a few major events in terms of participant surprise and potential impact. Therefore, the variables distinguish the characteristics that enable projects to respond to regular events, forming a more ordinary response capacity, from those enabling the project to respond to major events, forming a superior response capacity, which supports an effective response in almost any circumstance and degree of impact severity. The presentation of response capacity variables contrasts the properties that enable these two levels of response.

Cohesion refers to the extent that participants are likely to remain loyal to the project and jointly seek solutions to the problems caused by unexpected events, rather than succumb to opportunistic or panic-inspired centrifugal tendencies

(Hirschmann, 1970). We further assume that cohesion can result from adhesion or coercion. In turn, *adhesive cohesion* can have a *pragmatic* origin, in the presence of stimuli that are robust enough to preserve participants' interest after the unexpected event. In other words, the intertwined network of stimuli and interests still gives those wanting to save the project the possibility to convince others that participation will be profitable or to depict the project as a compulsory passage point, say, because of the impact it may have on their reputation. However, a detached calculative attitude, assumed by the pragmatic cohesion mechanism, is not likely to withstand major unexpected events that severely impact expected project benefits. Moreover, psychology research suggests that the perception of project stimuli does not deteriorate gradually, with the realization that project problems cannot be solved, but shifts suddenly from hope and adhesion to a new reference point in which actors fear their own demise and are ready to take any radical step to avoid it (Lopes, 1987; March & Shapira, 1992). Such sudden shifts can trigger a chain reaction from other actors, and a disintegration spiral for the entire network. Therefore, pragmatic adhesion only provides an ordinary cohesion level. In our view, stronger cohesion results if actors are *embedded* in a network of strong links, with routines that focus on solving problems, rather than blaming others, and favor open information exchange and deep personal involvement (Granovetter, 1985). Rather than feeling left to face consequences on their own, embedded actors perceive a security net, trusting the reactions of other actors and expecting reciprocity from them (Gulati, 1995; Uzzi, 1997; Poppo & Zenger, 2002). The more such expectations and routines are taken for granted, based on past cooperation, the stronger their resilience to post-event unfreezing and the likelihood that they will shape, from the outset, the actors' reflexive response to the event. A favorable structuring condition for embedded adhesion is a pattern of interactions between actors that is more intense and more encompassing, but also relatively stable.

If some participants do not adhere to the project on their own, they can also be *coerced* against their will, for example, by threatening legal action or other credible sanctions. Typically, coercion is enabled by a contract that includes important penalties and by a functioning legal environment. However, initial contractual couplings can acquire different emergent properties function of the relevant structuring processes. At one extreme, a low-deviation process takes contracts negotiated during planning as given and avoids reopening them, except when needed to coerce actors. This *formal* structure can be justified on grounds that it avoids diluting the symbolic stimulus and the strength of contractual levers in subsequent negotiations. Nevertheless, empirical evidence shows that coerced participants often engage in all-out confrontation and hold projects hostage in lengthy legal battles (von Branconi & Loch, 2004). Formalism increases the chances that this would happen. First, actors who are denied the opportunity to discuss the contract will more likely categorize it as a negative stimulus and would increase their preparations for an eventual litigation. Second, with fewer interaction opportunities, no routines will emerge for conveying mutual expectations and concerns as circumstances evolve, which increases the chances that post-event coercion will be seen as unfair because its onslaught appears more sudden and its locus of control is seen as external (Billings, Milburn, & Schaalman, 1980). Finally, with fewer episodes during which the contractual language and meaning are discussed, there is a higher chance that some event-related interpretation will remain ambiguous, providing a pretext for legal wrangling. Hence, a formal path provides an ordinary level of cohesion only.

The other possibility is a *governed* coercive structure, in which participants (mainly the owner) exert a constant effort to clarify the language and meaning of objects expressing binding commitments between participants, such as contracts and agreements, or of compulsory actions (procedures, instructions). This property may be rooted in a formal dispute resolution process, but it consists of routines and practices that enrich and adjust initial agreements and partitions, such as regular meetings to clarify and record new commitments and to interpret and renegotiate responsibilities, etc. (Stinchcombe & Heimer, 1985; Poppo & Zenger, 2002). The emergence of this property is facilitated by a more deviant structuring process. In turn, it not only reduces the ambiguity of the contractual coupling but leads to perceptions of contract stimuli, such as post-event potential losses and liabilities, as more equitable and less surprising, which legitimates coercive action in the eyes of affected actors. Hence, governed structures provide a stronger coercive cohesion.

Flexibility refers to the freedom that a structure allows for acting in the face of unexpected events, namely to change the project goals, schedule, market strategy, technical solutions, participants, contracts, capabilities and organization. It also has two varieties, configurational and sequential. *Configurational* flexibility is a property inspired by the literature on technical and organizational architectures (Baldwin & Clark, 2000; Sanchez & Mahoney, 1996) as well as that on boundary objects (Star & Griesemer, 1989), which captures the extent to which activities in different parts of a project can be carried on independently of each other. Akin to loose coupling (Orton & Weick, 1990) or modularity (Simon, 1981; Ulrich, 1995), it frees "local" action by preventing the propagation of consequences to the entire project. Its opposite, tight coupling or integration, is caused by major task, resource or technical interactions between parts of the project (Eppinger et al., 1994; Schilling, 2000). This kind of flexibility can be planned in technical, financial, and contractual design, but emergent structuring also affects this property. In less deviant structuring, actors consider objects resulting from planning as well as preexisting technical, capability and (inter)organizational fault lines as given, producing isomorphic networks that ensure an *implicit* separation and coordination of actions (Sanchez & Mahoney, 1996; Galunic & Eisenhardt, 2001). However, this kind of separation provides an ordinary flexibility level, because it tends to reproduce reflexively the fault lines included in "punctualized" objects, such as blueprints, contracts, and organizational charts, and in received "facts," such as the customary way capabilities are divided in sectors and firms. One example is the typical separation of roles and capabilities between project owners and contractors for a project, which not only cuts across important interactions but also hampers the flows of knowledge across contractual interfaces. Particular bidding processes and contract forms may even institutionalize this fault line in a given firm and sector (Hobbs & Andersen, 2001). Other examples include communication couplings embedded in information systems, which assume a certain partition of competencies and mediate the interactions between groups of actors in selective or even distorted ways. However, major events probe more deeply or alter in subtle ways the interactions between different parts of a project (Henderson & Clark, 1990), and prompt participants to find new ways of isolating the affected activities into a self-contained subset and to buffer the rest of the project from changes made in this subset (Söderholm, 2008). Rethinking separation is more effective or even possible at all if, during structuring, participants develop and constantly adjust a rich shared language and meanings about key project interactions, maintain strong ties that span across implicit activity divides, including contractual interfaces, and question routinely the overall technical and organizational architecture of the project (Hansen, 1999; Dougherty, 2001). If they become ingrained in the project organization, such ties, routines, and couplings enable a more *heedful* coordination between participants even in the wake of major events that trigger reflexive responses (Weick & Roberts, 1993; O'Sullivan, 2003).

If a confined response is unfeasible, projects can also attempt a holistic one, or even search iteratively for complete solutions. *Sequential* flexibility, the property that enables such responses, was inspired by the strategic literature on innovative and dynamic environments (Thomke & Reinertsen, 1998). It refers to the extent that post-event actions are unrestricted by past decisions and commitments. Its opposite is path-dependency, in which case change is difficult or requires an important lead-time because of high sunk and switching costs. This kind of flexibility can be built in a *proactive* manner, even from the planning stage, by scheduling some decisions as late as possible, reducing irreversible commitments, and proactively cultivating alternate options for action (McGrath, 1997; MacCormack, Verganti, & Iansiti, 2001). As discussed in the introduction, a particular source of rigidity can be a long-term, fixed-price contract with predefined specifications. Therefore, a cost-plus contract, as well as other ways of uncoupling the future from past decisions, such as contractual mechanisms for processing change orders that define how the cost of changes should be determined and how the responsibility for supporting them should be apportioned, can reduce rigidity. However, proactive sequential flexibility grows out of specific measures and depends on the imperfect anticipative capacity of actors, whereas major events are surprising and usually fall outside the areas covered by such measures. This means that proactive measures only provide an ordinary flexibility level. The alternative is the emergence, during structuring, of an *agile* organization. Its properties consist of networks that include polyvalent and experienced practitioners who can rapidly detect an event and assess the post-event situation; of practices that enable timely and speedy decisions; and of interaction routines that delegate the decisional authority or enable actors to rapidly escalate an issue, even across contractual interfaces, to the hierarchical levels or actors with the appropriate powers (Eisenhardt, 1989b; Jelinek & Schoonhoven, 1990; Volberda, 1996). Other factors include cultural assumptions that value the readiness to change rather than focusing on the past, as well as language and meanings with enough richness and nuance to enable actors to detect deviations and convey them fully across communicational couplings.

Resourcefulness is the response capacity component related to the ability to identify actions that would most effectively address the unexpected event and to make available significant additional resources for implementing these actions (Thomas, 1996). Resourcefulness has two components as well: sustaining and creating. *Sustaining* resourcefulness captures the ability of the project organization to provide funding, skilled personnel, and other rare resources for the additional activities needed to respond to the event. In most cases, these activities are an obvious extension of the regular project activities that were going on before the event, such as building an additional structure. One possibility is for such resources to be accumulated inside the project. The *cumulative* process can be initiated in the planning phase, for example, by including contingencies and other reserves in the project budget and by providing cost-saving stimuli and allowing economies to be retained as reserves. It can also be expressed in the emergent structure, through practices that help participants increase the efficiency of their work and via interaction routines that set aside and enable the reallocation of savings to other activities. However, such reserves rarely attain 30 percent of the budget of complex projects, whereas responding to major events frequently requires 50 percent and more additional funding (Floricel & Miller, 2001). Therefore, cumulative processes provide only an ordinary level of sustaining resourcefulness. Much larger amounts of additional funds and rare resources can be acquired if the emergent project structure can absorb new resources, including by redrawing project boundaries. This *absorptive* capacity (a term inspired by Cohen & Levinthal, 1990, but used with another sense here) depends on the development during structuring of a project network with direct links to powerful actors and stakeholders (Burt, 1992). However, it also relies on a practice of manipulating symbolically the project stimuli in ways that can convince these actors to significantly supplement project resources. These abilities are enhanced by the emergence of routines for evaluating resource needs in real time and of interaction scripts that facilitate the resource flows between participants (Zahra & George, 2002). But when an obvious extension of current project activities is not sufficient for solving the problems posed by the event, the project can rely on *creating* resourcefulness, namely on its ability to propose novel solutions. One way this goal can be achieved is by *exploring* the external environment for a ready-made solution or for specialists that can develop one. This capacity is expressed in the project network by a combination of internal actors that are sufficiently skilled and experienced to recognize and understand useful ideas and competencies, and, on the other hand, of many links to a diversity of external actors (Burt, 1992; Miliken & Martins, 1996; Hargadon & Sutton, 1997). However, such external solutions and skills may simply not be available, which means that exploring provides only an ordinary creative resourcefulness.

The capacity to develop original solutions internally, by combining the available knowledge, skill, and ideas, can cover a broader range of eventualities and solve problems that are more complex. However, in the wake of major events, time pressures and stress create communication problems and favor conformism. Thus, such *innovative* capabilities depend, on the one hand, on the emergence during structuring of a strong capacity to combine various contributions, including external as well as internal ideas. In terms of network, this capacity consists of strong ties that cut across not only organizational boundaries, but also across professional groups, age cohorts, and other fault lines. These ties help develop a common understanding of problems and of other actors' contributions and enable the transfer of complex and tacit knowledge (Brown & Duguid, 1991; Dougherty, 1992; Hansen, 1999; Simonin, 1999; Reagans & Zuckerman, 2001). The constitution of these ties relies in part on an effort to build and work around objects that provide common representations of problems and solutions in ways that are, fully or in essence, self-evident to all participants (Carlile, 2002; Ewenstein & Whyte, 2009). On the other hand, to counter conformism, the emergent structure includes a network with a broad mix of actor knowledge and skills, practices that give participants the occasion to express their ideas freely and confidently, and stimuli that reward risk taking (Woodman, Sawyer, & Griffin 1993; Amabile, Conti, Coon, Lazenby, & Herron, 1996).

In conclusion, it is important to reiterate that on the side of pragmatic adhesive cohesion and formal coercive cohesion, implicit configurational flexibility and anticipatory sequential flexibility, as well as cumulative sustaining resourcefulness and searching creative resourcefulness properties are more related to planning and subsequent anticipation and suppose a less deviant (iron cage) structuring process. However, they usually work only for anticipated eventualities and regular unanticipated events. However, they do not allow a response to major events, or cause the project to settle for partial or suboptimal responses. The properties at the opposite end of each variable (in italics in Figure 2-1), which enable an optimal response to major events, result from more deviant structuring processes and are more ingrained as well as more distributed in networks, routines and couplings.

4. Project Performance

As Figure 1-1 suggests, the reaction to unexpected events, conditioned by the emergent structure and its response capacity, has a significant impact on project performance. However, such performance has several aspects, and the different components of the response capacity, as well as where a project is situated with respect to the extremes of each variable, may influence each aspect differently. One distinction with respect to performance is between short-term aspects, which can be evaluated upon project completion, and long-term aspects that become fully clear during its exploitation. In addition, performance may concern the benefits that the project creates, or the resource expenditures that were needed in order to obtain these benefits. Hence, we distinguish four typical performance dimensions: two short-term and two long-term. In each pair, one mostly emphasizes a cost aspect, and the other, a value aspect. *Completion* performance refers to the degree to which the resulting artifact is finished, compared to the initial scope, and whether execution duration and cost are below those anticipated initially. The *technical* dimension refers to whether, in light of initial targets, the project achieves all its functions, with a high level of capacity, efficiency, and other valuable characteristics, as well as innovativeness. The *operational* dimension concerns the degree to which the cost of operating and maintaining the project in the exploitation phase is below anticipations, as captured by its long-term reliability and ease of operation. The *value* dimension refers to the extent to which the benefits provided to sponsors, clients, and stakeholders are above those expected in planning. It is captured by the profitability and strategic positioning possibilities it provides for sponsors as well as by the social satisfaction with the project.

5. Preliminary Hypotheses About Influence Trajectories

All components are now in place that would allow us to connect theoretically the planning, response capacity and performance moments of a project. As mentioned in the Introduction, our main theoretical assumption is that a significant proportion of the influence that planning exerts on performance is indirect and mostly unintended, namely through its effect on the ability of the project organization to deal with unexpected events. Therefore, the following hypotheses present these theoretical connections in the form of influence trajectories (akin to the statistical concepts of mediator or path), which start with a planning variable, go through the most affected response capacity variables, and end with specific performance variables.

Knowledge. The way the planning process produces and uses knowledge is likely to affect the response capacity variables that are affected by knowledge coupling and interaction routines, namely the configurational flexibility and the creative resourcefulness of the emergent structure. When discussing planning, we mentioned that conceptual processes open fewer knowledge black boxes and follow the usual knowledge partitions. Therefore, they are less likely to create encompassing kernels of interaction that would eventually translate into richer language coupling and more intense knowledge sharing practices needed to attain heedful configurational flexibility. In turn, relying on implicit configurational flexibility diminishes the capacity to contain the changes needed in order to respond to the unexpected event. This will affect the completion performance by increasing the cost and duration of technical and organizational changes that need to be made in order to provide an effective response, as well as operational performance, because unsuspected interactions with the portions left unchanged in light of an implicit partition show up later and affect the project reliability and operability. By contrast, an experimental planning approach increases the configurational flexibility of the emergent structure, which enables confining the changes to a relatively small portion of the project and results in lower cost and shorter schedules, as well as better operational performance.

The second likely consequence of the knowledge aspect of planning is on creative resourcefulness. Conceptual planning is predicated on the idea that valid external knowledge exists, that it can be adapted to the project needs without opening the black boxes, and that planning outcomes based in such knowledge can be readily combined with other elements of the project concept. Such beliefs are more likely to translate into a practice of seeking external knowledge and expertise in the face of problems, and in problem solving routines that search for readymade solutions. By contrast, experimental planning is likely to produce specific concepts, for which little external expertise exists, and reduces the chances of finding relevant external solutions and expertise. Moreover, the initial interactions kernel is more likely to translate in internally-oriented problem solving routines and in networks that span internal fault lines, which are both typical for innovating creative resourcefulness. The consequences of the higher creating resourcefulness that emerges from experimental planning are more specific and better-integrated solutions, leading to an increase in the technical and value performance of the project. These considerations can be translated in the following trajectory hypotheses originating in the knowledge aspect of planning:

Hypothesis 1: Trajectory 1.1—Experimental planning is likely to increase the chances of emergence of heedful configurational flexibility, which, in turn, is likely to increase the completion and operational performance of the project.

Trajectory 1.2—Experimental planning is likely to increase the chances of emergence of innovative creating resourcefulness, which, in turn, is likely to affect positively the technical and value creation performance of the project.

Participation. The participation aspect of the planning process is likely to affect the response capacity aspects related to the nature of networks, namely the coercive cohesion and the creative resourcefulness. A pluralist planning creates a wider network but makes its links more fragile because the stimuli are not always clear, given the compromises required to bring the network together initially. However, this fragility is likely to have the paradoxical structuring outcome of forcing participants to repeatedly discuss their agreements to clarify and record their expectations and commitments. These discussions will likely induce governed coercive cohesion in the emergent project structure, with practices and routines such as regular meetings to clarify agreements, solve conflicts and balance burdens. In contrast, centralized planning is less likely to encourage contractual governance practices, because dominant players fear that, by discussing contracts, they weaken the levers enabling them to control other participants, in addition to giving the latter a chance to negotiate better terms.

In terms of performance, formal coercion, more likely in dominated projects, increases the likelihood that contractors will perceive the repartition of liabilities after a major event as being unjust and will engage in protracted legal battles, which will delay execution and will increase costs. This means that the completion performance of dominated projects is lower. Operational performance is also likely to be lower, because the dominant player will be forced to replace recalcitrant participants on the fly with other contractors, who may not have the same knowledge of the project. On the other hand, pluralist projects and the governed coercion they induce have more chances to avoid court battles and ensure participant cooperation in finding a solution to post-event problems, which would ensure superior completion and operational performance.

The second influence of participation is likely to result from the number of perspectives it brings to bear on the project. The higher number of such perspectives in pluralist planning leads to a richer language about the project. However, it also makes the creation of a nexus of shared symbols and meaning more critical for coordination, because no participant is a hub of communication flows. One way of achieving such shared symbols is by creating objects that carry self-evident symbolic, semantic, and coordinative implications for most other players (Carlile, 2002). These practices are likely to be reproduced during the structuring process, as subsequent entrants bring additional perspectives or dispute earlier views, bringing further nuance into the shared language and creating interaction routines that span the various fault lines between participants. Therefore, pluralist planning is likely to result in emergent structures with a higher internal diversity of perspectives and with links and couplings that are more able to convey complex knowledge, which means that they will be more likely to rely on innovative creating resourcefulness.

In contrast, in structures resulting from centralized planning, one actor will play the role of a coordinative hub between other participants, with fewer direct links cutting across organizational fault lines, and a smaller portion of the language will be shared by all participants. Instead, the practice of interacting with participants with different competencies will prepare the dominant player for seeking ready-made solutions or actors with the required problem-solving skills outside the project organization, which means that emergent structures resulting from centralized planning are more likely to rely on explorative creating resourcefulness.

In terms of performance, as mentioned previously, innovative creating resourcefulness will likely increase the technical and value creation performance of the project. These arguments can be translated in the following hypothesis about the trajectories that result from the participation aspect of planning.

Hypothesis 2: Trajectory 2.1—Pluralistic planning increases the chances of emergence of governed coercive cohesion, which, in turn, is likely to affect positively the completion and the operational performance of the project.

Trajectory 2.2—Pluralistic planning increases the chances of emergence of innovative creating resourcefulness, which, in turn, is likely to affect positively the technical and the value creation performance of the project.

Argument. Because it reflects the degree to which the plan justifies action with arguments about means-ends relation, it is likely that the nature of the argument will affect the response capacity variables that involve anticipation, namely sequential flexibility and sustaining resourcefulness. A decisional plan includes a more realistic assessment of risks, and therefore, it is more likely to include the options for alternative action, which are typical of proactive sequential flexibility. Moreover, because planned actions are solidly legitimated with knowledge about the means-ends relations, a decisional plan is also more likely to become a "black-boxed" object and to translate during structuring in a series of taken for granted assumptions about project elements and participants, building an anticipatory iron cage likely to resist the unfreezing by the event.

On the other hand, by setting subsequent structuring on a more deviant trajectory, a promotional plan is more likely to establish the fast decision-making routines that are typical for the agile end. Emergent structures with proactive sequential flexibility are likely to respond well to a broad array of events, most of which are minor, but could prove unable to instigate the wholesale restructuring of the project that is needed for most major unanticipated events. Used to orient action function of the anticipatory iron cage, project participants are likely to cling to past solutions and be unable to decide on an integrated wholesale change, typical of sequential flexibility, leading to a response that will be suboptimal in some aspects. On the other hand, projects with promotional plans start very early in structuring to revise their scope and activities. This enables the development of decisional routines. Moreover, because the language of the plan focuses participants on the attainment of overall goals or even on value, rather than on particular means, it is easier for these decisions to legitimate wholesale changes to the project. In terms of impact on performance, because they try to stick with a past coherent solution, projects with decisional plans perform well in terms of technical performance. However, because they will find it more difficult to effect a major restructuring, this solution will likely diminish the long-term value creation performance of the project. On the other hand, the technical solutions of the projects with promotional plans will tend to be somewhat improvised in the wake of unexpected events, which would suggest a lower technical performance, but they will also be more coherent with some overarching goal, which explains their higher value creation performance in the long-term.

The second impact of the plan argument occurs via sustaining resourcefulness. A decisional plan is more likely to make a realistic assessment of project costs and value creation, which means that sufficient funds as well as contingency reserves or cost-saving incentives are more likely to be included from the beginning. Furthermore, the project will have the necessary resources to respond to both minor events and to some major ones. However, because participants consider the project to be self-sufficient, it is unlikely that during structuring the project network will grow the necessary links to actors able to provide the significantly larger amount of resources needed to deal with major events, or that it will develop the stimuli manipulation practices that convince these actors to invest such amounts. By contrast, promotional plans will not provide enough funds but will create very early occasions for seeking additional resources, and hence for the emergence of the necessary links and practices. In terms of performance, the response of projects with decisional plans will be confined by the presence of a large yet fixed resource envelope. Such projects can have a good completion performance, because the envelope is likely to be sufficient for executing the initial scope of the project within the anticipated time. However, the project is not likely to have a good operational performance, because it will likely be unable to add significant new elements that appear as necessary after the unexpected event. By contrast, a promotional project will have a lower completion performance, because it will be delayed by the need to seek additional resources. However, it will be more likely to supplement the project scope with all previously unforeseen elements or even support a major restructuring of the scope. These considerations translate in the following hypothesis about the plan argument.

Hypothesis 3: Trajectory 3.1—A decisional plan increases the chances of emergence of proactive sequential flexibility, which, in turn, is likely to affect positively the technical performance but to affect negatively the value performance.

Trajectory 3.2—A promotional plan increases the chances of emergence of absorptive sustaining resourcefulness, which, in turn, is likely to affect negatively the completion performance but to affect positively the operational performance.

Risk. The way a plan addresses the project risks is likely to alter the network links, interaction routines, and language couplings that emerge from structuring in ways that are likely to affect the adhesive cohesion and the configurational flexibility of the project. An allocative plan is likely to create an intertwined network of stimuli for actor performance. However, it is also likely to lead to categorizations of other actors as having conflicting interests. In addition, the structuration processes that stem from allocative plans hinder embeddedness because they parcel work, induce actors to refer to the plan rather than to each other, and foster calculative routines because of the liabilities that each party is likely to bear. Therefore, allocative plans are likely to lead to project structures with pragmatic adhesive cohesion. In turn, integrative plans favor the categorization of other actors as having converging interests and generate more frequent interactions and reciprocity situations between participants, stimulating the emergence of the stronger links and the more problem-oriented culture typical for embedded adhesive cohesion. Given a diligent allocation of risk, the network of stimuli resulting from an allocative plan is robust enough to enable a project to deal effectively with many minor and even some major unexpected events. However, most major events fall outside the range of eventualities covered by this allocation; many stimuli are likely to become unattractive in these conditions, limiting project cohesion. In terms of performance, such projects are likely to result in lower technical performance, because of lower efforts by uncooperative participants, and lower value creation performance, because finding a solution to the event may call for compromises with respect to the initial project goals.

The second way that the risk approach included in the plan affects the project performance is via the configurational flexibility. Allocative plans are likely to set up a modular organization, because it is difficult to pinpoint responsibilities without, first, separating tasks in chunks that are as autonomous as possible from those of other participants. However, the project will be most likely divided in chunks that correspond to historic fault lines and contractor capabilities but not necessarily to the project needs. Moreover, the interfaces created by such allocation will likely restrict communications to aspects that are required procedurally or contractually. This blocks the development during structuring of coordination routines that help participants understand the interactions between different parts of the project (Hobbs & Andersen, 2001). Therefore, an allocative plan is likely to foster a structure with implicit configurational flexibility. On the other hand, an integrative plan is more likely to stimulate the emergence of heedful routines that are more likely to help participants redraw activities in ways that allow a local response to the event and buffer the rest of the project. In terms of performance, heedful configurational flexibility is likely to increase the completion and operational performance of the project. These considerations can be summarized in the following hypotheses:

Hypothesis 4: Trajectory 4.1—An integrative plan increases the chances of emergence of embedded adhesive cohesion, which, in turn, is likely to affect positively the technical performance and the value performance of the project.

Trajectory 4.2—An integrative plan increases the chances of emergence of heedful configurational flexibility, which, in turn, is likely to affect positively the completion performance and the operational performance of the project.

The hypotheses result primarily from considerations about similarity of contents and mechanisms between the elements of planning and response capacity. But, given the multiplicity of social mechanisms and the complexity of structuring and response processes that our theory assumes, these considerations have to be validated and refined by means of longitudinal empirical research before attempting to test them in a cross-sectional manner. The results of these tests and the refined hypotheses that they produced, will be presented in the next chapter. However, the theoretical development presented in this chapter produced several interesting conclusions presented in the next section.

6.   Discussion and Conclusions

One outcome of the theory development effort outlined in the preceding chapters is a higher confidence in the argument that planning influences performance through the deviant trajectories of subsequent structuring. More specifically, if the three mechanisms described in Chapter 1 are valid, planning is likely to result in an emergent structure with unintended and often unexpected properties, which will affect its ability to respond to the unexpected events that invariably affect complex projects. This possibility has a number of implications for project management research, particularly for research on the planning of complex projects.

First, it justifies the recent trend of approaching the subject with a non-normative perspective, which focuses on describing in detail the concrete planning practices used in such projects. This is supported by the assumption, which underlies our planning variables, that there are multiple facets to, and forms of, planning activities and plans. However, these variables also suggest carrying a more in-depth inquiry into the drivers of planning practices, such as various social beliefs about the rationality of social action. As the relatively low number of variables we use suggests, this inquiry may help researchers make sense of the diversity of practices and move beyond critical description toward more predictive theories.

A second implication for project management research is at the core of an eventual advance toward prediction—namely, the studies of planning would benefit from an effort to understand its true impact via an inquiry that would do away with the implicit assumption of the normative functional approach that planning determines subsequent activities and would focus on social processes as they unfold in project organizations. Our theory suggests that planning influences are multiple and complex, but they are still intelligible and amenable to theorizing. The three mechanisms introduced in Chapter 1, even if their conceptualization is still schematic and their interactions are yet to be fully understood, provide workable tools for theoretical analysis and empirical research on planning influences and subsequent processes. Each of these mechanisms opens the way to incorporating theoretical insights from other disciplines, but in a more sophisticated way, which would combine them with other explanations rather than considering a single aspect as an all-explaining law. For example, the stimuli of the actor-network mechanism open the way for insights from economics, the structuration mechanism opens the way to insights from various institutional theories, and the communication ecosystem mechanism is an avenue for accommodating insights from different system theories without losing sight of the social nature of processes. In terms of practical implications, this kind of research will map and increase awareness about what we call "second order implications" of any planning approach or practice.

The third implication for project management research concerns the life cycle patterns in project. The main conclusion derived from the application of our theoretical framework is that deviation from plans and ongoing structuring is the reality of projects, before and after unexpected events. For example, both the actor-network mechanism, which focuses on tradeoffs and on the fragile intertwining of project stimuli, and the structuration mechanism with its emphasis on marginal awareness and unintended consequences, give good reasons for a divergent evolution of projects. The communication ecosystems mechanism suggests convergence, but this convergence is evolutionary, with random variation and selection based on project survival rather than plan at its core. When adding unexpected events and responses conditioned in subtle ways by the emergent structure, the picture of project life cycle loses all resemblance with the traditional view of a plan that determines in a teleological way the activities and performance of a project. Therefore, it is important to continue to study projects from a descriptive process perspective and to include the consequences of almost continual macroeconomic, institutional, and sectoral transformations as well as the ongoing restructuring of the broader organizations and coalitions that sponsor the project among the key interest areas. In these conditions, project management is no longer the implementation of a plan but a continual steering of the project toward an acceptable conclusion. Closer attention to the concrete practices used to steer projects at the juncture of structural capabilities emerging from past actions and of events thrown at the project by the unfolding future will help advance theory in this respect.

This last observation opens the way for discussing the wider implications of our theoretical development, which we begin by first addressing implications for strategy. If it is assumed as we did following a strand of dynamic capabilities research that capabilities are embedded in ordinary organizational practices and processes, or, more broadly speaking, distributed all across the organizational structure, then strategy can be seen as a balancing act between building such capabilities through a process that is largely unintended, and leveraging the resulting sources of competitive advantage via deliberate actions that develop, consolidate and capture value. This balancing act attempts to anticipate the future, but it also has to cope with continuous deviations in organizational structure, as suggested by the three mechanisms discussed in Chapter 1, and with continuous change in the relevant external environments, such as market, technological, institutional and social. Compared to the previous conceptualizations, where organizational structures are reduced to the iron cage of markets and assets or, at best, are seen as path dependent "positions" that condition dynamic capabilities, this view sees strategy as more fluid yet dealing with quite stable underlying logics. The understanding of these logics and the way they condition action is one of the best chances for creating a predictive link between the strategic intent and the performance outcomes.

This brings us to the second set of broader implications, which concerns organization theory. The study of complex projects is an extraordinary laboratory for the study of organizations in general, because it allows researchers to disentangle intention, with its underlying rationality, from action with its structuring mechanisms. One fruitful avenue for organization theory is to consider the same mechanisms but ask what is different in ongoing organizations. Are mechanisms such as the thoughtless reproduction of past structures or selection by organizational imperatives dominant over the more generative manipulation and negotiation of the actor-network mechanism, or on the contrary, the deviant components of all three mechanisms produce continuous structuring, transforming organizations into continuously unfolding complex projects? Our theoretical development suggests, in line with the views that highlight the improvisational nature and the continual adjustment of practices, that the second answer is closer to the reality of contemporary organizations.

The final implications are metatheoretical. The way the mechanismic approach worked out in our theoretical development suggests that the goal is no longer the identification of a catchall explanation that transpires in all phenomena. It is a quest for the identification of multiple salient strands, of a sort of "superstrings" with invariant local properties and plausible explanations, which are embedded with other less prominent strands in various social processes, as well as for understanding how these superstrings combine to produce observable systemic processes. Like the superstrings of physics, social mechanisms have strange properties, for example they appear to be instable and have a tendency to appear and disappear in a seemingly random manner, which seems to throw explanatory attempts back to a chaotic state. However, paying careful attention to these properties enables the detection of second-order patterns that are quite stable in a probabilistic sense and open the way to making rough predictions about social phenomena. In other words, theorizing is not a progressive abstraction to one essence but the distillation of social phenomena to a small series of resilient monads. Of course, the longer and more complex logical chains that link these superstrings to observable patterns and systemic processes make the development of explanations more difficult and fraught with errors. This explanatory fragility and the need for a further refinement of concepts and explanations is the main reason for the qualitative empirical research following and presented in Chapter 3.

3

A Qualitative Empirical Investigation of Response Capacity, Its Antecedents, and Its Impact

1. Introduction and outline on the qualitative methods

The main goal of this stage of empirical research was refining and providing a preliminary empirical validation for the conceptual framework of this research and for the hypotheses developed theoretically. The qualitative stage relied on semi-structured interviews for data collection and used two main methods for the analysis of the resulting data: semi-grounded theorizing and, respectively, comparisons across multiple cases.

Data Collection

Data collection focused on the way complex projects react to unexpected events. The theoretical framework provided a series of themes to be followed in the analysis of projects, namely planning, the nature of the structure that emerges by the time the project enters its execution phase, unexpected events, the way the structure conditions the response to these events, and, eventually, the success of the project. These themes enabled the development of the qualitative data collection instrument presented in Appendix A, which consists of 15 issues of discussion (open-ended questions), grouped in four major sections: planning, execution, flexibility, and outcomes. The relatively low number and the open-ended nature of these questions are typical of the semi-structured interviews, which are the main data collection method in this phase. In this type of interview, the goal is to induce respondents to express rather freely their recollections, thoughts, and feelings with respect to the processes of interest (Patton, 1990). The goal is to document the events as participants perceived them, and to explore the interpretations participants have of these events and the possible connections they establish between them.

Using this instrument, we performed retrospective interviews with managers and participants in 17 complex projects. A first criterion for project selection was size (cost more than US$100 million), which is a correlate of complexity (Shenhar, 2001). The second criterion resulted from our desire to ensure that projects were truly complex and to increase the variety in the sample. Therefore, we focused on projects executed in specific classes of sectors, corresponding to each of the three typical knowledge reproduction cycles proposed by Floricel and Dougherty (2007), namely science-coevolution, technology-recombination, and experience-continuity. For simplicity, we named the corresponding classes of sectors as discovery, digital, and infrastructural. By focusing on these three types of sectors, we sought to increase the differences between projects with respect to the nature of their complexity and in relation to the degree and nature of the knowledge available to planners, to the environmental dynamics they face, and hence to the number and nature of unexpected events, as well as to the institutional requirements and sectoral traditions of diligence for planning. In addition, in line with the theoretical framework, for each class of sectors, one half of the projects were expected to be dominated by one organization (mostly intra-firm network) and the other half to be carried on by a balanced or pluralistic network of participants. By combining the second and third selection criteria, we obtained the case selection matrix depicted in Table 3-1. In addition, we wanted about one half of the projects in our sample to be in North America and the other one half in Europe. We also wanted to include in the sample projects that were both successful (to various degrees) and unsuccessful (e.g., never completed, disappointing results, etc.). At the time of the interview, all projects had to be recently completed or nearing completion, in order to ensure accurate recollections.

The total number of projects to be studied was expected to exceed the number (6 to 10) recommended by Eisenhardt (1989a) for multicase research. For each project, we sought, to the extent possible, to interview several participants in order to obtain complementary perspectives on the key decisions and on their rationales, on the changes sought during implementation, on the reasons that made such changes possible or impossible, and on the way all these aspects affected the response capacity and the performance of each project.

A number of projects were selected as a function of these criteria, based on personal contacts and from secondary data. Key project participants were solicited for an interview. In addition, participants could suggest other possible interviewees. To those who accepted to be interviewed, we sent the issues for discussion in advance. Interviews were performed between August 2008 and August 2009, and they were all conducted on the premises of interviewees' organizations. In the end, we studied 17 projects, 9 in North America and 8 in Europe. Each interview lasted between one and two hours and was recorded using a digital recorder and transcribed verbatim. For each project, we performed between 1 and 8 interviews, for a total

Table 3-1   The Initial Case Selection Matrix

Sector	Participation	
	Dominated	Pluralist
Discovery	Biopharmaceutical drug development	Biotechnology ventures
Digital	Telecommunication systems and equipment	Information systems
Infrastructural	Petrochemical and power plants	Airport and land infrastructures

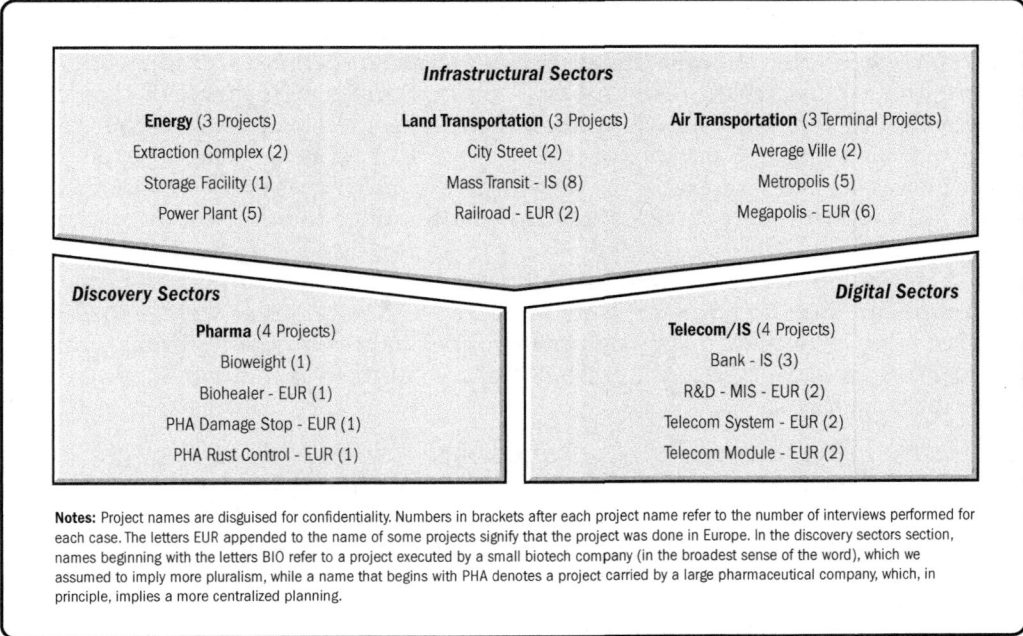

Figure 3-1   The Final Sample of Complex Projects

of 46 interviews (see Figure 3-1). The principal investigator participated in all but seven interviews, and, between the two of them, the first and the second author participated in all interviews.

Case Narratives

The first step in the data analysis was to write a narrative report for each case (Brown & Eisenhardt, 1997), which described the organization and the activities that occurred during the project. It included detailed timelines and figures outlining the organization and its evolution. The first draft of each case was prepared by a doctoral candidate or a master's degree student (see Foreword for credits), using a predefined template. In addition to the interview transcripts, case writers used various documents provided by the interviewees at the time of the interview, or obtained from company websites, or from general and specialized media. The principal investigator read these drafts and provided feedback to their writers, who produced a second, improved version. The narratives give a holistic perspective on the project, which helps situate and interpret the phenomena reflected in interviews and secondary data. These narratives were also sent to interviewees, providing them a compensation for the time and effort they spent. However, they are confidential to anyone else outside the research team, which was an initial condition for obtaining access to companies.

Semi-Grounded Theorizing Analysis

The cases were also analyzed by using a semi-grounded theorizing approach (Corbin & Strauss, 1990), in order to refine the theoretical framework. The original grounded theorizing method was developed to produce inductively theories in areas where theory is lacking. Resulting theories remain faithful to the data set, instead of forcing the data into the templates of a theory; they are substantive and relevant to a specific domain, rather than "grand" and abstract (Glaser & Strauss, 1967). In cases like ours, when prior relevant literature and an initial theoretical framework exist, Corbin and Strauss (1990) recommend a semi-grounded refinement of theoretical categories and relations. The grounded theorizing method relies on the content analysis for a very large number of interviews. The goal is to identify "exemplars" of the phenomena of interest, in the present case of properties of the emerging structures and to constantly compare them in order to understand their nature, context, relations, and implications. In the case of a semi-grounded approach, prior theoretical constructs are considered as an initial anchor of the analysis, and inductive techniques are used to refine existing categories and relations as well as to identify new ones. We also used an approach that was different from the traditional coding, in order to take advantage of the existence of case narratives that provided a holistic context for each case.

When all 17 case reports were nearing completion, all of them were split among the three authors of this report for a more in-depth analysis, which required a return to the interview transcripts. The cases were discussed in groups of three in weekly meetings; the grouping followed, to the extent that it was possible, the sectoral classification presented in Figure 3-1. For every weekly meeting, each researcher had to thoroughly revise and comment on one of the cases that were assigned, by completing the case study and significantly developing the findings and theoretical implications section (corresponding to "theoretical memos" in the grounded theorizing terminology). Researchers also had to read the other two cases scheduled for the same meeting as well as the comments that the researchers who were assigned the case made on them. During the meetings, each researcher presented, in turn, his case, while the other two commented. Researchers identified interesting situations as well as examples of the variables of interest. Cross-case comparisons and generalizations from the case discussed during the meeting were also attempted, as well as comparisons with cases and situations encountered in previous meetings. The grouping by sector was very helpful for detecting contingent factors that affected the processes that took place in projects. After each meeting, researchers prepared further theoretical memos outlining the theoretical insights that emerged during the meetings and circulated them to the other researchers. The initial comments and these memos were very useful in improving the definitions of the variables, for assessing their possible range in complex projects as well as in identifying possible relations and interactions.

Multicase Comparison

The last step in the qualitative analysis relied on a multicase approach (Eisenhardt, 1989a; Miles & Huberman, 1994). The aim of this analysis is to complement the semi-grounded analysis with a more holistic analysis, which focuses on the entire sequence of project activities and on the whole set of factors and interactions that determine the project outcomes (Langley, 1999). In essence, we first identified for each case the pattern of relations between variables. This was achieved by completing for each case a table (see Appendix 2 for the template we used), which conveys these patterns in a qualitative way and provides a preliminary quantification along the lines of the theoretical categories, using terms such as "most likely" and "clearly" in relation to a given property. The tables were completed by the three researchers after the discussion of all cases was concluded, which ensured that researchers has acquired an overall view of the cases. Each filled table was checked by at least one other researcher (generally the researcher who was assigned the case for discussion). At the end, the principal investigator checked all ratings for consistency. Then the patterns were compared across projects, mainly by cross tabulating the ratings to identify a pattern, and then by returning qualitatively to the cases that seemed to follow the pattern and those that seemed not to follow them. This provided a preliminary corroboration for the hypotheses presented in the previous chapter and enabled us to prepare a refined version of these hypotheses, which will be tested in the quantitative part of this research.

The following section presents the results of the "semi-grounded theorizing" analysis part of the qualitative research, which refined our understanding of the variables and the processes included in our theoretical framework.

2. Insights About Variables And Processes

The description of variables and processes in this section follows the sequence outlined in Figure 1-1 and the variable order presented in Figure 2-1. However, the case analysis has corroborated that the project initiation context is an important factor, which, as discussed in the conclusion of the planning section of Chapter 2, is an important contingent factor for the planning decisions. Therefore, we begin our discussion the findings that emerged with respect to the context, followed by the rest of the variables.

Context

A number of characteristics of the project context can influence its planning and execution. As anticipated, many of these are related to the type of sector in which the project takes place. One such aspect is the nature of the technical complexity affecting the project. For example, the technical complexity of the infrastructural projects that we studied was related to the ability to control the behavior of the artifacts that actors designed and built themselves. In three of the four discovery projects, the complexity was related to the ability to trick invisible natural phenomena that involved many causal strands and interactions. Finally, the complexity of the digital projects and a good part of the complexity of the MASSTRANSIT-IS project, which faced a hybrid of infrastructure and digital issues, was related to the ability to maintain the internal consistency between the various functions and operations performed by the technical systems. Other aspects were even more specific to the domain of activity. For example, for projects of similar size, airport terminal projects appeared, in principle, easier to separate into subprojects that could be executed independently (and even delayed) than the POWERPLANT project, which had to have all systems in place in order to perform its main function. However, beyond these differences, we would underscore several dimensions of the project context that seemed to affect planning. These could be treated independently of the specific sector, although some seem to be more prevalent in specific types of sector.

A first set of factors affected the *technical* complexity of the project. The first was the difficulty of the *natural environment* in which the project was being implemented. This factor affected only the infrastructural projects in our sample. Examples include soil conditions, whether the project was near or had to pass through areas with wildlife and other protected resources. For example, the MEGAPOLIS-EUR airport terminal project affected two rivers. The initial solution was to unite these two rivers and pass them through a tunnel, and then separate the flow and let it continue downstream in the older waterbeds. However, concerned parties and regulators considered this solution unacceptable because of the impact it would have on the wildlife and imposed a solution with separate flows, which caused an important rethinking of the project.

A second, more important factor was that the project had to be inserted in an already *"built"* environment, also sometimes called brownfield, be it other buildings and facilities, or information and management systems. For example, all three airport terminal projects were additions to existing and operating airports. Their planning and design not only had to cope with space and infrastructure constraints, but had to avoid disrupting the operation of the rest of the airport and to ensure a smooth transition when opening the new terminals. The planning of the information systems projects (MASSTRANSIT-IS and BANK-IS) had to take into account some continuing presence of old terminals and cards, as well as of old operating procedures and plan for training and transitions for users and operators. One of the most spectacular examples was CITYSTREET an upgrading project that had to cope with underground water, electrical, gas and other infrastructures, which were sometimes built over one hundred years ago, and with surrounding buildings that were historic monuments or included working retail operations.

Finally, a third important factor is the degree of project *novelty* for the sponsoring organization or of innovativeness in general (new to the world). All projects in the discovery sectors were innovations projects of some sort. However, some of them were less radically innovative or used a technology that had been successfully demonstrated by another division of the same company. The TELECOM-MODULE-EUR was also a new version of an older platform. Some infrastructure projects, such as EXTRACTIONCOMPLEX, were novel for the sponsoring organization and were considered pilot projects, while the IS projects were pioneers in North America (as opposed to Europe) and faced a lack of qualified programmers. The degree of innovativeness seems to be related with the use of an experimental approach, even for organizations used to dealing with innovation projects and with their stronger deviation during the structuring processes.

A second set of contextual factors concern the institutional complexity of the project. The first aspect concerns *regulation*, particularly its strength, and its novelty. Of course, regulations prescribed a lot of planning aspects in the biopharmaceutical sector. However, environmental regulation played a comparable role in almost all infrastructure projects. The RAILROAD-EUR project was the first major project to test a new environment-related legal framework in its host country, which increased significantly the uncertainty faced by the project. A closely related aspect is the *social and political interest* in the project. The brownfield projects were among the projects most affected by this contextual factor. For example, the concept of the MEGAPOLIS-EUR airport terminal project underwent the longest legislative inquiry in the history of its host country. The CITYSTREET project was constantly in the limelight not only because of the traffic difficulties it created but also because of the way it affected the retail and other businesses on the street. Like regulation, the social and political interest increases the chances that the planning will be more pluralist. Finally, a complex project can also be an occasion to try *new organizational and contractual forms*. The R&D-MIS-EUR project was such an occasion. It implemented a new management information system, which changed reporting requirements and information availability. Furthermore, it provided an occasion to shift the focus in the management of a key activity to the point of creating a new dedicated unit for implementing the project and subsequent developments as well as an entire division for managing its impact. Several other projects were an occasion for their respective owners to break with past organizational and contractual practices. The MEGAPOLIS-EUR terminal is an example in which the approach was new to the world, while RAILROAD-EUR was also done under a new organizational and partly political arrangement for the sponsor organization. The impact of all these contextual conditions will be underscored occasionally in the following discussion of variables and processes.

Planning

Knowledge. The cases studies brought in focus the fact that this variable, the kind of knowledge used in the planning process, refers primarily to knowledge about how to plan, structure, and manage a project. Hence, the *conceptual* end refers to the instances in which theoretical models of project management and of other relevant aspects, such as technical rules, are applied without need for validation or undue experimentation. POWERPLANT, CITYSTREET, TELECOMMODULE-EUR, TELECOM-SYSTEM-EUR, and EXTRACTIONCOMPLEX are all cases in which interviewees highlighted the fact that theoretical models of project execution were considered accurate predictors of cost and schedule; that there was a clear set of best practices and standard operating procedures; and that the project management team was experienced with such models and relied upon them to a large extent for planning. EXTRACTIONCOMPLEX, POWERPLANT, and CITYSTREET projects relied upon formal engineering models to determine the optimal scheduling and coordinating of different facets of the projects. The management concern in these cases was the optimal execution strategy with known technology, which suggests a belief in the substantive rationality of planning (Simon, 1978). The models they used were based on experience, and, as suggested in the theoretical chapter, they were "blackboxed," meaning that their validity and relevance was rarely called into question. The exception was the EXTRACTIONCOMPLEX case, which applied such models to a novel kind of project, for which some construction methods were unproven or had to be developed. As a result, the details of the conceptual planning models had to be verified (at times by external consultants) before they could be relied upon for planning decisions. The "blackboxed" nature of similar conceptual models for project planning and management produced two interesting structuring effects in a digital project, the TELECOM-SYSTEM-EUR; namely, the project director and the project manager, who had previous experience in two distinct divisions of the owner organization, each applied a different conceptual model and emphasized different aspects of planning. The result was a conflict between these two visions that was resolved only during the structuring process. In addition, the same project gives an example of how a conceptual approach leads to "blackboxing" in the development of the technical concept; namely the use of a technical solution from a supplier without checking its availability by the date when it will be required for implementation, which later caused a major unexpected event.

The examples may suggest that conceptual planning was used only for digital and infrastructural projects. In fact, we observed no correlation between the sector of activity and the type of process knowledge (conceptual or experimental). In biopharmaceutical projects, a sector where the nature of technical complexity and the extreme uncertainty it induces in projects, may suggest reliance on experimental knowledge even in project planning, conceptual knowledge was predominant, and its use seems correlated with the size of the sponsor organization. Models of optimal resource allocation played an important role in decision making at the portfolio level, determining which among several R&D projects should be pursued and which should be abandoned. Conceptual knowledge relating to the disciplinary composition of the project team, to the nature and scheduling of development, regulatory approval, and product launch activities, and to the logistics of marketing and distribution was also widely used in planning. Because the availability of conceptual knowledge made the tasks look more programmable, projects appeared amenable to planning by tools such as enterprise resource planning software. In fact, nearly all biopharmaceutical firms in our sample, including the sponsor of the R&D-MIS-EUR project, were familiar with or used the same well-known brand of portfolio and project management software adapted to pharmaceutical industry needs (the owner of the BIOHEALER-EUR project was the only exception). Interviewees praised the software for offering a detailed checklist of key planning issues. Because firms of different sizes used the same software in projects that were quite different, the underlying knowledge is probably quite generic, as anticipated in the theoretical chapter. In addition, interviewees reported that the software offered the possibility to adapt in part the templates for each project. However, some respondents complained that the software, and the information system it supported, did not always fit the specific needs of a firm or project, such as those regarding the detail level of information exchanged in distributed teams.

In contrast, the *experimental* production of process knowledge was used when planners did not have any conceptual models at their disposal, or found existing models irrelevant and insufficient for the given project. The need to produce their own specific knowledge was common for the three airport terminal projects in our sample, mainly because decades had passed since airport owners had completed the last projects of similar complexity. To address this relative novelty issue, all terminal project sponsors embarked on a tour of recent terminal projects completed worldwide. One of them also performed a broader study of megaprojects in general and leveraged the feedback from the public hearings process and the inclusion, on equal footing, of a number of reputable consultants in the project team to produce the needed knowledge. The owner of another terminal project even completed a pilot project of a smaller facility, in order to gain project planning and management experience. Identifying best practices and solutions, specifying quality and process control standards, or simply determining whether a particular assumption is valid, are all examples of knowledge that were obtained from such activities.

The technical complexity and novelty, which often means unknown parameters of the project, also requires some degree of experimentation or validation of concepts and procedures prior to execution. The terminal projects used various approaches for obtaining experimental knowledge, such as the off-site building of prototypes and simulation of the assembly process for of certain structures located in confined airport areas; testing built facilities using thousands of volunteers, who were assigned different roles and scenarios in special test days; and even building a full-scale functional prototype of the toilet rooms—a particularly sensitive aspect of customer experience—which were tested by various persons, including airport executives. In one case, the architectural concept of the terminal underwent at least three major iterations in early planning, because of the obtained feedback, followed by several layout changes even during construction. In some terminals that had to deal with concurrent demolition and construction, the scheduling of certain activities followed an incremental approach, which took into account the information obtained with respect to the difficulty and duration of some demolitions as well as about the interference with other activities and operations on the site.

Concerning technical aspects, pharmaceutical projects are particularly interesting examples, because they resorted to conceptual models for the basic breakdown, staffing, and ordering of activities, but the decision to begin the project and the selection of specific technical objectives and activities were based on knowledge obtained via an experimental approach. In particular, laboratory or clinical experimentation was required in order to determine whether the project could be pursued, and if so, what its objectives should be (e.g., improving bioavailability etc.). The conceptual project management processes, a gating approach with each stage being of uncertain duration or success, matched the experimental approach used in technical activities. Planning horizons were relatively short, for example, the project budget was assigned yearly rather than from the entire anticipated duration, and spending could be curtailed as soon as "showstopper" knowledge was produced.

In certain cases, the novelty or lack of models was so severe that the entire project or a major phase was considered an experiment of sorts, with the obtained knowledge to be used for planning and designing subsequent projects and phases. The RAILROAD-EUR project had to face a new fiscal situation for the given country and a novel public financing philosophy somewhat influenced by the PPP approach, and a new environmental regulation (yet to be tested in courts), as well as a new set of EU technical standards (still untested in practice). The project leaders had to create a new type of company to finance and to execute the project, and to go to courts in order to see whether they would side with the project or with those who objected to a specific part of its design and contested the environmental permit. The new EU standards had to be considered as well in the technical solutions of the project. This typically led to major changes in the planning and organizational approach as the project went on, and especially between two phases of the same project. The fact that the organizations that used extreme experimentation, MASSTRANSIT-IS for example, which had to deal not only with an unfamiliar technology but to step up the coordination between several municipalities that were to share the resulting infrastructure, were more than ready to change seems to support the argument advanced in the theoretical section that experimental planning creates fewer inertial "facts." However, we will discuss more about these changes in the sections about structuring and response to unexpected events. The projects that relied on an experimental approach, particularly MEGAPOLIS-EUR, also seem to have developed richer communication couplings and stronger links between participants, which seems to support the other contentions we made in the previous chapter.

Process participation. As expected, the projects we studied differed with respect to the participation in the planning process. In *centralized* processes, the core project team and the sponsor organization had a greater decision power compared to other project participants, such as contractors, input suppliers, and even the client; stakeholders, such as regulators, unions and environmental activists, had relatively little leverage over the project. As we observed in the POWERPLANT project, such power can derive from size, specific institutional arrangements, and from a tradition of interactions with the other stakeholders. Dominant partners also seem to prefer such control, because it appears to ensure that the project is carried out according to their wishes. For example, if the central player is also the client and expected to operate the facility for many years, centralization appears to this player as the solution for building the facility to the proper specifications and for achieving operational characteristics such as reliability, safety, and efficiency. However, in such situations, successful dominant players seem to know how to draw on the expertise of the other partners, in order to compensate for their own lack of internal expertise. This was not the case in the BIOHEALER-EUR project, in which a strong centralization was observed with respect to planning several aspects of product development and regulatory affairs, in spite of the project team's lack of experience in such matters. The project team had initially decided that its product would be sold as an over-the-counter product and they had generated relatively little clinical data prior to launch. However, this lack of evidence ultimately compromised the intended business model because it prevented the product from being covered by national drug insurance programs.

Many centralized projects are internal projects performed by large organizations. One refinement with respect to the initial definition of the participation variable, which resulted from our case studies, is that centralization can also be stronger or weaker inside an organization. For example, in one of the two large pharmaceutical companies in which we studied projects, the project portfolio management committee concentrated the ultimate responsibility and decision power for the fate of a project, while in the other, project decisions seemed to result from a more diffuse political process. However, in this respect, the TELECOM-SYSTEM-EUR, which was performed by a large organization, offers an interesting example of faux internal pluralism, which we call relayed centralized planning. In this case, the responsibility for planning the project was passed from one department to another within the division; namely from business development to operations to project management. Each of these departments applied a different conceptual template for planning, and then bestowed the results on the subsequent department, without consulting them in decisions beforehand. Therefore, instead of establishing links that may eventually become embedded and of harmonizing the language couplings between different participants, this process cut into the continuity of interactions and created many conflicts, as each participant approached planning differently and did not understand the rationales of previous decisions.

On the other end of this variable, there were more projects with a *pluralist* planning process in our sample. One of the main reasons for such pluralism was the large number and importance for project stakeholders. The geographical extension of the project or the density of affected parties situated nearby increased the number of important stakeholders. The larger the project site, the more likely it is to implicate a greater number of stakeholders by mere virtue of the fact that the project "runs through their territory," as evidenced in the CITYSTREET project. Here, the entire lanes and sidewalks of a busy commercial artery had to be dug up and replaced over several miles in order to place new electrical, sewer, water, and gas lines. Similarly, the more a project creates externalities such as noise and water pollution or traffic congestion, the larger and more diverse is its set of stakeholders. The public hearings for the MEGAPOLIS-EUR airport terminal project lasted almost one and one half years, heard several hundreds stakeholders and experts, and made nearly a hundred site visits. This eventually resulted in several hundreds of planning recommendations that conditioned the approval of the project. In such situations, increasing the pluralism of the planning process can be seen as a means of hedging risks against third party opposition to a project. For example, the RAILROAD-EUR project passed through several communities but could hardly avoid affecting some wilderness areas. By suitably accommodating demands for environmental preservation and by involving each municipality along the service line as project co-owners and decision makers with respect to the construction of the respective rail stations, the sponsor organization ensured that the support of municipalities for the project would offset the diminished opposition of environmental stakeholders.

A second reason for increasing the pluralism of the project was that the projects required so many different kinds of expertise that these were difficult to bring together under the roof of a single organization, even of a very large organization. This was the reason why, for example, the owner of the MEGAPOLIS-EUR involved representatives of contractors and consultants in the executive committee, in the core team, and in planning decisions at several other levels. In the case of the BANK-IS project, the expertise was provided by some certification bodies, while a certain assurance and guidelines for the implementation schedule were provided by an industry association. The BIOWEIGHT project was made possible because of strong relationships with external scientific advisory boards and consultants. To the extent that such relationships, which were also present in the BIOHEALER-EUR project, result in special teams with special powers, while the project also maintains centralized planning in other areas, the process participation is perhaps more aptly characterized as "hybrid" rather than clearly pluralist or centralized.

Another reason for increasing the project pluralism was obtaining the needed financial resources. In this case, pluralism can be manifested through customer involvement in a project. A typical situation was seen in the TELECOM-MODULE-EUR project, in which an innovation project was initiated and the specifications were adjusted almost at the request of an important, but by far not unique, client. However, an even stronger example of client-dependence was found in the case of two projects in which a capacity was built by virtue of a long-term service contract for a single client. In the case of the STORAGEFACILITY project, the client not only had the right to determine the specifications of the facility, which had to fit the requirements of its own facility that was constructed nearby at the same time, but the entire project schedule was contingent upon the decisions and construction advance of the client.

In the case of TELECOM-SYSTEM-EUR, the client put significant pressure on the project owner organization, including via personal links between the highest-placed executives, and insisted on the respect of the promises made with respect to the implementation schedule when the project was sold. Another way of obtaining resource was co-ownership through joint ventures, as seen in the EXTRACTIONCOMPLEX project, which increases pluralism structures, but the actual control still depends on the partner that has the most expertise. The MASSTRANSIT-IS project, initiated by a coalition involving a large number of companies, shows that the degree of pluralism varies even in projects with many partners. In this project, we observed an initial attempt at "democratic" planning, in which all partners had an equal say, even if they had organizations of different sizes and levels of expertise. Eventually, a more centralized approach was adopted, in which the largest partner organization—much larger than any of the other partners—had a corresponding decision weight and took a lot of responsibility in planning, developing specifications, issuing the call for proposals, selecting contractors, and so forth.

Contrary to what we expected, the networks of pluralist projects did not seem more fragile than the centralized projects. The partners and other stakeholders stayed with the project, which can be contrasted with the tendency of the more centralized projects to dismiss or replace contractors. Moreover, in the case of TELECOM-SYSTEM-EUR, the increase of pluralism from the stronger involvement of the service client led to an increase of the cohesion of the project network, both with the client and inside the owner organization. As we expected, however, in some of the most pluralist projects in our sample, such as MEGAPOLIS-EUR and MASSTRANSIT-IS, the participants with different perspectives we interviewed used a very rich language and expressed very similar views of the project and of its different events.

Argument. With respect to this aspect of the plan, our sample was almost equally split between promotional and decisional plans. Cases that involved the implementation of a new or unknown technology in order to achieve strategic goals led to the development of strongly *promotional* plans. Under these circumstances, it is not the technical plausibility or the thoroughness of the plans that is emphasized, but rather the importance of attaining a particular outcome. For example, describing the justifications for the MASSTRANSIT-IS project interviewees presented a logic that was not fully supported by detailed objective analysis; the initial budget and schedule for implementation also proved to be unrealistic. In a similar vein, in the TELECOM-SYSTEM-EUR project, there was little risk analysis and technical complexity evaluation prior to signing an agreement with a major client. In projects performed by startups, the issue of innovation was compounded by inexperience, and by hasty decision making because of the precarious nature of firm resources. As a result, planners did not take the time to fully appreciate the implications of irreversible decisions and to verify the plausibility of certain assumptions. For the BIOHEALER-EUR project, exploiting a recently patented technology seemed like the logical step in the growth of the sponsor company, even though the proof of concept had not been completed and regulatory requirements had not been adequately investigated. The project directors proceeded largely on the assumption that the new technology would be endorsed by a category of healthcare professionals, because it created a new and superior category of nonprescription health products, which could be recommended to consumers by such professionals rather than medical doctors. As discussed previously, the directors failed to recognize that one of the key elements of feasibility—reimbursement by public health insurance—was conditional upon clinical data demonstrating the efficacy of the product. This became clear late in the project life cycle, when managers, who had little experience in regulatory affairs, hired a consulting firm, which explained to them that additional clinical research would be the only means of ensuring such coverage.

Another situation where highly promotional planning occurs is when the project is seen as strategic, usually when there seems to be high growth in a sector or geographical area, which creates a drive to obtain a strategic foothold in the growing market. At the time of our interviews, many energy industries were such markets, resulting in projects that expanded capacity in large increments or sought to exploit untamed sources. In these projects, exemplified in our sample by STORAGEFACILITY and its client company's nearby related project as well as by EXTRACTIONCOMPLEX, plans emphasized execution deadlines rather than feasibility. An interesting situation occurred in the latter case, whose plan cannot be characterized as promotional overall, namely the detection of important cost overestimations during planning. These were attributed to mistakes, and estimates were lowered accordingly, but the results show that even the higher initial estimate was in fact a significant underestimation of project cost.

In the case of STORAGEFACILITY, the client, a relatively new company in the business, was also overly optimistic not only of the economic perspectives of its client project but also of its own capacity to carry out the implementation of such a project. Hence, this client was forced to constantly change project specifications and deadlines and ended up relying on its service provider and owner of the STORAGEFACILITY project for advice. The latter also seems to have itself entered into this combination of projects with an overly optimistic outlook on the growth of the energy sector in the geographical area in which the project was situated, and with a promotional-type strategy of using the project as a first step for establishing a foothold in that area. However, it had the wisdom to develop a clear contract that specified in detail the initial technical parameters of the project as well as a way to calculate the additional cost of any change or delay asked for by the client, which ensured that the project did not result in a financial loss for the owner even though it was never finished. Our interviewee's remarks about this contract suggested that clarity and detail, the hallmarks of a decisional plan, not only help decision makers to assess the project idea but also create an object (in the sense of the actor-network theory) that impacts subsequent actions, by becoming a better yardstick for any subsequent changes and conflicts.

All projects that were based on promotional plans led to significant increases in cost estimates, very early in the project life cycle and throughout its duration, as well as to important changes in technical specifications, in the project organization, and, in some cases, in contracts. They were often plagued by conflicts. This seems to support the argument proposed in the theoretical chapter that promotional plans lead to more intense structuring processes and to larger deviations from the initial plans. However, even in projects that had detailed plans otherwise, promotional arguments, such as the contention that the few hundred kilometers covered by the RAILROAD-EUR project will become a key transportation link between Asia and Europe, seemed to ensure that projects with marginal or even negative profitability perspectives were implemented.

On the other end of this variable, project plans characterized as decisional included detailed and formal studies establishing the project rationales. Airport expansion projects best characterize this situation. They were based on careful estimations of demand for terminal space relying on forecasts of growing passenger volume and of stricter requirements for compliance to international security standards. An additional reason for the use of detailed plans in these projects were the important constraints they faced, such as confined space and the requirement that service in existing terminals and runways should not be disrupted during construction. Detailed plans for progressive demolition and construction were therefore prepared, making the execution strategy as much a criterion for adopting the project as the need for expansion. Moreover, the legitimacy of terminal projects depends largely on the stakeholders that will be affected by it and on the regulatory agencies or even courts that oversee its impacts. Therefore, the quality of the plans became a symbolic argument used to legitimate the project. For example, policies that were to apply to specific construction activities (e.g., audits) were prepared in order to obtain stakeholder acquiescence and to reduce the likelihood of unforeseen opposition to the project.

A similar situation occurred in the pharmaceutical projects that we studied. In this kind of project, regulatory approval was needed to not only commercialize the new products but also just to start clinical trials, because these may affect the health of participating patients. Therefore, a plan that was not prepared with due diligence and according to the required scientific and ethical standards had little chance of receiving regulatory approval. Even inside large pharmaceutical firms, the "survival" of the project within the R&D portfolio was conditioned not only by the plausibility of the scientific arguments about the underlying technology, but also by the quality of projections about market size and positioning sustainability, penetration levels, and the chances of regulatory approval. Hence, decisional plans appear to be a means for key stakeholder cooptation in this industry as well. However, promotional plans did not seem to bother the venture capitalists who approved funding for the two biotech projects in our sample, which suggests that this kind of partner may be accustomed to different criteria and standards.

Our interviewees made interesting observations about the extent to which plans can be decisional. For example, interviewees in the POWERPLANT project pointed out that they faced a tradeoff between the additional cost and delay required with certainty in order to obtain more precise information, in this case about soil conditions, and the more remote possibility to incur additional costs if the soil conditions proved worse than expected during construction. In this situation, they often preferred to limit the information-production activities and to take a chance on the soil conditions. The results of the project proved them correct, because even if the soil conditions turned out to be much worse than expected, they did not lead to a spectacular increase in cost and delays. Likewise, an interviewee who participated in the PHADAMAGESTOP-EUR project pointed out that, in conditions of many competing projects, there is another tradeoff between a possible lack of essential details and information overload caused by abundant detail. These observations and the abovementioned role of contractual details suggest that detail plans are indeed objects that play an important role in the project network, which may minimize deviation but not necessarily by creating an iron cage as we supposed in the theoretical chapter.

Risk approach. This characteristic of the plan was one of the issues that triggered our interest in the response capacity of projects. It is therefore interesting to underscore that none of the projects in our sample used *allocative* approaches such as build-operate-transfer (BOT) or public-private partnerships (PPPs). The only projects whose contractual structure was somewhat closer to the models of the 1980s were the long-term service contracts in the TELECOM-SYSTEM-EUR project (public client) and STORAGEFACILITY (private client). However, even in these cases, the client eventually agreed to changes and delays in the former project, and the contract protected the contractor more than the client in the case of the latter project. As the interviewee from the STORAGEFACILITY project said, "The customer had to make decisions; there were financial implications of the decisions they made. . .." Even in the case of the RAILROAD-EUR project, which is the only project where the government established a special purpose company (a step typical for past allocative formulas), this structure was not adopted in order to push risk to private partners. All financing was provided by the Ministry of Finance of the given country to ensure that the entire sum was guaranteed to be available from the beginning rather than allocated on a yearly basis through the budget of the Ministry of Transportation, which would subject it to budget cuts in case of government change. In most of the other projects in which risk allocation was preferred, owners went only as far as concluding contracts with very detailed specifications, fixed price, and in which the contractor was required to post a significant bond or a deposit (as much as 50 percent) to be held in escrow. The owner of the POWERPLANT project and the coalition leader in the MASSTRANSIT-IS project used the leverage provided by such contracts in order to coerce contractors into obeying their orders. In most other cases, fixed price contracts were part of a menu of contracts and were used in general only for the relatively low-risk portions of the project. Another allocation strategy, used even in cost-plus contracts, was breaking the project into smaller parts and imposing clear milestones and deadlines to the respective contractors or teams, which made it easier to keep them accountable.

However, most other projects seemed to opt for an integrative approach to diffusing the risk stemming from uncertainty and unexpected events. One of the most pervasive means was cost-plus (cost reimbursement) contracts. Such contracts insulated contractors against unforeseen contingencies, by allowing them to pass on additional unforeseen expenses to the client, and ensured that they make a profit. The unforeseen increases in costs were ultimately shouldered by the entire project budget, rather than by the profit margin of a single contractor. An additional integrative measure was to employ construction management (where the client directs the supplier to build certain structures). Because they do not provide from the beginning a set of clear, detailed specifications that must be fulfilled and allow the contractor to be paid on a cost plus basis or according to some other variable cost scheme, the client ultimately bears the burden of cost overruns. This approach was used in the METROPOLIS airport terminal project and in the first phase of the EXTRACTIONCOMPLEX and AVERAGEVILLE airport terminal projects. In the latter case, the project, shifted to a more allocative plan, with fixed price contracts in the second phase when management had acquired more experience and process knowledge.

In the MEGAPOLIS terminal project the project owner used multiple cost-plus contracts, but went beyond this and concluded a special agreement with all first-tier contractors. The agreement stipulated that the owner agreed to support all risks, pay all additional costs, and ensure that contractors will make a profit. In exchange, contractors agreed to identify risks and signal them as soon as possible rather than incorporate risk margins in the contracts, to focus on jointly solving problems with the other participants, and give their best effort and people for the project.

It is interesting to note that planned structures can also be more or less allocative even in internal projects. For example, in the PHADAMAGESTOP-EUR project, carried out by a large pharmaceutical company, tasks and budgets were strictly allocated between various involved units, often situated on different continents, and strict procedures had to be followed by each of them. On the other hand, in the PHARUSTCONTROL-EUR, the company established a life cycle team, in which representatives of different disciplines and units shared the responsibility for the entire project throughout most of its duration. In the BANK-IS project, all members of the project management team assumed joint responsibility for the project. The risk is therefore borne by several individuals (partners) in a centralized structure. The TELECOM-MODULE-EUR case also demonstrated highly integrative planning, because several teams were required to assume joint responsibility for meeting the evolving needs of an important client. In general, when cost control for a particular project seemed to be the main concern, such as in the case of the PHADAMAGESTOP-EUR project, highly allocative planning (in the form of detailed budgets) was preferred. In contrast, where cost-control was not the major concern, for example in the R&D-MIS-EUR project, a more integrative structure, which emphasized collaboration and lacked a detailed allocation of responsibilities, was put in place.

In projects with integrative plans, relations were usually collaborative and led to the development of stronger links and richer communication couplings, as assumed. For example, the MEGAPOLIS-EUR project seems to be a good example of owner collaboration with consultants and contractors. But relatively strong links also emerged between the client and the owner of the STORAGEFACILITY project, which were related by a contractual arrangement that was allocative in what concerns the cost of the service provided by the owner (service provider), but in which the client assumed most construction risks. The fact that the contract protected the owner from cost overruns caused by client decisions and delays, made construction similar to the situation in the MEGAPOLIS-EUR project, in which owners assumed all risks relative to contractors. The parties were also forced to collaborate by their mutual dependence for the functioning of their respective projects.

Structuring Processes

One of the more interesting findings of our empirical research is the confirmation that complex projects undergo important structuring processes, in which deviations start as soon as the first plans are developed but continue throughout the execution phase and even after the project exploitation begins. We coded the nature of structuring deviation using the broad categories of "intense" and "moderate" deviation and found that in most of the projects we studied (11 out of 17), deviations with the initial planners' intentions were intense. In general, structuring episodes that lead to intense deviation from plans are triggered by a precipitating event, most typically internal problems or conflicts but also external events, not necessarily unexpected, which induce the realization that something in the organization, capabilities, personalities, technical solutions, etc. of the project is dysfunctional and compromises the likelihood of its successful completion. This, in turn, triggers the changes in salient structural elements, such as stimuli and language couplings, which were more easily observable with the kinds of methods we used, but also disrupt existing routines and trigger new routinization processes. The following are some of the most visible examples of structuring elements that we observed just in the MEGAPOLIS-EUR project (included are only examples that did not result from unexpected events, which will be discussed in a later section):

- Four CEOs led the project successively; each of them emphasized different priorities;
- One of them started a gradual shift from one-person leadership to management by committees;
- Mid-way through execution, the unitary project organization was changed into a program with 4 groups, 16 projects, and many subprojects;
- After construction started, the main client decided it will become the sole occupant of the terminal, requesting changes in the design of operational facilities;
- Other important changes to the architectural design continued throughout the execution;
- Labor shortages required that a large number of workers be brought in from all over the world;
- Construction managers stated that many more transportation routes and accommodations were needed on the construction site;
- A certain construction sequence initially as unidirectional was later changed for a radial one, which, in turn, was later abandoned in favor of the initial solution;
- Designed and built solutions also underwent continuous but more minor changes, enabled by a special approval process;

An external event that affected both this and other airport projects, was the September 11, 2001 terrorist attacks, which not only required airport authorities to accommodate security requirements, but also gave regulatory bodies a greater role in the design and even funding of projects, because they were to finance the changes and because a larger number of security personnel would be working in their facilities. The design focus shifted to some extent from passenger experience (e.g., convenience, aesthetics) to compliance with government regulation. Most consequences of this event on the projects in our sample trickled down gradually and led to important structuring episodes. In the response processes section, we will discuss other effects of the same event, which influenced the same projects in a more direct and unexpected way. Another typical external source of structuring is long regulatory approval delays. For example, in the case of the RAILROAD-EUR project, rather than let the personnel go during the more than a year delay, management asked its technical experts to rethink certain technical solutions, which led to significant improvements and even cost savings. In other cases, the structuring event was outside contestation, and it led to changes in organizational routines that increased the participation and recognition of external actors. In both RAILROAD-EUR and CITYSTREET projects, the project management team initially assumed a strong, internally focused coordinating role, but it later encountered resistance from affected parties. Opening up the project to these stakeholders, for example, by organizing a special information office on the street being affected by the latter project, allowed these projects to prevent many problems and delays.

A frequent internal problem is the inadequacy of the existing organizational routines for the given project. The TELECOM-SYSTEM-EUR project was assigned to the operating division of the sponsor firm, which was used to manage projects executed only inside its home country. The project in question, however, concerned a global network. The routines of the operating division, as opposed to those of a global project office of the same organization, were inadequate for this project. For example, instead of testing a device in several countries, it performed simulated tests in the home country. Moreover, it did not know how to deal with local telecom partners in many parts of the world. The problem was not really solved until the project experienced major delays and a crisis ensued, which will be discussed in the response processes section. The TELECOM-MODULE-EUR was confronted with two problems. First, the customer would continually request changes to the product being developed for them. Second, the project team did not have enough human resources to make all these changes without disrupting other projects. This prompted the team to make two major changes to its work routines that were inspired by the experience of other projects. First, it introduced the concept of streamlining—the team added new features only if it had available resources. Second, it introduced the concept of integration center engineering—any desired change had to be compatible with existing functions and with other required changes. The team ran several tests, and, if the level of compatibility was high, the change was accepted, if not, the product was released without that new feature.

Conflicts among various participants were another internal source of deviation. In the case where the conflict was with employees and project contractors, the point of contention was often a level of service, performance, or compatibility that was untenable. An example is the MASSTRANSIT-IS project, in which a conflict emerged between two suppliers responsible for two key subsystems, which also were direct competitors on the market. The contractors were under contractual obligation to ensure that their respective pieces of equipment were compatible, but even though one of them was designated as system integrator, the other ignored its advice because of communication problems resulting from differences in language, measuring systems, and standards. Therefore, these contractors were unable to coordinate their work and blamed each other for equipment noncompatibilities. The problem was compounded by the fact that the client had supplied detailed specifications (a sort of language coupling) that were inappropriate and insisted that contractors equally share the responsibility for any problems and delays (network stimuli). Only after the owner assigned one manager to the task of overseeing this aspect of the project, and later started resorting to contractual levers, such as penalties, intentionally delayed payments, etc., the integration between the two contractors improved.

A lack of competence on the part of a manager was also a source of deviations. Replacing the manager often results in new routines that put a project back on track for meeting its objectives. For example, participants in the BANK-IS project realized that a manager responsible for a certain part of the project failed to put in place an adequate quality assurance (QA) process, in fact the person didn't really know how to put in place such a process. Software and other products that were being developed could not be tested in an environment that was realistic enough for the developers to be able to reproduce and correct problems. The manager eventually resigned and was replaced. The new manager put in place the needed process. Implementing it added costs and delays, but ultimately resulted in a capacity to debug problems before they resulted in catastrophic failures. Working with a QA process also made it possible to obtain many critical certifications required for project success.

In other cases, the problem was just one disgruntled manager, who became a nuisance, or a conflict involving two individuals with incompatible personalities. These problems were solved by firing or replacing the respective persons. In the TELECOM-SYSTEM-EUR project, the pursuit of perfection (resulting in undue delays for the customer) is what ultimately caused a manager to be replaced. Another conflict pattern was observed in the TELECOM-SYSTEM-EUR as well as in the BIOWEIGHT and R&D-MIS-EUR, in which the main issue was the area of authority that a management team or manager could have in directing others. In many cases, managers were replaced to create a less hierarchical and more collaborative set of routines. Although such changes allowed projects to be completed more harmoniously, they rarely, if ever, enabled the project to be completed according to the initial schedule and budget.

The requests for technical changes were also an important source of structuring episodes. We mentioned earlier the many changes to the MEGAPOLIS-EUR project. MASSTRANSIT-IS is another example in which the many ownership partners, as well as the different departments of the main partner's organization constantly produced new requirements that they wanted included in the project specifications. The participants even invented a name for it: the "Since-we-are-doing-this-anyway" Syndrome. This problem, compounded by the leader organization's lack of experience in managing IS projects of similar scope, eventually led to a crisis that resulted in a major organizational restructuring to which we will return in the response processes section. The STORAGEFACILITY project, in addition to the changes that the client constantly requested after the long-term service contract had been signed, had to cope with a new round of important change requests quite late in the execution process. These changes stemmed from the fact that the client hired operators for its own facility, and these operators found major flaws in the design of the client facility. The requested changes were so important and costly that a conflict ensued inside the client organization, between the operator camp and management, so much so that the service provider had to arbitrate between the two, an interesting change in the interaction routines between the owner and the client.

Other important sources of restructuring are reorganizations of sponsor organizations during, or just before the start of the project. For example, the owner of the EXTRACTIONCOMPLEX project was a part-owned subsidiary of a foreign multinational company. When the first stage of the project was nearing completion, the multinational decided to acquire full ownership of the subsidiary and transform it into a division. Among other changes, the multinational brought in new executives and experts, many from its home or other countries. The ensuing change in planning and design routines led, in the second stage, to more detailed plans, and more detailed and rigorous testing and approval procedures (often involving experts outside of the project management team).

While intense deviations may save a failing project, the gravity of the changes they produce are often met with resistance and skepticism. In some cases, the affected parties question the motives of the initiating parties, while in other cases desired changes are implemented only after delays or added costs. For example, in the MEGAPOLIS-EUR project, the process of shifting the sequence of construction activities undermined the collaboration rhetoric and led to the discontent of the contractors responsible for the project, who were not consulted prior to these decisions. This led to subsequent delays and, as some respondents suggested, the attempt to meet the project deadline by compressing the schedule of some of these activities later led to major operational problems.

With the examples that illustrate the many structuring episodes encountered in the cases that we studied, we can now safely argue that there is enough corroborating evidence for our hypothesis that the evolution of project organizations follows a trajectory resembling the structuring detour depicted in Figure 1-1. Therefore, we can now turn and examine the evidence we obtained on the characteristics of the emergent project structure, particularly the response capacity properties that condition is a reaction to unexpected events.

Response Capacity

As discussed in the theoretical chapter, we consider that an adequate response to unexpected events requires a structure with high cohesion, flexibility, and resourcefulness. A first conclusion that we can draw from our research is that the interviewed managers found the questions referring directly or indirectly to these variables relevant and were able to provide interesting insights. We discuss these three variables with their dimensions and extremes in turn.

Cohesion. The variable "cohesion" indicates to what extent project participants would collaboratively work to find a solution when facing unexpected events. We found a lot of both implicit and explicit evidence in projects about the presence of this characteristic. Its importance was revealed by the fact that some project management teams, apart from the expected contractual forms or collaboration procedures, purposefully and consciously took specific actions to strengthen their cohesion.

In some cases, the project initiator used predominantly coercive means to impose its view to the other participants, either by referring to specific stipulations in the initial contract or by using meetings to inform rather than consult its partners. In other cases, adhesive cohesion played the leading role, all unexpected events being approached in a collaborative manner. However, both forms of cohesion were present in all projects.

Adhesive cohesion. The *embedded* adhesive cohesion occurred in three main forms: preexisting, built from the beginning, or developed during the project. All these forms could be found in most projects, but sometimes one form predominated. Examples of preexisting adhesive cohesion include cases in which the same project team that worked in prior similar tasks or projects is allocated to the current project (especially in internal projects, but also for the POWERPLANT project). This situation is also likely when contractors and suppliers are preferred for their past positive collaboration with the owner organization. For example, EXTRACTIONFACILITY used the same suppliers as in previous projects, and BANK-MIS used many contractors and consultants with whom they had collaborated in the past. In all these cases, strong links had been developed between members, the collaboration capacity had been already tested, and the level of uncertainty regarding the partner's performance is reduced to a minimum.

The embedded adhesive cohesion was sometimes purposefully built from the beginning of the project. For example, in all airport projects, partnering sessions were held to increase the team spirit and to teach participants to see themselves as a team and not as a group of individuals representing different organizations. In most projects, the embedded cohesion was continuously developed during the project through team collocation, as spatial proximity favors friendship and frequent information exchanges. Another approach was intensive communication, used, for example, by the CITYSTREET project, which developed a specific strategy and set up an office in order to optimize stakeholder-oriented communication. Mentoring was another method that enabled new members or smaller teams located overseas to be quickly integrated into the project, for example, in the TELECOM-MODULE-EUR project. These are other approaches that were used: meetings of the core team and with different other participants; embedding representatives of the core team in various organizational units that participated in the project, to create at least one strong link to each of these units; integrating representatives of contractors, partners, clients or other functions in the core project team; enabling the project management team to build a large number of strong connections to a diversity of external organizations; and so on.

In respect to the embedded cohesion, we found two interesting occurrences. The first concerns the PHARUSTCONTROL-EUR project, which, like the other project carried on by a large pharmaceutical company, can be characterized metaphorically as a "lean entity thrown in the organizational meat grinder." The project was provided with just enough resources to perform the required activities, while most participants, even members of the core team, remained in their respective functional units, and the resources were allocated periodically based on results from the previous period, with the priority of cutting spending as soon as the project appeared no longer viable. In this situation, the core team, in spite of its constant travel and efforts to maintain strong links with the many participants and units located around the word, failed to maintain the needed embedded cohesion. We characterize this phenomenon as overstretching the project network over the preexisting organizational and political canvas and suggest that it leads to low project cohesion in the face of unexpected events. Similar situations occurred in the BIOHEALER-EUR project, in which managers ended up sending an unprepared junior clerk to deal with a supplier; in the BANK-IS project, in which the addition of a major client by the department of marketing without consulting the team led to internal discontent; as well as in the TELECOM-SYSTEM-EUR in which the contract concluded with the client in the beginning had already prestretched the capabilities of the project team and the supporting organizational units. This is likely to be a growing trend in the context of globalization and projects done by multinational firms.

It is interesting to note that the owners of the MEGAPOLIS-EUR airport terminal project not only took purposeful measures from the beginning of the project to increase the embeddedness of various participants, for example by integrating consultants and contractors in the core team, on a status that was equivalent to that of its own employees. They also ensured that this team disposed of abundant internal resources and all needed competencies, in order to avoid overstretch. They also avoided overstretch by including special ceremonies in which work in an area was handed from one contractor to the next and through other means of developing local collaboration routines. In this way, embeddedness was preserved until almost the very end, when a certain acceleration and a change of building sequence some-what affected it. On the contrary, the managers of the EXTRACTIONCOMPLEX project realized that they did not have enough resources in the core team in the first phase, and they took steps to ensure an adequate level for the second phase.

The second finding is that some forms of embedded adhesive cohesion might have a negative effect when some project participants hold out or refuse to share the reciprocity, openness, and other interaction routines that contribute to embedded cohesion. The example in question is the RAILROAD-EUR project, in which the owner belonged to a national culture that sees trust as an implicit value in joint endeavors. Consequently, the project management team did not take into consid-eration any risk related to "schedule delays caused by contractors." Unfortunately, for the project, not all participants had the same approach regarding trust, and some foreign contractors experienced major schedule delays. For this reason, a rather com-mon problem had a more important impact on the project schedule and budget than it should have had. In general, national cultural differences affected the adhesive cohesion of project participants. As another example, the MASSTRANSIT-IS project suffered because of communication problems between parties generated by the use of different systems of measurement units; different languages and imperfect transla-tion; different meanings of words belonging to the same language, but spoken in two different countries, etc. In addition, in the POWERPLANT project, major conflicts occurred between the main contractor and craft workers unions because of the differ-ent perspective on managing industrial relations brought by this foreign contractor.

On the other end of adhesive cohesion dimension, *pragmatic cohesion* relies on providing appropriate stimuli to ensure project collaboration. For example, the TELECOM-SYSTEM-EUR project had a structure with three dedicated teams, and "transversal resources" that were supposed to serve all three teams as well as other projects. The interviewee complained that in the initial phase, when the project was not visible to the higher management in the sponsor organization, the transversal resources were not responsive. The situation changed only after the project became a priority of top managers, who strongly signaled to these "resources" that they should pay attention to the demands of dedicated project teams. A similar pragmatic orientation seemed to prevail in the pharmaceutical companies, because of struc-tural conditions in the host organizations. In the PHADAMAGESTOP-EUR project, the reason was that the owner firm used systems that strictly allocated resources and responsibilities, which led to a culture of internal political games. The reason in the PHARUSTCONTROL-EUR project was a recent history of rapid growth by acquisitions and a policy of preserving the autonomy of the acquired units.

Apart from the internal intertwining of stimuli that enjoins participants to have the project successfully completed, pragmatic cohesion was often tributary to external (with respect to the project) reasons, such as the owner's importance and the public exposure provided by the project. For example, in the POWERPLANT project, the owner was a major regional player in the energy infrastructure industry. Contractors were highly motivated to adhere to the current project, knowing the potential of their client to initiate future projects in which they would like to be involved. Likewise, in projects with significant public exposure (such as the airport projects), participants tended to avoid any negative impact on their reputation, which could result from being associated with unsuccessful projects and inappropriate or not socially desirable behavior.

Coercive cohesion. This kind of cohesion results when some project players, usually the owners, force other participants to collaborate even if they do not want to do so, most often by leveraging enforceable contracts and rules. As mentioned in the theoretical chapter, the approach in which these contracts and rules are defined in the beginning and revisited only in case of problems is called *formal* coercive cohesion. Formal coercion is confrontational, and the indicators we found include a pattern of using the contract to pressure contractors, even with known imperfections in specifications, including the use, or threat to use the advantage provided by security deposits (MASSTRANSIT-MIS) or warranty bonds (POWERPLANT).

Because in projects with formal coercive cohesion the initial contract is the owners' only means for solving a problem, contractual details become very important. Inadequate contracts can dramatically affect the performance of projects. For example, in the RAILROAD-EUR project, the owners put their faith in embedded adhesive cohesion, but they would have liked to resort to the contract against the foreign contractor, when the delays mentioned above occurred. An incomplete and unclear contract prevented them from receiving any compensation.

At the other end of the coercive cohesion dimension, managers see contracts as a lively working tool and revisit it repeatedly. This kind of governed coercive cohesion is more subtle, and, if used properly, it allows owners to impose their will without resorting to confrontation or legal battles. In projects with a high level of governed coercive cohesion, project leaders try to constantly clarify the meaning of contractual clauses and specifications, and more generally, to explain their intentions and the reasoning behind their actions. Multiple meetings at different levels are used to communicate their point of view and to air eventual objections. Thus, the AVERAGEVILLE airport project management team held numerous meetings to clarify design misunderstandings, when they needed to cope with conflicts between architects and constructors. Another tool used in a governed approach were dispute resolution mechanisms, including contract renegotiations if conditions put one side at a marked disadvantage with respect to other parties to the contract.

Some projects used other kinds of procedures to define terms and conditions that were not defined in the initial contract. For example, in the BIOWEIGHT project, manufacturers signed quality agreements, to make sure they understand each other's responsibilities. In the MEGAPOLIS-EUR airport project, the owner took all the risk and guaranteed the reimbursement of all costs incurred by contractors. However, the owner elaborated jointly with contractors a list with disallowed costs to avoid eventual misunderstandings and misuses of funds.

It is interesting to note that the case studies revealed that this dimension applies to internal procedures as well. For example, the PHARUSTCONTROL-EUR project (one of the examples of overstretch discussed earlier), was characterized by a rather formal application of organizational procedures, which imposed tight deadlines and a result orientation, focused on risk analysis and stopping risky projects. However, the core project team attempted to introduce elements of a governed approach in order to reduce the negative impact of such structures. For example, when problems led to persistent tensions, they created a sort of "war teams," in which everybody reflected on a solution, including project leaders. They also organized meetings with the project champions and with the all-powerful portfolio committee in order to clarify their expectation.

Flexibility. This variable measures the leeway that the emergent structure gives actors to implement the desired response to a negative unexpected event. Flexible structures limit this impact to a specific project area, or to a moment in time.

Configurational flexibility. This kind of flexibility is best expressed by the term modularity, which means that the project is divided into parts, whose independence enables project participants to contain the effect of an unexpected event to only one part and to respond to this event by modifying that part or arranging it differently with the project. The projects we studied divided the main project in several phases, subprojects, and further down to activities. For example, the RAILROAD-EUR project was broken down into four main parts, each corresponding to a specific geographical area and further into several other subprojects. When the project faced major delays in obtaining permits for one geographical subarea, this structure enabled the team to limit the negative impact of the event at that small area and all other projects and subprojects could be developed as planned. However, the benefits of separation are limited by the interactions between the different parts of the project, which enable the negative impact of an unexpected event to propagate to other parts of the project. As mentioned in the theoretical chapter, the extent to which language couplings and interaction routines between actors include a rich understanding of these interactions defines the different extremes of the configurational flexibility dimension.

On the one hand, configurational flexibility can be achieved *implicitly* through an initial partition of the project in accordance to tradition, preexisting organizational and technical fault lines, or based on a rough understanding of interactions. This was, for example, the case in pharmaceutical companies, in which the project partition paralleled organizational divisions into units and functions, the customary disease and disciplinary fault lines, as well as other separations imposed by regulation. These fault lines were so powerful that they continued to create problems in spite of a series of special measures that aimed to develop rich couplings through the following measures: assigning to each member of the core team the task of coordinating a special functional team; giving these functional teams the responsibility to coordinate operational teams in their respective units; performing systemic risk estimations in each phase several times per year; and using an effective data interchange system. This last point highlights that the information systems are another source of implicit partition. The other project carried out by a large pharmaceutical company, PHADAMAGESTOP-EUR, seemed to have suffered from its effects. Our interviewee complained that the information system did not allow for information exchange with the level of detail that would be sufficient for teams that are working on different continents.

Another source of implicit partition can be the contractual interfaces, which may stem from the limits of internal capabilities and of those of the various contractors but may also follow other considerations. For example, in the MASSTRANSIT-IS project, the conflict between the two contractors (discussed earlier), could have been avoided if the entire scope, which obviously was not easy to separate, would have been awarded to just one contractor, especially since both had all required capabilities, or could have subcontracted, in turn, the parts in which they did not feel at ease. However, the desire to have more control and other obscure considerations prevented the lead partner to do so. In the RAILROAD-EUR project, the coexistence of multiple subprojects in the same area made it difficult for the project team to establish clear areas of responsibilities and favored opportunistic behavior of contractors; they starting blaming each other for delays and inappropriate quality of work.

Finally, an example from the technical sphere illustrates the importance of a rich understanding for configurational flexibility. Due to labor shortages, the EXTRACTIONCOMPLEX project used a modular design, which would enable most subsystems to be built and assembled on an external facility, located near a populated area with a larger workforce pool. These subsystems would then be transported in the construction site and installed. However, the engineers that designed these subsystems were not properly trained and did not have the required experience for this type of design, which led to multiple difficulties. In the second stage, they were replaced by engineers with a more appropriate set of skills.

This consideration brings us to the other end of the dimension—the *heedful* configurational flexibility. As discussed in the theoretical chapter, after unexpected events, it may be necessary to quickly rethink the separation of activities, in near crisis conditions and in a situation in which new interactions may emerge between various parts of the project. This kind of response is possible only if the structure already includes the rich couplings and routines discussed. An example of the difficulties that can emerge from such a situation is the AVERAGEVILLE project, which struggled to stay on schedule when the construction was delayed, because the initial schedule has overlapped the building of the new terminal, the demolition of an old one, and ongoing operations in a way that did not take into account all possible interactions.

In this respect, the MEGAPOLIS-EUR project provided an example of a constant effort to cultivate a heedful configurational flexibility, and of the emergence of routines that reduced it. The measures came on top of the use of a strong project management capability and of a practice of intimate involvement in project activities, which enabled better coordination of separate subprojects. For example, the project used a procedure for the progressive shaping of a detail-integrated plan for construction, so decisions could be delayed until an adequate understanding of interactions emerged. It also used a sophisticated risk management procedure, which encouraged various participants to think of the many possible interactions between them and of their consequences, hence establishing a richer language coupling. The team paid a lot of attention to site logistics during construction and required contractors to work the interfaces among them. As the project approached the ramp-up to operation, they paid attention to the integration between the systems teams and the operating teams. Moreover, the former were asked to avoid systems innovation, in order to take advantage of the experience from previous projects and to perform extensive tests, including during the volunteer test day mentioned previously. On the negative side, interviewees mentioned that project routines and communication couplings did not ensure that all decisions were documented and communicated to all interested parties. Moreover, the communication chain with third tier suppliers was often too long. The project also had troubles with succession, as people changed before their scope run out. Finally, as was mentioned before, too little time was allowed at the end for system integration. These routines may have been responsible for the difficulties that the project had to respond to during a major unexpected event (to be discussed below).

Sequential flexibility. This kind of flexibility minimizes the dependence of current response actions on the decisions and actions taken in the past. One possibility for achieving it is through *proactive* strategies that delay irreversible decisions and open alternative options for action. A good example can be found in the TELECOM-SYSTEM-EUR project, where the scope was defined gradually, starting with only 60 percent in the planning phase. Also, in AVERAGEVILLE and METROPOLIS projects, the design was completed in several steps—the so-called 30/60/90 percent approach, which allowed designers to receive and incorporate feedback from constructors, and to include changes that became necessary later in the project as a result of various unexpected events. The MEGAPOLIS-EUR project used a *"loose fit envelope design,"* also called *"progressive fixity approach,"* during the design phase, which enables the incorporation of changes quite late in the process. However, proactive flexibility depends on the ability to anticipate problems, and hence it diminishes if experts are asked for advice too late, as it was the case with the BANK-IS project, or if the consultants hired are unable to foresee the obstacles, as was the case in the BIOWEIGHT project.

However, even the best experts and consultants are not able to foresee all possible events that may affect the project. In addition, the proactive measures may slow down or limit some subsequent choices. The alternative is, therefore, the *agile* sequential flexibility, which increases the speed with which new effective decisions are made. This was cultivated through clear and fast decisional procedures, via decision-making autonomy, and fast and efficient problem solving processes. For example, the TELECOM-SYSTEM-EUR project, performed by a hierarchical and control oriented organization, enabled the project organization to escalate problems to the highest decisional levels and shift to a crisis mode with an incredible speed. In the AVERAGEVILLE project, clear areas of responsibilities and decisional procedures enabled leaders to quickly react when unexpected events threatened the project. Moreover, having fewer intermediaries speeds-up and makes more efficient the problem solving processes. In this sense, the managers of the POWERPLANT project preferred to hire directly all contractors, avoiding subcontracting, to maintain a shorter communication chain and a direct control over their partners and project activities. In the case of METROPOLIS, trade contractors enjoyed a large autonomy to change work processes and methods, while still delivering the same output. Smaller teams, such as those in the BIOHEALER-EUR, BIOWEIGHT, the second phase of AVERAGEVILLE, and some subprojects of the MASSTRANSIT-MIS project, and higher team autonomy, such as that observed in RAILROAD-EUR and METROPOLIS projects, were also associated with faster decision processes. Finally, in the TELECOM-MODULE-EUR project, a project management procedure enabled leaders to reallocate resources to the most stringent activities at given moment.

Resourcefulness. This feature of the emergent structure supports the implementation of responses to unexpected events. It provides access to additional financial, human, or time reserves, as well as to creative response solutions.

Sustaining resourcefulness. One facet of resourcefulness is the ability to provide the project with the needed additional funds, personnel, and time. One possibility is to set aside reserves from the beginning and to continue to accumulate them during the project life cycle. As an example of this *cumulative* approach, is a common project management practice to reserve 8 percent to 10 percent contingencies to mitigate foreseen and unforeseen risks. Some projects used even larger amounts. For example, for the airports in our sample, reserves were over 20 percent of the budget. Among these, METROPOLIS had a particular approach, apart from the regular 15 percent visible contingencies allocated for foreseeable risks, the project director had access to another 15 percent management reserves, specifically prepared for unexpected events. The availability of the latter was unknown to other participants, so they will not rely on these funds and will make all possible efforts to stay within budget. Other projects also protected the planned schedule and the completion date with time reserves. The POWERPLANT project allocated three months for unexpected delays, which were eventually not used. AVERAGEVILLE allocated six months for each of the two phases, and, when the team managed to finish the first phase on time, the project was particularly successful in the eyes of the public at large, as it appeared to be completed six months ahead of schedule.

However, in some cases, it is impossible to maintain such reserves and the project team even has to purposefully diminish the cumulative sustaining resourcefulness of the project. For example, in the CITYSTREET project, under stakeholder pressure, the team shortened the project schedule from 22 months to only 13 months. This was compensated for by having longer working days (until 9 p.m.) and working weekends, but the project had no time reserves for unexpected events. We already mentioned previously that projects in the pharmaceutical industry are kept quite lean. Moreover, we found that most projects in our sample tended to cost significantly more than initially foreseen. Yet, only projects that allocated higher-than-usual financial reserves managed to finish on budget. However, for most projects, it is difficult to justify such reserves, which means that projects have to obtain additional resources after the fact.

In such cases, and when accumulated resources are not sufficient for project completion, the project had to rely on its *absorptive* sustaining resourcefulness. In the first place, resource absorption means good access to additional internal resources. This is easier when projects are considered high priority by the sponsoring organizations, as was the case for the BANK-IS and MASSTRANSIT-IS. The TELECOM-SYSTEM-EUR is a special case again, because, after it went into the crisis mode, it appeared able to attract a significant amount of additional resources. Second tier executives were calling the project manager every week to ask whether something was needed for the project. While this case, in which the best resources are allocated to the project only after the problems, is somewhat unique, the pharmaceutical companies seem to institutionalize similar levels of absorptive resourcefulness. Approaches vary from lean projects with little internal leeway and an easily overstretched network, having unlimited access to additional resources and expertise, to semiautonomous projects, which have access to a dynamic resource envelope. This situation can be contrasted with the cumulative situation of airport projects, which are highly autonomous. These projects received all the needed funding and significant contingency reserves from the beginning, and could reallocate savings to other activities of the same project. It should also be noted that the access to internal resources can be eased by the visibility of the project to external stakeholders, such as potential investors and pressure groups (e.g., patients associations), as was the case for PHARUSTCONTROL-EUR and PHADAMAGESTOP-EUR. The second aspect of resourcefulness, the access to external resources, is facilitated by the connections established by the project team. For example, through the members of their board, airports had good connections to many large companies, and could obtain additional resources.

Thanks to the high level of absorptive resourcefulness, several projects easily almost doubled their budget and schedule. This was the case for these projects: RAILROAD-EUR project, which received more government funds; the EXTRAC-TIONCOMPLEX project, which received additional funds from the partners in the joint venture that owned it; and BIOWEIGH, which received more financing from venture capitalists. However, the latter was able to do so only after the biotech startup that owned the project cut down or spun-off other parallel projects and activities. Moreover, in cases such as BANK-IS and POWEPRLANT, the ability to attract or dispose of additional resources was limited by other internal projects that were going on at the same time. In the case of MEGAPOLIS-EUR and EXTRAC-TIONCOMPLEX, the ability to attract additional human resources was limited by the number of large external projects that were happening at the same time, forcing them to try to recruit personnel from abroad.

Creating resourcefulness. Project participants also have to propose solutions to the problems posed by unexpected events. On the one hand, they can find and adapt an existing idea or to identify someone who has the ability to provide a solution. On the other hand, they can develop an entirely original solution on their own. These two options form the extremes of the creating dimension of resourcefulness.

The first option relies on the *explorative* capabilities of the project network. The case studies show that, in large organizations, a first level of these capabilities is provided by links to internal experts in the broader organization, while a second was to bring in experts from outside it. For example, participants in the TELECOM-SYSTEM-EUR project had a practice of "escalating" technical problems to internal technical experts. If the latter were unable to provide a solution, they, in turn, "escalated" the problem toward the suppliers of the equipment that caused the problem. In the MEGAPOLIS-EUR project, one approach was to replace internal engineers that were unable to find a solution for a given problem, for example, resulting from a planning condition imposed by regulators, with engineers that were more specialized in that type of problems. Like many other large firms, the owner of the POWERPLANT project had a large number of excellent internal experts that were not part of the project team. These were solicited to participate in finding a solution. However, most of the time, they created teams that also involved external experts or asked the latter to provide the solution. Our interviewees in that company appeared to believe that involving as many external consultants as necessary, as often as the situation requires, is a sure recipe for success even for serious unexpected issues, when the solutions call for breaking a world record. Yet they also noticed that external experts mostly disagreed between them about the origin of problems and about the best solution. Hence, team members needed the competencies required to choose between these solutions or, less frequently, to combine them into a new solution.

Similar solutions were used in the projects of large pharmaceutical companies. For example, the PHARUSTCONTROL-EUR team had access to an advisory committee of experts and consultants, while PHADAMAGESTOP-EUR benefitted from its owner's practice of forming dedicated teams to respond to each event. Because of their more limited internal resources, smaller pharmaceutical firms, such as BIOWEIGHT, had a practice of developing a ramified network of external consultants.

In the digital projects in which the technology to be implemented had been already used elsewhere, external consultants were a constant source of ideas, for example, by providing insights about how the system works in other companies in the case of R&D-MIS-EUR, in other countries in the case of BANK-IS, or in other cities in the case of MASSTRANSIT. A less common approach was used by BANK-IS—namely, of developing a database with technical problems and solutions to share specific knowledge within the team.

The second option of creative resourcefulness relies on the *innovative* capability of the project team. An example of solutions that this capability can provide to a complex problem is offered by the EXTRACTIONCOMPLEX project. To attract the necessary work force, the project management team tried multiple approaches, such as searching for workers outside the region and even overseas; using modular off-site building; building a new town, with its own airport and leisure facilities close to the construction site; using a fly-in fly-out approach from regions that did not experience labor shortages, to minimize the period of time people would have to stay far from their families; providing higher salaries and benefits; and scheduling the peak construction activity so it will not coincide with the peaks of other projects taking place in the area, and so on.

Despite the difficulties caused by overextension, the firm that owned the PHADAMAGESTOP-EUR project made a special effort for developing the innovative capacity of its organization. Project teams held regular meetings to address emerging issues and, in difficult situations, used techniques such as brainstorming and collective decision making to base the final decision on different perspectives and to develop creativity within the team. The interviewees remarked that, several times, very interesting solutions were proposed by answering a question asked by a participant who had the least knowledge about the discussed topic. This suggested the importance, as well as the difficulty, of letting everyone participate in the process, for example, by encouraging individuals who have a less outgoing character but excellent ideas to speak up. This seemed to require a personal effort from managers and from every team member, in addition to the cultural effort by the company. The latter strived to develop a culture of creativity, which supported the initiatives emanating from project teams and specific individuals and encouraged managers to be sensitive to individual differences. However, this was complemented by a practice of internal challenging, whereby ideas proposed by one team were confronted with the ideas of other employees in order to be sure that the concept was stable before approaching the higher management or external experts for approval.

There were also projects with a low innovative capability. For example, in the MASSTRANSIT-IS project, managers constantly rejected the new, innovative technical solutions proposed by their suppliers. When one feature of the system had some technical problems, the managers decided to simply drop out that feature. In addition, they considered the constant cross-function communication, which also leads to innovation, a waste of time. As a result, toward the end of the project, the core team was split into four hermetic departments. Members of each department were asked to focus on their specific task and to communicate with personnel from the other department only at the level of department leaders.

Unexpected Events

As expected, all projects in our sample experienced a large number of unexpected events during the execution phase. In fact, almost 60 percent of the projects experienced one or a few events that could be qualified as severe, which could have, or in some cases did, jeopardize the completion of the project. The rather unexpected finding was the salience of events that can be said to have an "internal" origin, which includes mistakes, conflicts, and technical problems, as well as of events that were somewhat expected but proved to be much more severe than expected.

Table 3-2 presents a typology of unexpected events based on two dimensions: the predictability of the event, and its source. Among the events that were predicted is the case of POWERPLANT, in which numerous geological tests and estimations had been made in the planning phase, but when the team started the actual construction, the soil proved more friable, its composition more unfriendly, and the solid ground located much deeper than predicted. Similarly, in the EXTRACTIONCOMPLEX project, while the shortage of craft workers had been predicted,

Table 3-2   Typology of Unexpected Events

Predictability of the event	Source of the event		
	Internal (estimation errors, conflicts)	External – related (other projects, autonomous actors)	External – unrelated (macroeconomic, political processes)
Worse than predicted	• Geological conditions issues • Errors in estimating project costs • Optimistic schedule • Technical incompatibilities • Quality issues • Key members departure/relocation	• Lack of qualified workers • Frequent change of technical specifications from client • Strong opposition to project implementation • Major delays in obtaining permits due to environmental issues	• Economic crisis
Unpredicted but predictable (omissions)	• Communication issues with overseas division • Contractor-related schedule delays • Compatibility issues of systems delivered by different suppliers	• Future change in regulations • External interdependent project delays • Unfavorable regulator response • Major client change of requirements • Major client bankruptcy	• Decrease in the price of the project output
Unpredictable	• Identification of toxicity in later animal tests	• Cancellation of governmental approval	• September 11, 2001 terrorist attacks

the construction activity in the region began to increase exponentially over time, which led to labor shortages and wage levels that were much higher than anyone had initially foreseen.

Other events could have been predicted, but they were not, because of omissions in planning. For instance, the RAILROAD-EUR project leaders did not expect any contractor-related schedule delays, while BANK-IS and STORAGEFACILITY teams did not foresee the problems experienced by the external projects with which they had to interoperate.

Finally, some events were simply unpredictable, as assumed in the theoretical chapter. In the PHADAMAGESTOP-EUR project, all tests had been done in conformity with regulations and organizational procedures. However, some later routine tests on animals identified a toxicity that had not been discovered in all prior tests. Eventually, the project had to be completely abandoned. Similarly, METROPOLIS project leaders had obtained all necessary governmental approvals for the design of security-sensitive areas. When construction was already well advanced, all of a sudden, the project manager was informed that governmental officers reevaluated the project and withdrew the earlier approval, meaning that the project has to be substantially redesigned.

With regard to their source, we classified events as internal, external-related, and external unrelated. Events internal to the project are generated by errors in planning and estimating, conflicts within and between teams, inefficient communication flow, quality issues, and so on. They are the most frequent types of unexpected events, but, among all categories, the project team has the best control over these. Even so, their impact is sometimes significant. For example, the MASSTRANSIT-IS project was delayed more than one year because of major compatibility issues between the technical systems delivered by the two main suppliers of the project. The POWEPLANT project was also affected by important conflicts between one major contractor and unions.

The second source of events is found in the external environment, but in projects or actors related to the focal project. For example, the MASSTRANSIT-IS and R&D-IS-EUR projects faced a serious resistance to implementation from some departments. The RAILROAD-EUR project had major delays in obtaining construction permits for one specific geographical area due to complaints and even actions in court of some environmentalist groups. Because these events are often conditioned by the actions taken by the project itself, a change in the project can reduce or eliminate the impact of these events.

Finally, some events that occurred in the external environment, but which are not related to the project, can also affect the project. A spectacular example is the economic crisis, which affected, among others, the value performance of airports projects, as the number of passengers increased slower than expected and, consequently, so did the revenues. In the STORAGEFACILITY project, the crisis affected the owner of the client project, which declared bankruptcy and stopped the project. Another example is the September 11, 2001 terrorist attacks, which determined governments to require stricter security measures, which had to be implemented in all airports. New facilities had to be incorporated in the airport building design.

Reaction Processes

The case studies also enabled us to better understand the reaction process that takes place after the unexpected events. Many respondents recalled that the first reaction was on the emotional level. The first emotional impulse often leads participants to misrepresent the problem. For example, in the EXTRACTIONCOMPLEX project, participants initially perceived technical issues as being much more difficult to solve than they turned out to be. Another reaction is ignoring or rejecting the events. For example, the team of the BANK-IS project first refused to reschedule the project so that it can meet requirements of a new, large client signed-up by the marketing department. It only did so, when forced by executives.

However, in general, this emotional event is followed by a mobilization of resources. The impacted teams and project leaders meet and start looking for solutions. As a frequent first outcome, the project manager designates specific persons or forms specially dedicated teams to manage the response. Examples include the crisis cell formed to deal with the September 11, 2001 terrorist attacks inside the METROPOLIS project; personnel reallocation to manage stringent problems in TELECOM-SYSTEM-EUR project; and the formation of sub-teams for each event in PHADAMAGESTOP-EUR.

Another frequent step in the reaction process is involving representatives from affected parties as well as external experts. As mentioned previously, in order to find the most appropriate solutions for the multiple geological issues they faced, POWERPLANT project leaders organized meetings between core project team participants and experts from the owner firm, from contractors, from external consultants, as well as with the local community. This step helps in the understanding of problems as well as in finding a solution, especially since, in some cases, the emotional reaction prevents the project team from understanding up front the impact that the event will have on the project. For example, after the September 11 terrorist attacks, government authorities opened discussions regarding the implementation of additional security measures in airports only several weeks after the event, and the requirements became effective one year later or even more.

As we anticipated via the emphasis we put on the cohesion variable, unexpected events frequently lead to conflicts. Approaches to solving these conflicts ranged from amiable discussions between parties in the case of RAILROAD-EUR, to the moderation and sometimes pressure of higher hierarchical levels, as was the case in the POWERPLANT and MASSTRANSIT-IS projects, and even the involvement of an external arbiter in the case of METROPOLIS. It is interesting to note that thanks to the steps taken to embed participants the MEGAPOLIS-EUR project had few conflicts for a multibillion dollar project, and almost all were solved amicably, in the spirit of focusing on problem solving rather than blame. Respondents recalled only one event after which the owner had to force a contractor to take responsibility for an error and support the cost of corrective action. However, as the launch date approached, delays led to a more dictatorial mode, expressed in the acceleration of the schedule, and the imposition of the radial construction pattern over contractors' objections. However, a culture of blaming others developed only after the opening day, when a major event affected terminal operations.

With respect to changing the pattern of relations between participants after an unexpected event, a very interesting reaction is the instauration of a dictatorship in the MASSTRANSIT-IS project. The schedule of this project started to experience significant delays because of the democratic decision-making procedures that gave all partners an equal say in spite of their different role and financial contributions, and because of the continuing attempts to include new functions and features. Eventually, these delays led to a crisis. Therefore, it was decided that the leading partner would have the ultimate decision power, after consulting the others. Moreover, a consultant that had already worked on the project was appointed as a sort of dictator. The consultant, in turn, imposed five principles, which, among others, ensured that only a trimmed down set of specifications will be implemented and that no other additions to this set will be allowed. All additional features and functions were to be considered for a possible second phase of the project. In these conditions, the project was finished relatively quickly and functions properly.

Another interesting change in the pattern of relations between participants was the shift into the crisis mode that took place in the TELECOM-SYSTEM-EUR project. As already mentioned, the problems experienced by the project came to the attention of the top managers of the owner company, including via privileged relations that they had with the top managers of the client organization. This resulted in a special attention to this project, even from a second-tier executive, who was put in charge of supervising the project and activated a line of command made of mid-level managers, which ensured that decisions were made fast and that the project had all needed human, material and financial resources. All participants maintained a cooperative mode and avoided finger pointing.

Many other reactions involved major redefinitions of project elements. The most frequent example was the re-estimation of the project budget and schedule. For example, the budget of the EXTRACTIONCOMPLEX project was increased significantly, while the schedule of the STORAGEFACILITY project was delayed repeatedly. The activity sequence was also changed in many cases. For example, one part of the RAILROAD-EUR project was delayed for several years, while other parts were accelerated. Likewise, in the second phase of AVERAGEVILLE, the demolition-construction-operation sequence was further split and overlapped. The TELECOM-SYSTEM-EUR managers convinced the client that the initial in-service date was unrealistic and determined jointly with the client the sites where the system will be implemented in priority, while also negotiating with the previous provider the continuation of service until the new system was operational (for which the new provider supported all costs). Finally, some projects required finding new technical solutions in the place of those that did not work, as well as redesigning and even rebuilding certain parts in order to solve the problems. Again, the TELECOM-SYSTEM-EUR project developed creative technical solutions for two technical problems, one of which stemmed from the reliance on equipment that was not yet available for sale.

In general, the response to events was effective, even though in some cases it involved a significant financial effort. For the METROPOLIS project, changing the design when the government required it involved significant funds, but in the given situation, the response was highly effective. On the other hand, the PHADAMAGESTOP-EUR team managed only to efficiently close the project after the tests involving the drug they were developing revealed toxicity in animals.

Their response was highly ineffective compared to initial goals, but effective in dealing with the event. Similarly, the STORAGEFACILITY team did not complete the project, but successfully put it in the preservation mode, awaiting a rebound of energy prices after the economic crisis.

Performance

The projects that were part of our sample provided us with a good variability with respect to performance on all four dimensions proposed in the theoretical chapter. This enabled us to perform the comparative analyses of trajectories whose results are presented in the next section.

Completion. Out of 17 projects, only 13 were entirely completed. Two had sub-projects postponed for future phases, because of cost and schedule issues (TELECOM-MODULE-EUR, MEGAPOLIS). Another one was stopped and prepared for long term preservation (STORAGEFACILITY), because the related project of the external client was stopped. Finally, one project was fully stopped, because of some potential negative effects on patients, discovered in tests (PHADAMAGESTOP-EUR). It should be noted, however, that both STORAGEFACILITY and PHADAMAGESTOP-EUR were not stopped because of poor project management performance.

In terms of budget and schedule delays, only the three airport project teams managed to finish on budget as well as on or even ahead of schedule. A good completion performance was obtained by the POWERPLANT and CITYSTREET teams, which finished on time and with less than 10 percent over budget. The EXTRACTIONCOMPLEX project was finished on time, but with significant (50 percent) cost overrun. All other projects experienced both budget and schedule overruns. At the extreme, the RAILROAD-EUR, MASSTRANSIT-IS, and some pharmaceutical projects almost doubled their schedule and budget. The TELECOM-SYSTEM-EUR had the most important delay, as it lasted 20 months, rather than 4 months as planned initially.

Technical. Apart from the two projects that were stopped and the other two that had functions postponed for future phases, all projects fully reached their initial goals and performed all planned functions. Some projects were local innovations, as they introduced systems that had been used before elsewhere, but were entirely new for the given organization (R&D-MIS-EUR) of for the given geographical area (MASSTRANSIT-IS, BANK-IS). Other projects were the first of their kind for the given organization or team (all airports and EXPLORATIONCOMPLEX). The RAILROAD-EUR project was the first large project to fulfill the requirements of the new National Environmental Code. During the development of some projects, such as POWERPLANT, certain solutions constituted worldwide innovations and records.

Operational. For most projects operation costs are as predicted, clients are satisfied with the output, the system functions reliably, and no significant accidents or malfunctions have occurred. However, apart from the two projects that were stopped and thus never operated so far, some projects did experience various problems: including technical bugs (R&D-MIS-EUR, MASSTRANSIT-IS, AVERAGEVILLE), slightly higher operation costs (MASSTRANSIT-IS), and some accidents and incidents (EXTRACTIONCOMPLEX).

To ensure a good operating performance, project teams paid particular attention to the opening or launching date, the day in which the project will start operating.

Multiple tests, mock-ups, and simulations were done in all projects. Some projects even performed pilot tests (BANK-IS) in a local community, or volunteer test day involving thousands of people and all participating organizations (METROPOLIS). While most projects involved operations representatives in the project team from the beginning, some also created dedicated teams (EXTRACTIONCOMPLEX, METROPOLIS) for the ramp-up and launch. Despite taking similar measures, the MEGAPOLIS terminal opening day was perturbed by a malfunction of a key system. The problem could not be solved immediately, so the whole air traffic to that terminal was affected. In what concerns the project reputation, this event was a disaster, and, even though the problem was solved in a matter of weeks (but with high cost), a successful project from all other points of view became all of a sudden a failure in the eyes of the public.

Value. The value performance of a project includes elements such as financial returns, competitive gains, and social satisfaction. All projects are recently completed, so data about financial returns were available only in a few cases when writing this report. Apart from the TELECOM-SYSTEM-EUR project, which had good sales but poor profitability, all others seem profitable. However, contextual factors had a significant impact in some cases. The expected increase of passenger flow was smaller than expected in the airport projects, most likely due to the financial crisis from 2008–2010. The same crisis and the significant decrease in energy prices affected revenues of EXTRACTIONCOMPLEX and STORAGEFACILITY.

In terms of social satisfaction, perceptions vary widely across projects, and sometimes the same project is evaluated differently by different stakeholders. Projects with high public exposure have been closely scrutinized, while others remained almost unknown to the large public. Among the former group, the increase in transport capacity and public comfort enabled by the terminal, RAILROAD-EUR, and CITYSTREET projects was positively perceived in general, exceptions included complaints about the noise (airports), environmental issues RAILROAD-EUR, and inherent discomfort associated with the presence of a construction site in the middle of the city (CITYSTREET). Perceptions were lower in the case of the EXTRACTIONFACILITY project, which had to face constant complaints from environmentalist groups. Operations at its site were suspended several times due to the illegal presence of activists.

Most projects contributed to the strategic advance of the sponsor organization by increasing its production and operation capacity (POWERPLANT, airports, RAILROAD-EUR), by increasing the product portfolio (PHARUSTCONTTOL), enabling operations in a new industry (EXTRACTIONCOMPLEX) or geographic area (PHARUSTCONTROL), or significantly changing/upgrading the technology in use (MASSTRANSIT-IS, BANK-IS, R&D-MIS-EUR).

The higher confidence in our variables and a better understanding of their range, which emerged from the qualitative results reported in this section, prompted us to attempt to corroborate the hypotheses developed in the theoretical section by comparing the trajectories of influence between variables that were observed in all projects. The results of this effort are reported in the next section.

3. Preliminary Results Concerning Influence Trajectories

As mentioned in the Methods section, we rated all projects on all theoretical variables. This enabled us to perform a rough detection of covariance between

	Adhesive (embedded)	Coercive (governed)	Configurational (heedful)	Sequential (agile)	Sustaining (absorptive)	Creating (innovative)	
Argument (decisional)				−	−		
	+	−			−	+	+ **Completion**
Knowledge (experimental)			−	−	−	+	
	+				−		**Technical**
Participation (pluralist)		+	+	+		+	−
	+					−	− **Operational**
Risk (integrative)	+	+	+	−		+	
				−	+	−	+ **Value**

Figure 3-2   A Summary of the Relations Between Variables Identified Across All Cases

different classes of variables, using a combination of cross-tabulations, correlation, and even regression. This enabled us to suspect, with some degree of confidence, the presence of the relations between variables that are summarized in Figure 3-2. This image is rather difficult to understand, but we will attempt to clarify it briefly. First, the relations refer to the variables listed on the left, across the bottom and on the right. For the planning and response capacity variables, the word in brackets designates the "high" end of the variable (the "low" end is omitted). In the central matrix, each cell has an upper and a lower part. The upper half shows whether there is a relation between the planning variables listed on the left and the response capacity variables listed across the bottom. The lower half shows whether there is a relation between the response capacity variable listed across the bottom and the performance variables listed at the right. The signs in the rightmost column, which do not correspond to any response capacity, signify the presence of a "direct" relation between planning and performance. Please note that the planning variables are not listed in the usual order and that the performance variables are shifted half a line down in relation to the planning variables, to enable the creation of this compact figure. All signs in brackets indicate the presence of a relation and its sign.

Figure 3-2 shows whether the relation between a planning variable and a performance variable can be explained by a trajectory that goes through a response capacity variable (or two), as well as to assess whether the absence of a relation can be explained via two trajectories that go through different response capacity variables but cancel each other's effect. The results, grouped by planning variables, are presented in the following subsections.

Knowledge

As can be seen from Figure 3-2, the knowledge variable of the planning process appears to be related to the completion performance dimension of the project. This seems to confirm one of the influences proposed by hypothesis 1 in the theoretical chapter. However, as can be seen in Figure 3-3, the trajectory of influence does not go, as argued theoretically, through the increase in configurational flexibility, but via the cumulative sustaining resourcefulness. In light of our case studies, this direction can be explained by the fact that projects using an experimental approach, and the associated initial lack of knowledge can be easily transformed into a stimulus for participants to be more careful and to include reserves in their budget and schedule as well as to save money and time whenever possible and add these to the reserves. This, in turn, enables projects to complete the entire scope, within the allotted time and budget.

All airport projects, which were the only ones with an almost perfect completion performance, seem to have followed this influence trajectory. The examples that followed the trajectory with the reverse values of the variables, namely, conceptual planning to absorptive capacity to lower completion performance include PHARUSTCONTROL-EUR, STORAGEFACILITY, TELECOM-SYSTEM-EUR,

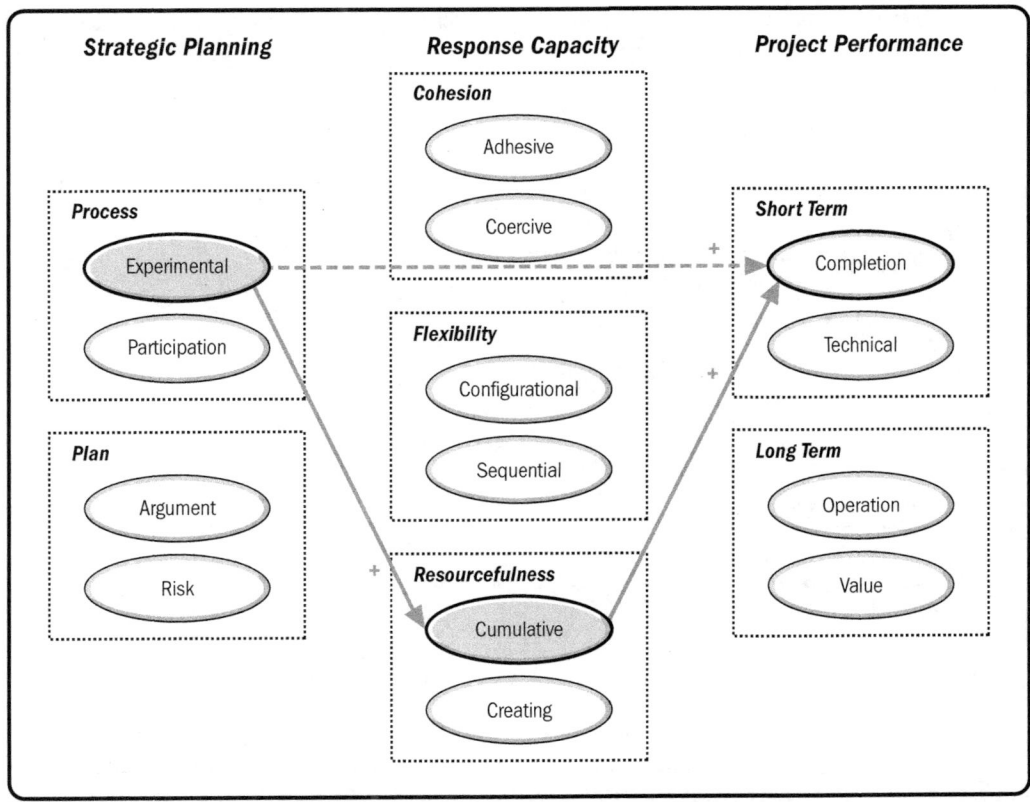

Figure 3-3   Influence Trajectory from Planning Knowledge to Completion Performance

TELECOM-MODULE-EUR, EXTRACTIONCOMPLEX, and POWERPLANT, although the latter is the only one having clearly conceptual and absorptive ratings. This suggests that a conceptual approach creates overconfidence, which means that the project does not accumulate enough resources and has to rely on subsequent absorption, and hence it will appear to exceed the initial budget and time limits, and sometimes to push parts of the scope to subsequent projects. It is also interesting to note that this pattern corresponds to one of the pharmaceutical companies' projects, because this pattern fits the description of lean projects planned according to conceptual models, sometimes imposed by regulation, which most of the time do not complete their scope.

There was no other direct relation between planning knowledge and the other three dimensions of the project performance. However, the investigation of influence trajectories using Figure 3-2, suggests that the absence of relation (in fact only a weakly positive relation) between planning knowledge and value performance may be explained by two trajectories that cancel each other out. As shown in Figure 3-4, cumulative resourcefulness influences negatively the value performance. However, experimental planning knowledge also influences positively the proactive sequential flexibility, which in turn influences positively the value performance. The effects largely cancel each other and result in a weak overall influence of experimental

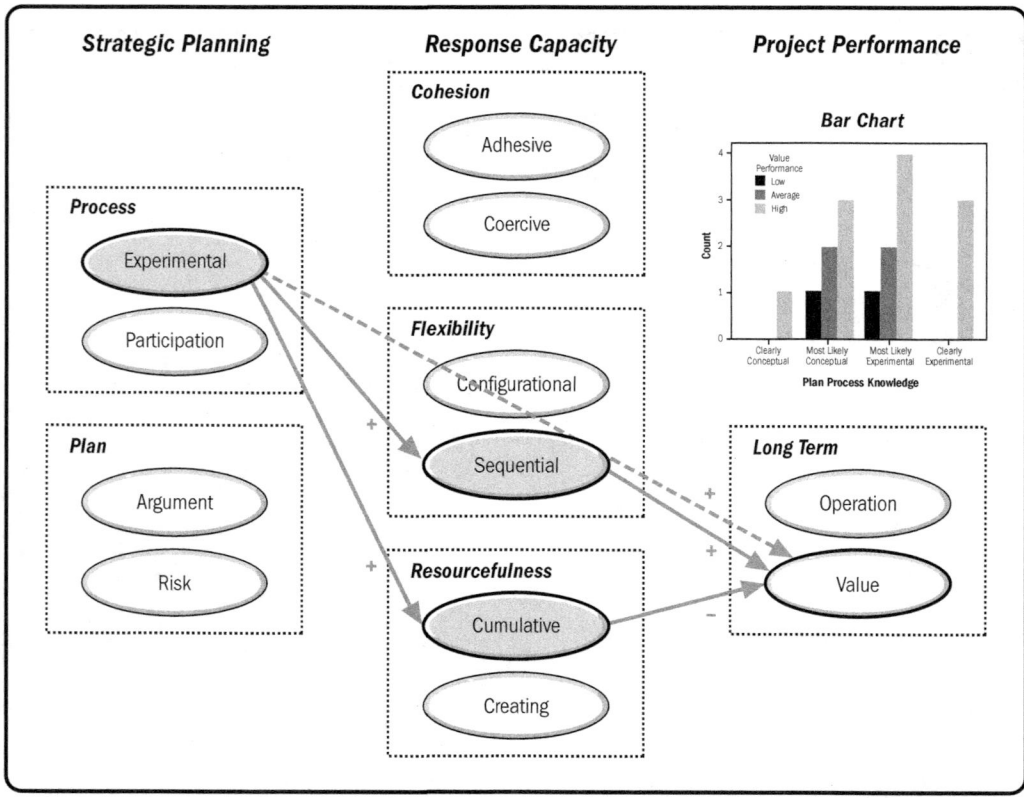

Figure 3-4   Mutually Cancelling Influence Trajectories from Planning Knowledge to Value Performance. The bar chart depicts the less clear relation between planning knowledge and value performance.

knowledge on value performance. The influence of experimental knowledge on pro-active sequential flexibility also has a plausible explanation in light of our case studies. Like in the case of cumulative sustaining resourcefulness, the uncertainty created by the initial lack knowledge is a stimulus for participants to develop ahead of time alternative courses of action. The negative impact of cumulative sustaining resourcefulness on value performance may stem from the fact that a practice of staying within the (generous) budget and schedule, rather than being forced to seek additional resources may limit the ability of projects to access significant amounts of additional resources and may force participants to compromise and cut corners with respect to the value-creating elements.

The TELECOM-SYSTEM-EUR project provides an example of this trajectory at the opposite end of the variables. After a conceptual planning, the project faced negative experiences, which forced it to pass into a crisis mode, with a highly agile decision mode and highly absorptive resource procurement. The successful resources absorption (money from higher management and time from the client) enabled project participants to solve all problems, but the decisional agility did not guarantee the best decisions in the long term (they had to re-stitch the strategic aspects later). The EXTRACTIONCOMPLEX project seems to have gone through a similar pattern. However, clearly conceptual projects, such as POWERPLANT, can have a high value performance in a stable environment, which the sponsor organization largely controls.

We can conclude with respect to the planning knowledge variable that it seems to affect the variables that are related to anticipation, and it does so in the sense of increasing the response capacity elements that are related to anticipating the future and compensating for its uncertainty in a prudent way, such as cumulative resourcefulness and proactive sequential flexibility. In turn, while benefitting from a certain cushion of resources, project participants would most likely act within the limits of this cushion, which may prove insufficient. These considerations become the new working hypotheses with respect to planning knowledge, to be validated in the quantitative part of this research report.

Participation

Figure 3-2 suggests that the participation variable is strongly related to the technical and operational performance. More precisely, centralized, rather than pluralist, planning seems to be related to high performance on these dimensions. We predicted a relation between participation and operational performance as well as technical performance, but with the opposite sign, namely that pluralist planning increases, rather than diminishes, the operational and technical performance. For technical performance the influence goes, as we predicted, via the creating resourcefulness, as can be seen from the results of qualitative research depicted in Figure 3-5. However, for operational performance, we predicted a trajectory mediated by the coercive cohesion variable. Instead, results suggest that the (reverse sign) influence occurs via the development of explorative creating resourceful-ness. In light of our case studies, the relation between centralized planning and explorative capabilities has a simple explanation. The same network centrality that enabled a player to dominate the planning process, later also enables the same player to rapidly identify and recruit experts with the required problem solving competencies. These external (to the project) experts also seem to be more effective in solving these kinds of problems rather than value creation problems.

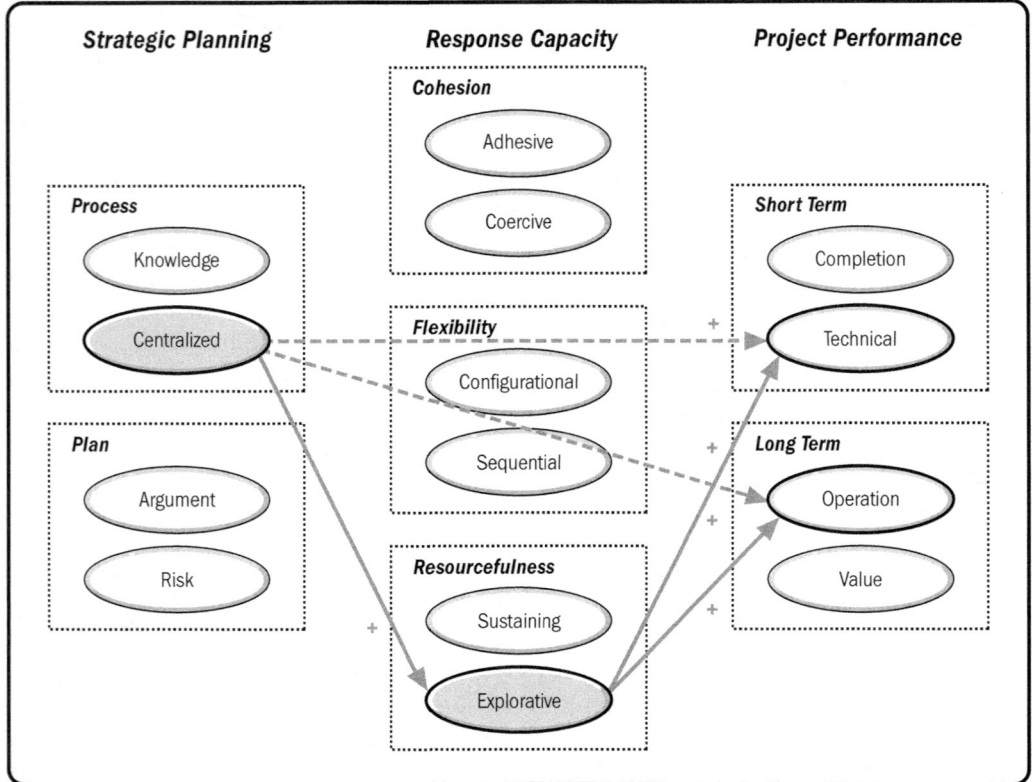

Figure 3-5   Influence Trajectories from Planning Participation to Technical and Operation Performance

PHARUSTCONTROL-EUR, BIOHEALER-EUR, AVERAGEVILLE, and POWER-PLANT correspond to the pattern depicted in Figure 3-5, with its double performance effect. However, only the owner of the last one played a strongly dominant role in project planning. STORAGEFACILITY, MEGAPOLIS-EUR, PHADAMAGESTOP-EUR, and R&D-MIS-EUR are examples of the pattern with reverse values (more pluralist planning, a higher innovative capacity, but lower technical and operational performance). It should be noted that our hypothesis 2 predicted that pluralist planning will lead to the emergence of innovative creating resourcefulness, but rather, with a positive effect on technical and value creation performance. Moreover, the influences of planning participation on the response capacity variables depicted in Figure 3-6 seem to correspond perfectly to those proposed in hypothesis 2. As we can see, pluralistic planning appears to stimulate the emergence of governed coercion and of innovative capacities. However, the effect of governed coercion on completion performance appears to be negative. This may happen because the discussion and clarification routines with contractors may slow down activities and dilute the stimulus to act that would stem from a formal attitude to contractual relations, leading to delays and to situations in which it is difficult to identify who is responsible for supporting consequence and for taking corrective action. In parallel, there is a positive, yet unanticipated effect of the innovative capacity on completion. It may be explained by the fact that completion performance is influenced more by some sort of ad hoc yet

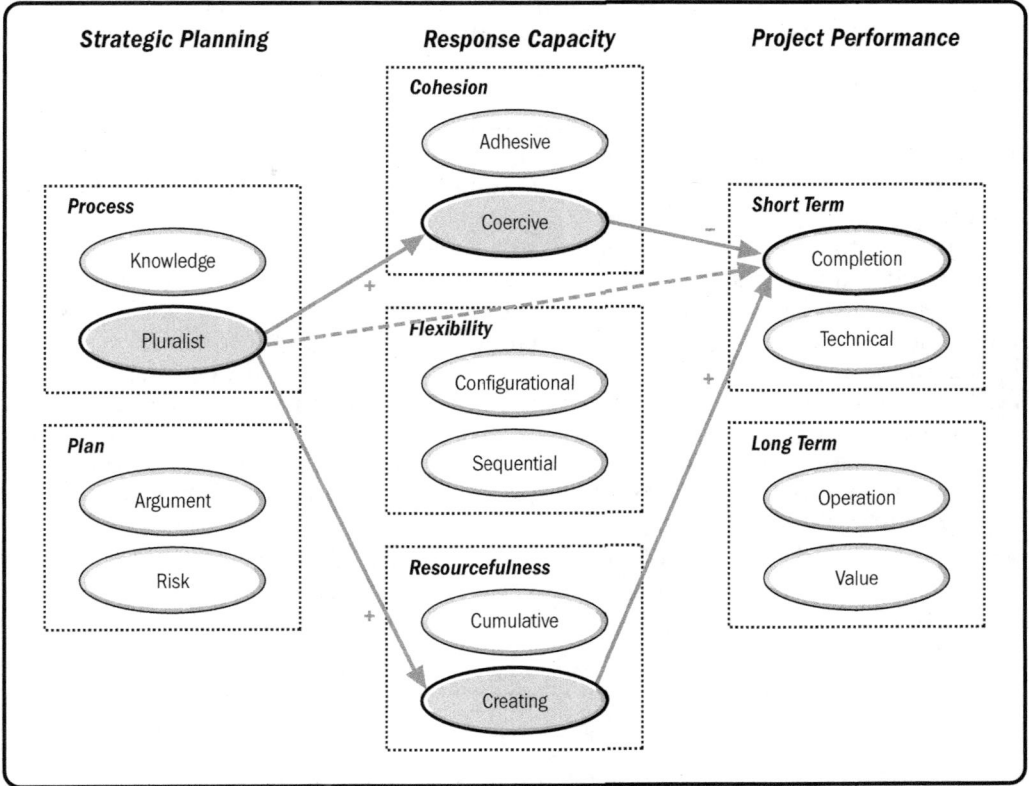

Figure 3-6   Mutually Cancelling Influence Trajectories from Planning Participation to Completion Performance.

project specific resourcefulness, while technical and operational performance may be more dependent on sources of more generic (scientific and technical) knowledge as well as of varied experience, which external experts can more easily provide.

The net effect of the two trajectories depicted in Figure 3-6 is that there is no discernible relation between planning participation and completion performance. Also, there is no effect on the value performance, and no trajectory that relates the two.

The patterns uncovered with respect to the planning participation variable suggest that, in our theorizing, we were right on the mark with respect to the impact this variable will have on the response capacity variables. Indeed, the interaction routines and communication couplings planted during pluralist planning seem to enhance the capabilities that depend on such routines later on, namely governed coercion and innovative resourcefulness. However, we were far off the mark with respect to the impact that these capabilities have on performance. The emerging understanding is that explorative capabilities may be more effective in solving technical and operational problems, as it brings in a systematic set of specialized technical ideas and skills, which cannot be replicated via brainstorming, while the innovative capabilities may be more effective in solving completion problems. As for the governed coercion, it does not seem to have the anticipated positive effects, except, as our case studies appear to suggest, for the participants' satisfaction with the process. Instead, it may affect negatively the completion of projects. These considerations form our new working hypotheses with respect to the planning participation.

Argument

Figure 3-2 suggests that the nature of the plan argument is related to the completion performance of the project, more specifically that a decisional argument increases this performance. Moreover, this influence appears to be mediated by the sustaining resourcefulness variable (In Figure 3-2, we added an influence from the knowledge to the same variable to underscore a certain commonality that will be discussed later). As seen in Figure 3-7, a decisional plan increases the cumulative sustaining resourcefulness, which in turn affects positively the completion performance. This is exactly one of the two influence patterns included in Trajectory 3.2 (but formulated starting with a promotional plan there), which seems to partly confirm hypothesis 3. Once again, the three airports are examples of the pattern starting with a decisional plan leading to cumulative resourcefulness and high completion performance. Examples of the same pattern with the reverse signs (promotional, absorptive, poor completion) are PHARUSTCONTROL-EUR, BANK-IS, TELECOM-MODULE-EUR, and EXTRACTIONCOMPLEX, which are almost invariably internal projects of large organizations, with a degree of innovation or novelty. Together with the influence that comes from planning knowledge, this pattern suggests that a good completion performance relies on putting in place a process for the production of project-specific

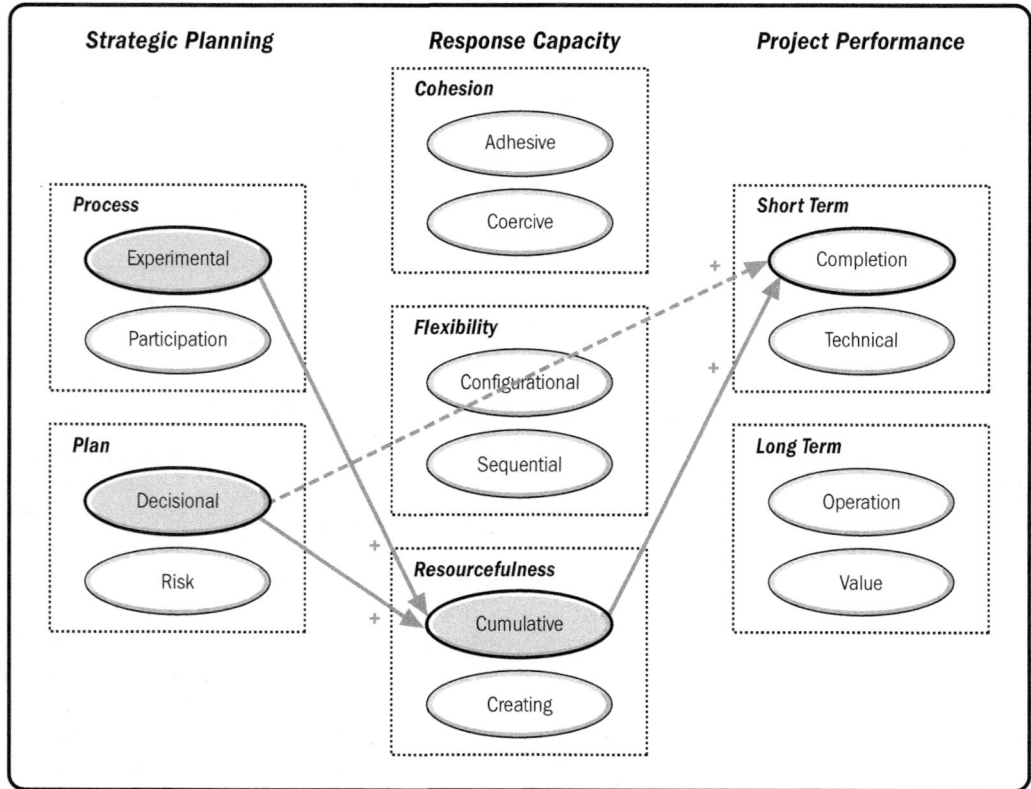

Figure 3-7   Influence Trajectory from Plan Argument to Completion Performance

knowledge, and, in the basis of this knowledge, to develop a diligent decisional plan. This will result in an organization that will accumulate sufficient resources to ensure a full and timely completion of the project.

Hypothesis 3 also predicted, among others, that a decisional plan would increase the chances of emergence of proactive sequential flexibility, which in turn will affect positively the value performance. This pattern is confirmed by the results of the qualitative research. However, as Figure 3-8 suggests, a decisional plan is also likely to stimulate the emergence of cumulative sustaining resourcefulness, which, as we have seen above, in our discussion of the influence of planning knowledge, has a negative impact on value performance. With this additional unanticipated influence, the overall impact of the plan argument on value performance becomes only weakly positive. Examples of projects with decisional plans that led to the development of proactive sequential flexibility as well as of cumulative sustaining resourcefulness are all three airports as well as BIOWEIGHT. However, all of them had good value performance. The example with the reverse values, starting with a promotional argument—in this case the importance of obtaining the business of the client in question and, thus, consolidating the owner's position in a new market—is TELECOM-SYSTEM-EUR with its crisis mode relying essentially on agile decision and massive resource absorption.

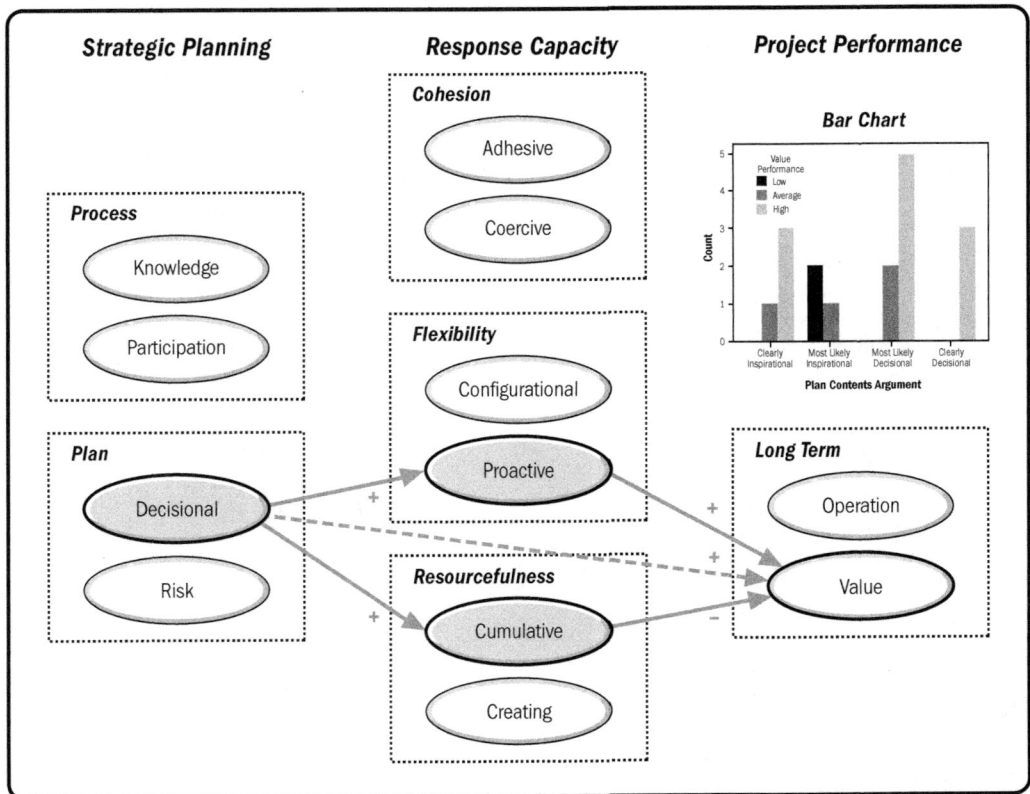

Figure 3-8   Mutually Cancelling Influence Trajectories from Plan Argument to Value Performance. The bar chart depicts the less clear relation between plan argument and value performance.

In conclusion, about the plan argument variable, we would underscore that the hypotheses anticipated correctly the impact this variable will have on the response capacity variables. However, the impact of the latter on performance variables is less well anticipated. We also note that it appears to be, at least in our sample, a perfect parallelism of influence trajectories between the plan argument variable and the planning knowledge variable, two quite distinct variables. This parallelism may occur because a decisional plan is the object that usually carries the fruits of anticipation efforts, and, as such, is likely to include the stimuli for the creation of reserves and options for the future. In other words, a decisional plan is a complement of the initial lack of knowledge in certain projects, while a promotional plan may be the complement of an overconfident conceptual planning process. However, the parallelism between the two variables may also result from the predominance in our sample of projects that contrast these two variables.

Risk

Figure 3-2 suggests that the plan risk variables influence the value and operational performance of projects. More specifically, an integrative approach to risk has a positive influence on these variables. As Figure 3-9 suggests, the influence on operational performance happens through the development of an embedded

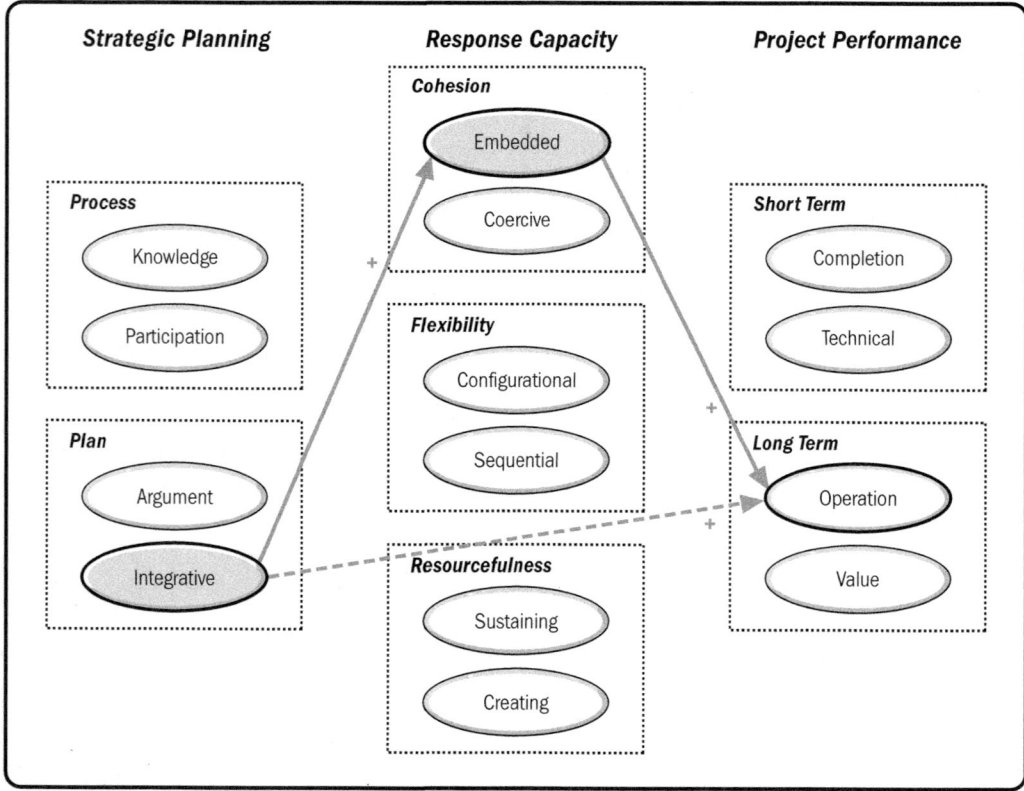

Figure 3-9   Influence Trajectory from Plan Risk Approach to Operation Performance

adhesive cohesion, which is not how we predicted (via configurational flexibility). The BIOHEALER-EUR, RAILROAD-EUR, TELECOM-MODULE-EUR, BANK-IS, POWERPLANT, AVERAGEVILLE, CITYSTREET and METROPOLIS projects seem to follow this trajectory connecting an integrative plan, embedded adhesion and high value. However, POWERPLANT and BIOHEALER were not rated as clearly integrative (only as most likely integrative), while CITYSTREET and AVERAGEVILLE were not rated as clearly embedded. This leaves RAILROAD-EUR, BANK-IS, TELECOM-MODULE-EUR, and METROPOLIS as the projects that most clearly follow this pattern. MASSTRANSIT-IS, STORAGEFACILITY, and TELECOM-SYSTEM-EUR are examples of trajectories in which the variables take the opposite values (allocative, pragmatic, lower operational performance).

In turn, as can be seen from Figure 3-10, the influence of the risk approach on value takes place via the development of proactive sequential flexibility, which, again is not how hypothesis 4 predicted. In fact, the influence of the plan risk approach variable on sequential flexibility, especially the fact that an integrative approach leads to proactive flexibility, is also quite surprising, as hypothesis 4 predicted instead an influence on the configurational flexibility. Considering the case studies, particularly MEGAPOLIS-EUR, in which owners insisted on the proactive identification and airing of risks by contractors, this influence does not seem implausible. However,

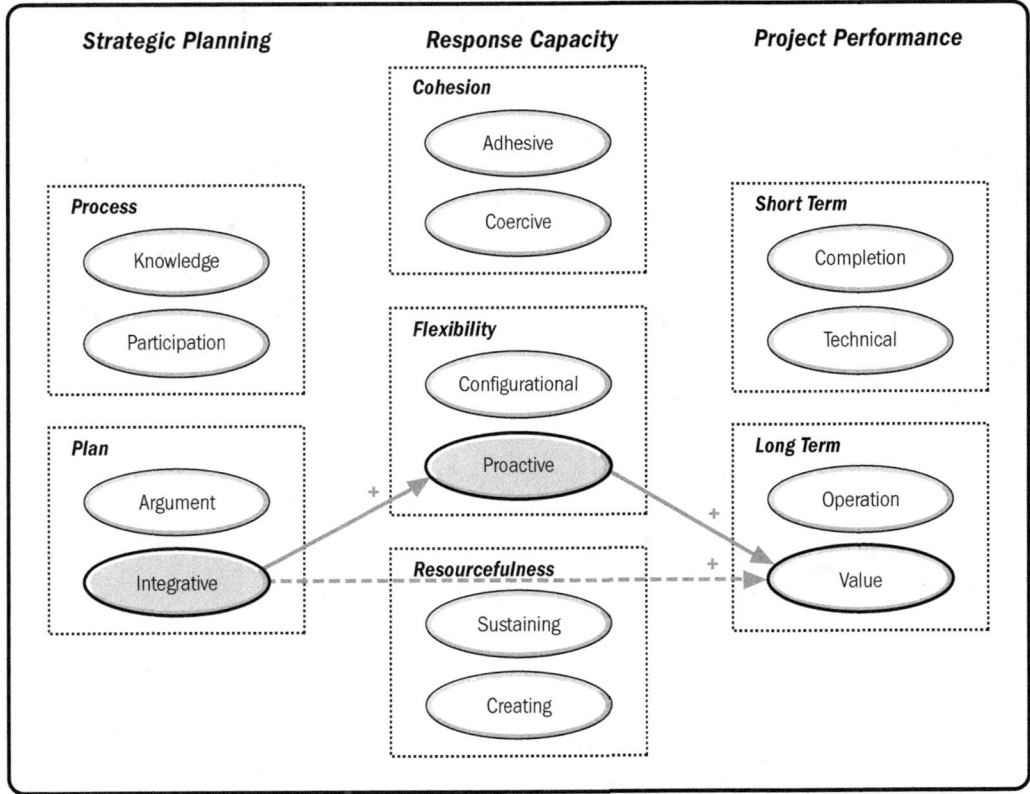

Figure 3-10   Influence Trajectory from Plan Risk Approach to Value Performance

this project did not exactly follow the trajectory depicted in Figure 3-10. Instead the representative projects include PHARUSTCONTROL-EUR, BANK-IS, TELECOM-MODULE-EUR, POWERPLANT, AVERAGEVILLE, R&D-MIS-EUR, METROPOLIS and BIOWEIGHT. However, POWERPLANT and PHARUSTCONTROL are not clearly integrative and none of them is clearly proactive. Examples of the pattern in which variables take the contrary values (allocative, agile, lower value) are STORAGEFACILITY, TELECOM-SYSTEM-EUR, and PHADAMAGESTOP-EUR, the latter the lean project prototype.

Another influence predicted in hypothesis 4 was nearly confirmed by our results. Indeed, the influence trajectory presented in Figure 3-11, from integrative plan to embedded cohesion and to technical performance is as predicted. However, the direct relation between the integrative plan and technical performance is not very strong. As can be seen from the embedded graph, two projects, which are in fact TELECOM-SYSTEM-EUR and MASSTRANSIT-IS, were rated as having a clearly allocative structure but also as having a high technical performance.

Another finding with respect to the plan risk approach is the pattern of mutually cancelling influences depicted in Figure 3-12. Through its role in increasing the

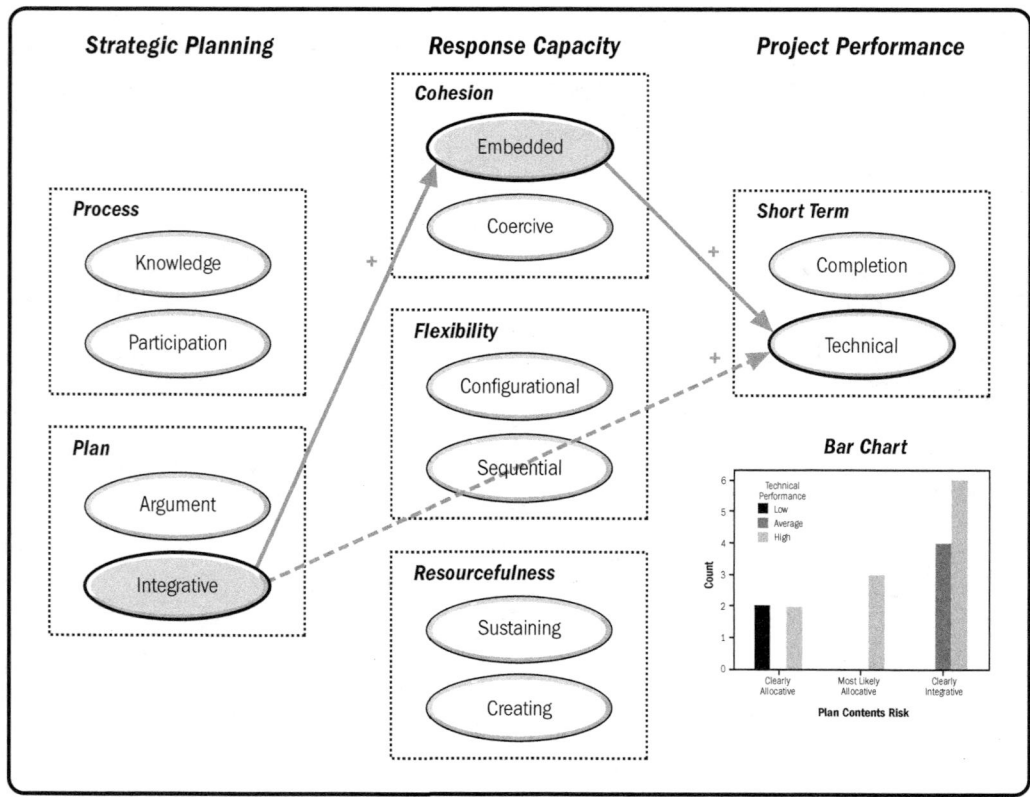

Figure 3-11   Influence Trajectory from Plan Risk Approach to Technical Performance

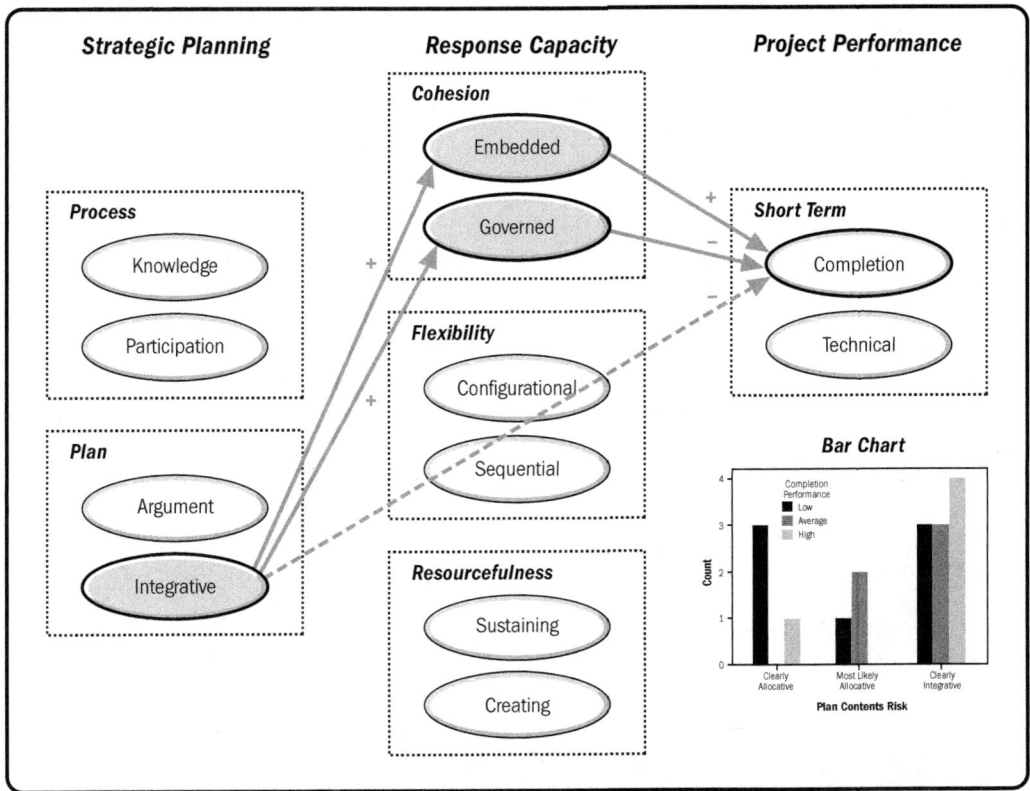

Figure 3-12   Mutually Cancelling Influence Trajectories from Plan Risk Approach to Completion Performance.

embedded adhesive cohesion, an integrative risk approach appears to have a positive influence on the completion performance, which we did not predict. However, integrative plans also seem to affect positively the emergence of governed coercion, which, as we have already seen, has, in turn, a negative impact on completion performance. Therefore, overall, the impact of the integrative plan on completion performance seems slightly negative. Examples of this pattern that join an integrative plan, through an embedded and governed cohesion to completion performance are RAILROAD-EUR, BANK-IS, and TELECOM-MODULE-EUR. All of them have low completion performance, which suggests that embeddedness may give some project participants an occasion to drag their feet and obtain additional funding because of unexpected events.

The overall conclusion with respect to the plan risk approach is that this planning variable has a strong impact on the project. Moreover, at least in our sample, integrative approaches seem to have a positive impact on performance, while allocative approaches seem to have a negative impact on performance. The main influence of this variable occurs via its relation with the embedded adhesive cohesion, which in turn has a positive impact on three out of four performance variables—namely, completion, technical, and operation. In addition, the risk approach influences positively the value performance via its role in increasing the proactive sequential flexibility. These trajectories seem to confirm the attention we paid to this variable from the introduction to the theoretical chapter, as well as, in a sense, the importance we attribute to the emergent project structure and its capacity to respond to unexpected events.

4. Discussion and Conclusions

By considering various dimensions of planning, we attempted to identify relationships describing how planning configures response capacity and how response capacity may in turn affect project performance. The "trajectories"—configurations of planning, structure, and performance—that we identified seem to support our key hypothesis that some projects flourish, where as others apparently falter because of constraints created by the structure of a project emerging from its planning. If we return to the entire set of planning variables and response capacity mediation, we see that each planning variable has at least one significant influence on a performance variable. Table 3-3 (upper part A) recaps these influences. The plan risk approach appears to have the strongest impact. As we anticipated, the integrative approach appears to be related more often to the positive performance, by opposition to an allocative approach. It seems to work especially by strengthening

Table 3-3   Summary of Influences of Planning and Response Capacity Variables on Project Performance (*italics* highlight situations when theoretical predictions were not confirmed)

A. Planning Variable	Strong influence	Weak or mixed influence
1) Risk approach (integrative)	· Operational · Value	· Technical · Completion
2) Participation (centralized)	· Technical · Operational	· Completion
3) Knowledge (experimental)	· Completion	· Value
4) Argument (decisional)	· Completion	· Value
B. Response Capacity Variable	*Positive influence*	*Negative influence*
1) Adhesive cohesion (embedded)	· Completion · Technical · Operational	
2) Coercive cohesion (formal)	· Completion	
3) Configurational flexibility		
4) Sequential flexibility (proactive)	· Value	
5) Sustaining resourcefulness (absorptive)	· Value	· Completion
6) Creating resourcefulness (explorative)	· Technical · Operational · Value	· Completion

the embedded cohesion but also by enhancing the proactive flexibility. In turn, these response capacity properties affect project performance over the long term, in terms of value creation and operation indicators. Participation in the planning process is second in terms of performance impact. Here, contrary to our expectations, it is a centralized approach that appears to have a positive impact, particularly through the exploring creative resourcefulness as well as the formal coercive cohesion (both of which we did not see as providing the highest level of response capacity). Its impact is stronger on the "hard" performance aspects of the project. The planning knowledge, the experimental approach in particular, also seems to influence performance, in particular completion, but to some extent the value creation. Its contribution seems to occur by fostering the proactive flexibility and the cumulative resourcefulness of the project organization (both of which we also did not see as providing the highest level of response capacity). Finally, the plan argument, in particular via the decisional approach, as predicted, seems to influence positively the same performance dimensions as knowledge, essentially by enhancing the same response capacity properties. In sum, with the exception of the participation variable, the predicted "ends" of the planning variables seem to influence positively the performance dimensions. However, they do not seem to work via the anticipated response capacity dimensions and extremes.

This turns our attention to the results regarding the response capacity variables, presented in Table 3-3 (lower part B). Quite often, the influences we observed from the planning variables to the response capacity variables were as predicted. When this was not the case, the case studies provide plausible explanations for the observed pattern. However, our theoretical predictions regarding the influence of response capacity trajectories on performance variables are less well supported by the results. For example, with regard to cohesion, in line with our anticipation of its positive role, embedded adhesion appeared to affect positively three performance dimensions. However, it was formal, rather than governed, coercion that had a positive impact, affecting two performance dimensions. In addition, in terms of sequential flexibility it was the proactive extreme, rather than the agile extreme, which had a positive impact on three performance variables. In terms of sustaining resourcefulness, results are somewhat mixed, with the absorptive end and the cumulative end, our favorite, having each two positive impacts. Results are even less encouraging with respect to creating resourcefulness, with the exploring end having three positive impacts, and the innovating end, our preference, having only one. These somewhat unexpected results suggest that a closer look at the processes of reaction to unexpected events may be necessary. However, an important result is the fact that influence trajectories, including mutually cancelling trajectories, go through almost all response capacity variables that we proposed. The exception is configurational flexibility, which was "avoided" by all influence trajectories, calling attention to the fact that this variable was perhaps insufficiently theorized, or that the criteria for coding were not sufficiently clear, or that the number of cases or the particular selection in our sample did not enable the detection of influences involving this variable.

Overall, the qualitative empirical research increases our confidence in the theoretical framework and further refines our hypotheses based on a deeper understanding of the processes that occur in complex projects. The results seem to support the broad lines of the arguments advance in the introduction to the theoretical chapter. That is, the planning of complex projects is better understood as a kernel for the development of organizational capabilities rather than as the definitive construction of an iron cage that curtails deviations. Particularly interesting in this sense is the rich evidence on the severe structuring processes that these projects undergo. Moreover, results corroborate the idea that the emergent structure, particularly its response capacity, plays a nontrivial mediation role between planning and project performance. Therefore, it warrants the special attention that we have given it in our theoretical framework and empirical research. However, its impact will be understood even better, if the attention given to the response processes will be as high as that given to structuring processes.

The quite unexpected detection of mutually cancelling trajectories, suggested an interesting practical implication, namely, that the planning approach can be adjusted in order to increase the chances of success of dimensions of performance that appear most important to project sponsors. Of course, the relatively low number of cases, and the inherent imperfections of qualitative research do not allow us to argue that the results presented in this chapter are definitive. To further increase our confidence in the response capacity theory, we undertook to advance our empirical research by means of a quantitative survey based on a large sample of complex projects that were recently completed worldwide. The results of this survey are presented in Chapter 4 of this report.

4

A Quantitative
Empirical Exploration
of Influence Trajectories

1. Introduction

The qualitative phase established the relevance of the theoretical framework and improved the definition and the understanding of the range of the variables referring to project planning, response capacity, and performance, as well as to trace some of the influences among these variables. The purpose of the quantitative phase is to increase our confidence in this theory and its generality, by using a larger and more geographically diversified sample of projects as well as methods that are less dependent on researchers' judgment. We used psychometric scales to measure project participants' perceptions about our variables.

2. Quantitative Methods
Scale development

Reliable and valid scales are a necessary precondition for empirically estimating the relationships between the theoretical constructs. Given the newness of the theoretical constructs used in this research, we had to develop a new set of reliable measures for them. Schwab (1980) suggests three basic steps in the item development process—namely, the generation of individual items, the combination of items into scales, and the psychometric evaluation of scales. Based on our refined theoretical framework and on language obtained from interviewees in the qualitative part of the study, we generated at least five items for each end of the theoretical dimensions. This increased the chances to eventually retain a sufficient number of validated items per construct, and hence avoid content or reliability problems (Nunnally, 1976). With the exception of the demographics items, which were either categorical or open-ended text, all items were measured with seven-point Likert-type scales (for a detailed discussion of the advantages of Likert scales, see Meyers, Gamst, & Guarino, 2005, p. 23). In fact, each item presented the respondents with a statement, and respondents were asked to mark their degree of agreement with the statement, by giving a score from 1—"Totally disagree" to 7—"Totally agree." The use of the same type of psychometric measure throughout the questionnaire helped respondents concentrate on the questions rather than on understanding the different scales. A seven-point scale is the minimum size that enables the application of variance analysis (Birkett, 1986; Krieg, 1999).

After the first version was ready, we asked two reputed scholars who also teach and do project management consulting, as well as one scholar with recent practitioner experience with complex projects, and one project management practitioner to review the questionnaire. They had very few observations. These observations were incorporated in a second version, which was then administered to practitioners who participated in specific projects. The initial intention was to pretest the survey further on 15 respondents and then prepare a third version. Because the questionnaire is based on a solid theoretical framework and qualitative research, and the four pretest participants and early respondents understood the questionnaire in terms of the nature and wording of questions, and together with the low response rate and the approaching deadline for the report submissions, we decided to skip this stage and perform the statistical validation ex post, based on the entire set of responses. The final version of the questionnaire appears in Appendix C.

Data Collection and Sample

The output of the pretest was the final form of the survey, which was used for data collection. The survey was available to respondents on a secure site using the service provided by the U.S.-based company SurveyMonkey, via a paying account that UQAM has with this company. The advantages of this method are simpler logistics, elimination of manual data entry, with its possibility for errors, and a potentially faster data collection. In addition, we prepared a general information page, with free access, hosted by UQAM at the following address: http://www.gpi.uqam.ca/en/steering/68-response-capacity.html

Potential respondents were contacted via email. The team that conducted the survey consisted of the Principal Investigator, and, at different times, doctoral candidates Sorin Piperca and Kerstin Kuyken, as well as master's degree students, Adrien Sicard and Nicolas Dziasko. Before contacting the respondents, the team identified potential contacts, mainly project leaders and managers, as well as executives responsible for project planning and delivery. For each respondent, to the extent that it was possible, the team identified projects that they had managed as well as publications and interviews in which they were involved. This information was used to compose a personalized email message for each respondent. The model used for the emails is reproduced in Appendix D. The respondents who answered and indicated their interest to participate received a second email that communicated them the address of the survey as well as a code that enabled them to identify themselves without entering an email or other identifying information for the purposes of receiving the survey results and other feedback from researchers.

To ensure an adequate variability for independent, moderator, and control variables, respondents were recruited from a variety of industries. While the qualitative part of the study focused on specific industries corresponding to the three types of sectors discussed in Chapter 3, such as petrochemical, biotechnology, and telecom, the quantitative part, while maintaining an important share for the previous sectors, included a larger number of sectors. Also, the survey was conducted in North America, Europe, South and Central America, Africa, Asia, and Australia. The principal investigator sent from his email account, in his name, 707 personalized emails. For these emails, he identified over 75 percent of the addresses and projects. A limited number of these emails were repeated after a month. The emails sent by the PI produced the bulk of the responses. In addition, Sorin Piperca sent nearly 800 emails in his name, but these emails produced only six answers to the survey. Moreover, Kerstin Kuyken sent approximately 100 emails, most of them in German, but these did not produce results. The other students provided contacts or addresses to the PI. The survey was also advertised on the PMI-Montreal LinkedIn group and via the newsletters of Réseau GP Quebec and MISA (Quebec association for innovation in mining). Other associations, such as International Project Management Association (IPMA), Engineering and Construction Risk Institute (ECRI), and the Quebec Association for Innovation in the Chemical Industry (ADICQ) were contacted but with no success. The resulting sample included 71 responses, which suggests a response rate below 10 percent for the emails sent by the PI and less than 1 percent for the emails sent by doctoral students in their own name. This low rate of response can be explained by the recent downward trend in the rate of response for email surveys, which, as we learned recently, now is often as low as 2 percent. For example, a survey sent recently over the Internet to firms on specified industry association and business directory lists (Tucker, 2010) yielded a response rate of less than 2 percent, despite the use of many best practices described in Dillman, Smyth, and Christian (2009). The pool of our respondents was also limited by the relatively low number of complex projects, compared to, say, innovation projects. In addition, 32 respondents agreed to participate in the survey and received a code from the PI, but never actually completed the questionnaire, despite two reminders sent to each of them.

Nevertheless, we obtained a diversified sample, both geographically and in terms of the type and sector of the project. It includes a large proportion of fascinating cases of projects. Table 4-1 presents the countries in which respondents' projects

Table 4-1   Project Location by Continent and Country

North America (35)	United States	26
	Canada	9
Africa (6)	Undisclosed	4
	South Africa	2
Australia (3)	Australia	3
Latin America (6)	Argentina	1
	Brazil	1
	Chile	1
	Panama	1
	Peru	1
	Venezuela	1
Europe (18)	United Kingdom	6
	Ireland	3
	France	2
	Austria	1
	Denmark	1
	Finland	1
	Netherlands	1
	Norway	1
	Spain	1
	Sweden	1
Asia (3)	China	1
	Dubai	1
	Saudi Arabia	1

are located. The projects come from all continents. The areas that are underrepresented are East Asia, particularly China, as well as Eastern Europe, particularly Russia. This can be explained by the difficulty of identifying the right contact and of finding the person's email. However, we never received any reply, even negative, from the contacts to which we managed to send messages. The same situation applied for the respondents that we contacted in the Republic of Korea and Japan. Along with other factors, this suggests the possibility that English may have been a barrier for respondents in these countries. English-speaking countries are well represented in the sample.

Table 4-2 presents the industries (domains of activity) to which the projects belong. In this case, the sample is also well diversified. Compared to the qualitative research stage, we had more difficulties in obtaining responses from participants in pharmaceutical projects. We contacted participants in nearly all projects that succeeded in obtaining FDA approval for medicinal drugs in recent years. In this particular group of projects, we combined the initial email approach with a repeat email and, in many cases, with follow-up calls by Kerstin Kuyken, but still were not successful. Only one potential respondent promised to participate but did not keep that promise.

Table 4-2   Project Nature (Sector of Activity)

Type of project (sector)	Number of projects
Power generation (including offshore and nonconventional)	11
Road transportation infrastructure (highways, underpasses)	10
Information systems	6
Water and sewer infrastructure	6
Flood protection, remediation and dredging	4
Sports facilities	3
Port facilities	3
Oil and gas (including offshore)	3
Telecommunication infrastructure	3
Research facilities	2
Parks, streets and urban regeneration	2
Cultural facilities	2
Biofuel facilities (including demonstration)	2
Urban transportation (mass transit)	2
Railroad infrastructure	2
Airport terminals	1
Innovation projects	1
Tunnels	1
Hotels and tourism	1
Manufacturing facilities	1
Mining facilities	1
Ground improvement	1
Bridges	1
Office buildings	1
Educational buildings	1

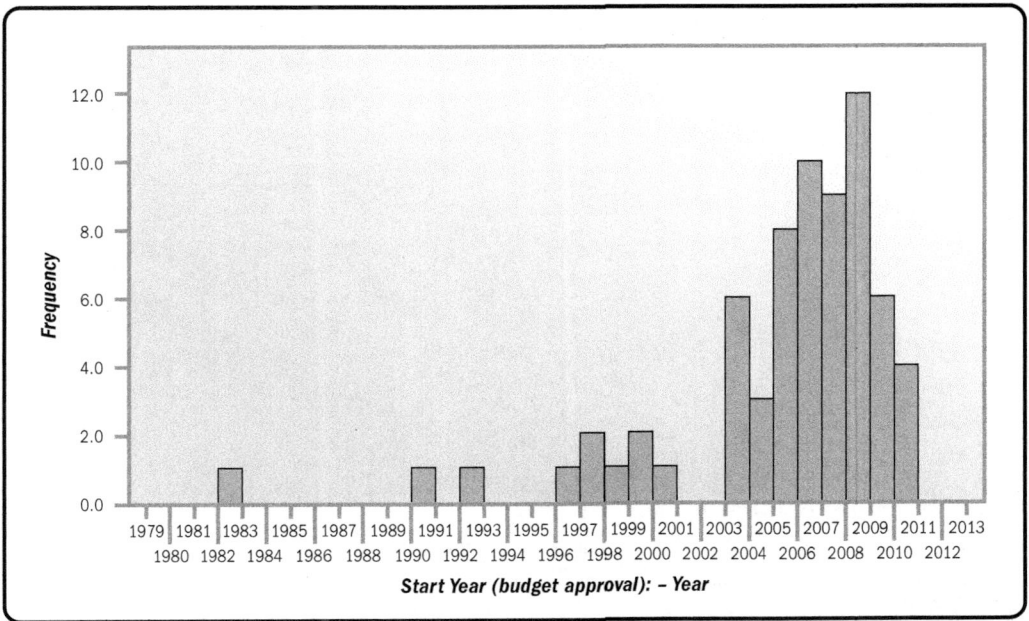

Figure 4-1　　　Project Distribution by Start Year

We asked the respondents to select either a project indicated in our email or another recently completed complex project in which they were closely involved. One concern was to obtain projects that were still fresh in the respondents' memory. In terms of starting date, measured by the year when the budget was approved the sample is distributed as depicted in Figure 4-1. Most projects that started in the 1980s and 1990s are in fact megaprojects that also lasted until recently. In this case, the possibility of forgetting the early events is minimized by the sizes of these projects and the attention the circumstances of their planning and execution continued to receive in the participating organizations and in the public arena.

In terms of duration, the projects in the sample were distributed as presented in Figure 4-2. The mentioned megaprojects also lasted very long, which means they were completed recently.

Total cost of the projects was distributed as shown in Figure 4-3. This categorical variable will be used as a control variable in certain analyses. Like the start year and duration data suggest, the cost data suggest that the sample included a small number of megaprojects, which cost over $10 billion. However, the sample also included a number of projects that were smaller but had other sources of complexity, particularly technical but also organizational and institutional.

Response Validation and Statistical Analysis

Responses were evaluated with statistical techniques for scale reliability analysis, such as calculating the Cronbach's Alpha. We aimed to have reliabilities of at least 0.70 for all scales, which is considered a good reliability level (Nunnally, 1976). In certain cases, a good reliability level was obtained by eliminating certain

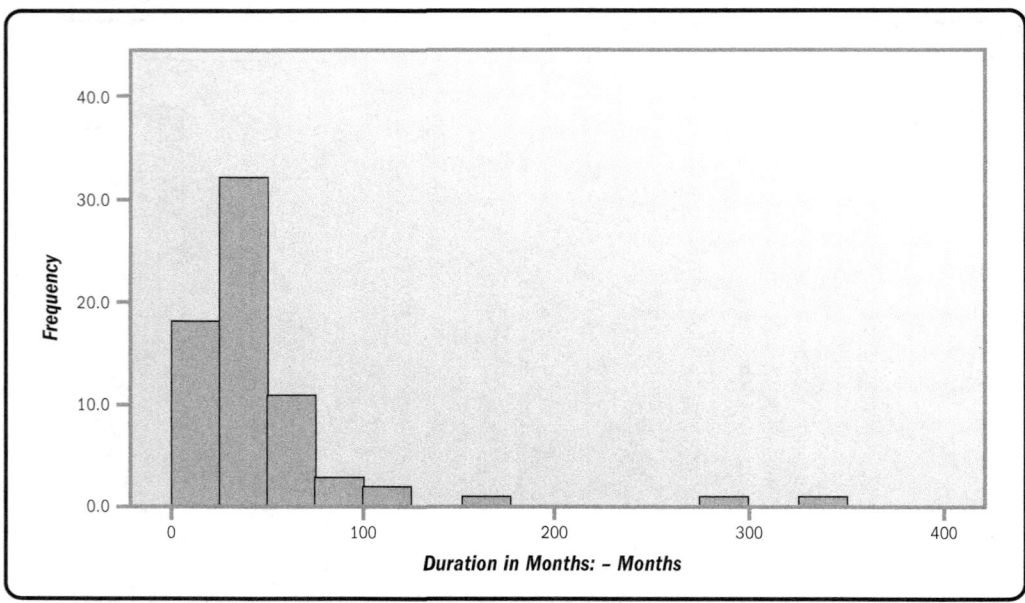

Figure 4-2   Project Distribution by Duration (in Months)

items from the scales. In some cases, we also used exploratory factor analyses procedures, which relied on the principal component procedure, with Varimax rotation methods, and aimed to validate the relation of items to theoretical categories and dimensions, as well as the orthogonality of the latter. Exploratory factor analyses and reliability tests were performed using SPSS software. The results for different scales will be presented in the Measures and Descriptive Results section.

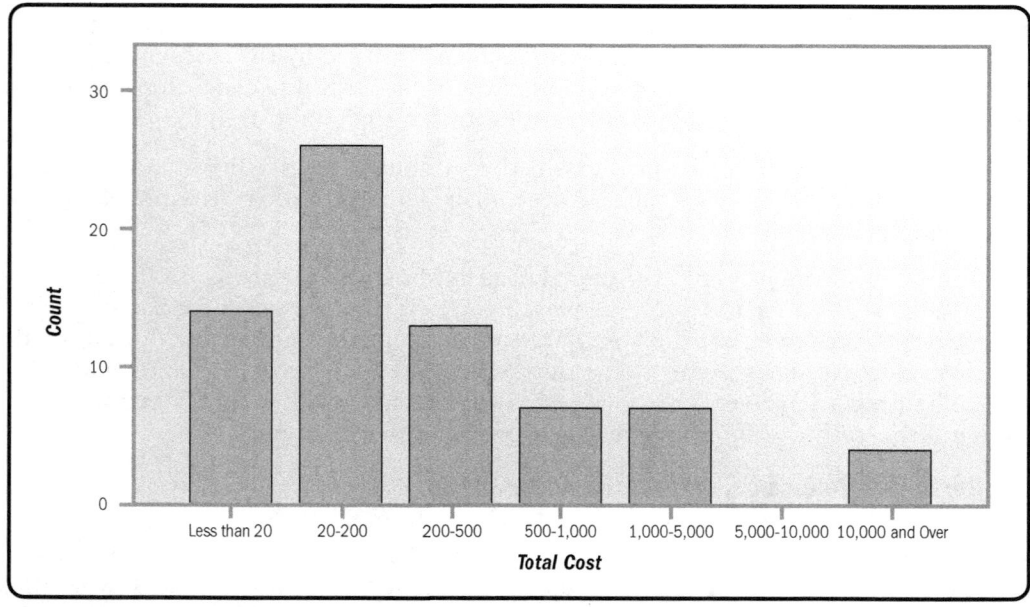

Figure 4-3   Projects Distribution by Total Cost in Millions (USD)

Testing our hypotheses relied on several statistical techniques. The following section presents results referring to separate variables, and, in particular, to the relations between variables referring to the same construct. These analyses enabled us to assess, for example, whether the various dimensions of the response capacity of a complex project are complements or substitutes. The subsequent section presents mainly two types of analyses used to detect the role of response capacity in the influence trajectories from planning to project performance. The first type is multiple regression analysis, which enables us to sort out the influence of multiple context, planning, and response capacity variables on each other and on several indicators of project performance. For example, we performed regressions of each stage in the influence trajectory on the antecedent stages, as well as of project performance on most other constructs. Among others, regressions enabled us to detect the mediation effect between strategy and performance variables of distinct response capacity variables. A second type of statistical method was discriminant analysis, which enabled us to assess the respective role of planning and response capacity as multidimensional constructs in accounting for intercase differences in project performance, also seen as a multidimensional construct. A discussion and conclusion section works out the implications of these findings and qualifies them in light of the methods that were used.

3. Measures and Descriptive Results

In this section, we present the results of the analyses, such as reliability assessment and principal component extraction, related to groups of items that measure the different constructs included in our theoretical framework, primarily "Complexity," "Planning," "Response Capacity," and "Performance." In addition to validating their measurement, these analyses enabled us to better understand the nature of these variables—for example, the synergies and tradeoffs that exist between various aspects of the response capacity of projects.

Complexity

This research deals with complex projects. Therefore, measuring the level and the nature of complexity, as participants perceived it at the beginning of each project, was an important aspect of this research. Complexity variables were used to assess whether the projects included in the sample were indeed complex and as independent or control variables in the models used to identify the influence trajectories and the relations between other variables. The latter use was suggested by the results of the qualitative research stage, in which we found that perceived complexity affected significantly the planning and execution of projects. The items used to measure complexity were derived from this research. We considered that each item in the scale is a separate source of complexity. We grouped these sources in three categories. The first category, "Technical complexity," refers to natural, manmade and performance obstacles or constraints that complicated the task of project planning, design and execution. Prior research as well as our case studies shows that such constraints require more innovative or more integrated, and hence more risky, technical solutions (Ulrich, 1995), as well as more careful planning and organization in order to take into consideration all interactions and minimize interference. The origin of technical complexity is considered internal to the project, as it is conditioned by the decision to choose the given project rather than other possible ones. The second category, "organizational complexity," refers

Table 4-3   Complexity Items and Composite Measures

Complexity items and composite measures	Min.	Max.	Mean	Std. Dev.
Technical: We faced major issues related to natural conditions (soil, water, weather etc.)	1	7	5.03	2.000
Technical: The project interfered with a sensitive natural area (wildlife, ecosystem, scenery)	1	7	3.79	2.027
Technical: The project had to fit with pre-existing technical systems or tight built surroundings	1	7	5.41	1.712
Technical: The project had to minimize the disruption to ongoing operations and businesses	1	7	5.22	1.969
Technical: Bold project goals forced us to use technical solutions that no one had tried before	1	7	5.45	1.717
Technical: Our challenge was maintaining full control over the behavior of the artifacts we made	1	7	4.34	1.797
Technical: We strived to gain influence over natural processes affected by many invisible factors	1	7	4.04	1.824
Technical: Our problem was ensuring coherent interoperation between scores of artifact functions	1	7	4.55	1.636
Organizational: The project was much larger than all other projects the owner had ever managed	1	7	4.19	2.254
Organizational: Project timing was conditioned by urgent needs or limited windows of opportunity	1	7	5.72	1.412
Organizational: During this project, the owner organization embarked on a major restructuring	1	7	3.85	2.160
Organizational: The project was the first to implement new project management processes and norms	1	7	4.06	2.104
Organizational: The project was seen as an occasion for trying new financial or contractual methods	1	7	4.43	2.032
Organizational: Conditions forced us to rely on contractors or personnel from many different countries	1	7	3.74	2.230
Institutional: Regulatory approval was a critical precondition for initiating or exploiting the project	1	7	5.31	2.017
Institutional: Key applicable laws and regulations were ambiguous or untested in practice	1	7	3.53	1.865
Institutional: The project was likely to become a battleground for political interests and militants	1	7	3.85	2.167
Institutional: The project was funded with public money or relied on government guarantees	1	7	5.01	2.236
Institutional: Project implementation depended on decisions made by foreign government entities	1	7	1.51	1.173
Institutional: The project output targeted a market whose emergence and growth were still uncertain	1	7	2.78	1.969
Institutional: The market we intended to serve was known for its severe swings in price and demand	1	7	3.25	1.935

to situations and constraints that originate within the organizations of project participants and lead to difficulties and risks for the project organization. The third category "institutional complexity" refers to conditions that originate in the external environment, and have the potential to create additional problems as well as interactions for the project.

Results in Table 4-3 show that for most items the mean answer was above 4, the center point for the 1 to 7 scales we used. The most common sources of complexity were urgency, boldness of goals, and the fit with existing systems and buildings, followed closely by minimizing disruption, public funding, and natural conditions. Moreover, despite the presence of less "popular," yet sometimes critical, sources of complexity, such as the approval of foreign government entities the average for the overall complexity index was above 4. Only two projects had a score that was less than 4 on the overall complexity index. We also computed a maximum complexity index, which is the largest score (from 1 to 7) obtained on any complexity item. Only five cases in the entire sample did not have at least one score of 7 among the complexity items. These suggest that projects in our sample had many characteristics that suggest a high level of complexity, and at least one aspect in which these characteristics were highly relevant for the project.

Because each of the items shown in Table 4-3 represents a distinct source of complexity, there was a danger that composite measures that simply added various items in a category would not be meaningful if items were not correlated to each other, as they should in a psychometric measure. Given that reliability analyses, which capture the correlation between items that attempt to measure the same construct, were low, this danger seemed real. In this situation, we had the choice of using individual items rather that scales including multiple items, or to attempt to identify the common underlying factors among all items measuring complexity. The latter approach also had the advantage of revealing the way respondents think about the complexity that their projects encounter. Therefore, we performed a principal component analysis, which extracted six factors, or "orthogonal underlying dimensions," from the 21 items presented in Table 4-3. It should be noted that a rotation method that could have extracted non-orthogonal factors produced essentially the same result. We named these orthogonal factors Change, Innovation, Emergence, Nature, Constraints, and International, respectively. The factors form a parsimonious set of complexity sources, which will be more likely to yield meaningful results than a priori categories and will be less tedious to follow than 21 individual items. The items that are most related with each factor are presented in Table 4-4, which also presents the correlations between these items and the respective factors. To make the presentation clearer, only the statistically significant correlations ($p < 0.05$) are presented.

Planning

The planning items were designed in accordance to the theoretical framework, which recommended four dimensions: knowledge, participation, argument, and risk approach. For each dimension, we identified two extremes, as explained in Chapter 2 (see Figure 2-1). Items included in the survey instrument captured both extremes of each dimension. The challenge was to assess whether jointly these items, or a subset among them, best captured every dimension. To make this assessment, we relied on principal component analyses. In the cases of all four dimensions of planning, the measure that was selected was the first unrotated principal component extracted after the elimination of certain items. The items that were intended to measure one end of the dimension have correlations with this factor that are all either positive or negative, while the items that were intended to measure the opposite end have correlations with the opposite sign.

Planning knowledge dimension. A principal components analysis of the set of items included in the survey (please see Appendix C, questionnaire section II-a, for the entire set of items) suggested that the first unrotated principal component captures very well this "conceptual vs. experimental" dimension. Items intended to capture the conceptual end, located near the beginning of the list, had high positive loadings on the factor, while the items intended to capture the experimental end of the dimension, located toward the end of the list had high negative loadings. We decided to eliminate two items—one located toward the middle of the list and the other at the end of the list—because their loadings on the principal component were not high enough or did not have the sign we anticipated theoretically. The resulting factor captures well the intended dimension, with higher scores signaling conceptual planning, and lower scores, experimental planning. Table 4-5 presents the contributing items and their correlations with the planning knowledge factor.

Table 4-4   Complexity Items, Factors, and Correlations Between Items and Factors

	Change	Innovation	Emergence	Nature	Constraints	International
We faced major issues related to natural conditions (soil, water, weather etc.)				0.726		
The project interfered with a sensitive natural area (wildlife, ecosystem, scenery)				0.799		
The project had to fit with preexisting technical systems or tight built surroundings					0.731	
The project had to minimize the disruption to ongoing operations and businesses					0.817	
Bold project goals forced us to use technical solutions that no one had tried before		0.366		-0.343		
Our challenge was maintaining full control over the behavior of the artifacts we made		0.834				
We strived to gain influence over natural processes affected by many invisible factors		0.698		0.431		0.261
Our problem was ensuring coherent interoperation between scores of artifact functions		0.869				
The project was much larger than all other projects the owner had ever managed	0.769					
Project timing was conditioned by urgent needs or limited windows of opportunity		0.256			0.686	
During this project, the owner organization embarked on a major restructuring	0.738		0.263			
The project was the first to implement new project management processes and norms	0.790	-0.259				
The project was seen as an occasion for trying new financial or contractual methods	0.639					
Conditions forced us to rely on contractors or personnel from many different countries						0.738
Regulatory approval was a critical precondition for initiating or exploiting the project	0.412	-0.388	0.285	0.542		
Key applicable laws and regulations were ambiguous or untested in practice	0.401		0.688			
The project was likely to become a battleground for political interests and militants	0.526		0.415	0.303		
The project was funded with public money or relied on government guarantees	0.598					-0.520
Project implementation depended on decisions made by foreign government entities						0.697
The project output targeted a market whose emergence and growth were still uncertain			0.786			
The market we intended to serve was known for its severe swings in price and demand			0.749			

Factor and item loadings (correlations)

Extraction Method: Principal Component Analysis; Rotation Method: Varimax with Kaiser Normalization

Table 4-5   Correlation Between Included Items and the Factor Measuring Planning Knowledge (Positive Correlations–Conceptual; Negative Correlations–Experimental)

Items used to extract the planning knowledge factor	Correlation
We fully relied on templates, models and data already existing in our organization	0.568
Past learning captured in rules and information systems was more than enough for us	0.754
Planning decisions followed directly from regulatory norms or industry standards	0.720
We brought in all needed expertise by hiring experienced managers or consultants	0.372
We had to produce lots of new data and models before being able to shape this project	-0.329
We used a pilot project or the early stages of this project in order to gain experience	-0.440
We carefully validated all our decisions based on simulation or external feedback	-0.524
The planning process went through several iterations that totally redefined the project	-0.476
The planning was full of twists and turns as a result of our learning and discoveries	-0.589

Table 4-6   Correlation Between Included Items and the Factor Measuring Planning Participation (Positive Correlations–Centralized; Negative Correlations–Pluralistic)

Items used to extract the planning participation factor	Correlation
One organization maintained a complete control over the entire planning process	0.818
Inside the lead organization, a single unit retained all the decision power for planning	0.817
One team was responsible for carrying out the entire planning process for this project	0.777
Planning was under strict formal supervision by an internal unit such as a project office	0.332
Numerous units within the lead organization had a strong say in the planning process	-0.373
Planning decisions were negotiated between a few equally powerful organizations	-0.448
Planning depended on input or sanction from key client, contractor or financial backer	-0.178
Every decision was scrutinized by regulators, certification bodies or political groups	-0.160

Planning participation dimension. A principal component analysis suggested that a few items measuring the "centralized" end of this planning dimension, as well as a few items capturing the "pluralist" end, did not have the expected relation with the participation dimension. Among these, we decided, however, to retain two items on the pluralist end, which had relatively low loadings on the factor but have the correlation has the right sign and captures meaningful sources of pluralism in light of our theory and qualitative research. After the elimination of the two remaining unsuitable items, a new principal component was extracted. Contributing items and their correlations with the planning participation factor are shown in Table 4-6.

Plan argument dimension. The items included in the survey in order to measure this dimension attempted to capture both its "promotional" extreme and the "decisional" extreme. We performed a factor analysis, which showed that a few items on the "promotional" extreme did not have the right sign. After eliminating these three items, the remaining items were used to extract a new factor that appeared to correspond to the meaning that we anticipated theoretically for this dimension. The included items and their correlation with the plan argument factor are illustrated in Table 4-7.

Table 4-7   Correlation Between Included Items and the Factor Measuring Plan Argument (Positive Correlations–Decisional; Negative Correlations–Promotional)

Items used to extract the plan argument factor	Correlation
Plan documents appealed to emotions in order to gain support for the project	-0.402
The plan maintained a degree of ambiguity even with respect to important issues	-0.606
The plan included detailed analyses based on multifaceted evidence for all issues	0.606
Plan documents spoke to the prudence and reason of those who approved the project	0.661
The plan included a thorough analysis and mitigation measures for all possible risks	0.815
The plan provided a realistic and comprehensive estimation of project costs	0.747
The plan provided decision makers with very detailed and comprehensive information	0.790

Table 4-8   Correlation Between Included Items and the Factor Measuring the Plan Risk Approach (Positive Correlations–Integrative; Negative Correlations–Allocative)

Items used to extract the plan risk approach factor	Correlation
The plan pushed all risks to other participants with fixed price and schedule contracts	-0.485
Suppliers and contractors had to provide significant warranties and performance bonds	-0.682
The owner assumed all risks in order to secure cooperation from other participants	0.801
Cost plus contracts, alliances or joint ventures were preferred as a way to build trust	0.607

Plan risk approach dimension. This dimension captures the difference between attempting, on the one hand, to allocate risk and responsibilities between different participants and, on the other hand, to induce participants to share risks and responsibilities in an integrated manner. Like in the previous dimension, the factor analysis suggested that some items did not relate to the others as expected, perhaps capturing other aspects that were not of significance for our research issues. After eliminating these items, we extracted a factor based on four items. These items and their correlation with the factor that measures the plan risk approach are presented in Table 4-8.

Response Capacity

Like the planning constructs, the response capacity constructs were intended to be reflected by dimensions with two extremes. Therefore, we also relied on principal component analyses in order to extract these dimensions from the corresponding items, as well as to understand how the items relate to each dimension. For each of the six dimensions of the response capacity construct, the questionnaire included five items for one end of the dimension and five items for the other end of the dimension, which assessed the nature of the response capacity properties and how they were achieved. These items were used to extract the principal components. In addition, the questionnaire also included three items for each dimension that were used to assess the magnitude of the response capacity property. For example, they were to assess how cohesive was the project organization at the peak of execution, in addition to the assessment of the sources of this cohesion provided by the two sets of five items. For the three items that were used to assess the magnitude of the property, we did a reliability assessment, by calculating Cronbach's Alpha. We also performed correlation analyses to understand how different variables relate to each other.

Adhesive cohesion dimension. The principal component analysis revealed that two items, one on the pragmatic end, and the other one on the embedded end, were not meaningfully related to the extracted factors. After these items were deleted, we extracted again two principal components again. Interestingly, it was the second extracted component that better reflected the theoretical dimension; the first one had positive correlations with all remaining items. The second component explained 22.3 percent of the variance of the eight items, compared to 33.0 percent for the first component. The second component became our measure of the nature of adhesive cohesion. The included items and their correlations with this component are presented in Table 4-9.

Table 4-9   Correlation Between Included Items and the Factor Measuring Adhesive Cohesion (Positive Correlations–Embedded; Negative Correlations–Pragmatic)

Items used to extract the adhesive cohesion factor	Correlation
Owners constantly adjusted the incentives in order to keep all participants motivated	-0.194
We all believed that the project advanced only if participants see a gain for themselves	-0.462
When requesting more effort, owners always made clear what others will get in return	-0.445
Everyone was constantly reevaluating the potential gains and losses from this project	-0.634
Many team-building and partnering sessions were held throughout project execution	0.372
All major participants occupied collocated offices or met face to face every week	0.492
Consultants and contractor representatives were fully integrated in the core team	0.645
Specific efforts and liaison positions helped integrate newcomers and remote teams	0.365

Regarding the strength of adhesive cohesion, the three items included in the survey formed a scale with a very good reliability (Cronbach's Alpha = 0.81). This scale, obtained by adding the three items was used in subsequent analyses. The items that compose it, as well as the descriptive statistics can be seen in Table 4-10. It is interesting to note that this scale is correlated with the factor we used measure the nature of the adhesive cohesion. The correlation, $r = 0.38$ is highly significant ($p < 0.01$). It suggests that the main source of adhesive cohesion is the strong embeddedness of project participants in the project organization rather than their self-interest and incentives.

Coercive cohesion dimension. The principal component analysis revealed that all items except one, which intended to measure the formal side of this dimension, were loading on the factor as expected theoretically. After eliminating the single item, we extracted principal components again and used the first factor, which explained 33 percent of the variance of the remaining nine items, as a measure for the nature of the coercive cohesion dimension. The retained items and their correlation with the factor are presented in Table 4-11.

We also computed an indicator of coercive cohesion strength based on the items included in the survey to this effect. The indicator has a good reliability (alpha = 0.77). The items included in scale, as well as the descriptive statistics for the items and for the scale, are shown in Table 4-12.

Overall cohesion statistics. We also computed a composite indicator of overall cohesion strength, which consisted of adding the items included in the adhesive

Table 4-10   Item and Scale Statistics for Adhesive Cohesion Strength

Items in scale for adhesive cohesion strength (Alpha = 0.81)	Mean	Std. Dev.
In case of problems, everyone focused on finding a solution rather than blaming others	5.11	1.65
When participants faced difficulties they obtained help from others without delay	4.02	1.45
Personal bonds and mutual trust kept participants united in the face of adversity	5.03	1.55
Scale	**15.16**	**3.97**

Table 4-11   Correlation Between Included Items and the Factor Measuring Coercive Cohesion (Positive Correlations– Governed; Negative Correlations–Formal)

Items used to extract the coercive cohesion factor	Correlation
Clients constantly explained the intentions and expectations behind contractual terms	0.435
Parties to a contract held meetings routinely to discuss concerns and to air objections	0.364
Owners were open to reinterpreting and renegotiating contractual responsibilities	0.661
A practice of promptly addressing and solving contractual disputes had emerged	0.710
Changes and new commitments were carefully recorded and added to agreements	0.657
Owners never discussed contractual provisions to avoid diluting their legal power	-0.629
Owners held contractors at arm's length by following initial agreements to the letter	-0.564
Owners never hesitated to threaten using all contractual levers at their disposal	-0.678
Formal criteria and procedures were strictly followed even when counterproductive	-0.316

cohesion strength scale and those in the coercive cohesion strength scale. The six-item scale (see the respective subscales for item descriptives) had an excellent reliability, with Cronbach's Alpha = 0.85. The mean for the scale is 30.59, and the standard deviation equals 6.83.

We also wanted to learn how various cohesion indicators related to each other. Therefore, we computed Pearson correlations between all these variables (Table 4-13). First, results suggest that the adhesive cohesion strength indicator is correlated with the adhesive cohesion factor ($r = 0.377$; $p < 0.01$), which means that embedded cohesion is the main source of perceived adhesive cohesion, while the pragmatic emphasis may, in fact, reduce adhesive cohesion perceptions. Likewise, the coercive cohesion strength indicator is highly correlated with the coercive cohesion factor ($r = 0.636$; $p < 0.001$), which suggests that governed coercion properties are highly correlated with coercive cohesion strength perceptions. Results also suggest that the factors characterizing coercive cohesion and, respectively, adhesive cohesion properties have a statistically significant correlation between them with $r = 0.359$ ($p < 0.01$). The adhesive cohesion strength indicator is also highly correlated to the coercive cohesion strength indicator ($r = 0.615$; $p < 0.001$), which is also reflected in the high reliability of the overall cohesion indicator.

Table 4-12   Item and Scale Statistics for Coercive Cohesion Strength

Items in the scale for coercive cohesion strength (Alpha = 0.77)	Mean	Std. Dev.
(Reverse) Relations between participants were adversarial even before major problems started	5.16	1.52
(Reverse) When problems appeared, leaders had a hard time imposing their decisions on others	4.80	1.62
The core team was often able to maintain adequate ties between the various groups	5.46	1.16
Scale	13.10	3.61

Table 4-13   Correlations Between Various Cohesion Dimensions and Indicators

Adhesive cohesion factor (embedded)	1			
Adhesive cohesion strenth	0.377*** 0.003	1		
Coercive cohesion factor (governed)	0.359*** 0.004	0.543*** 0.000	1	
Coercive cohesion strength	0.380*** 0.002	0.615*** 0.000	0.636*** 0.000	1
	Adhesive Cohesion Factor (Embedded)	Adhesive Cohesion Strength	Coercive Cohesion Factor (Governed)	Coercive Cohesion Strength

Note: *** $p < 0.01$

Flexibility

For this set of response capacity properties, we used the same approach as for cohesion variables; namely, we used principal components analyses to uncover the items that will help us assess the nature of the properties that have a theoretical interest for us. We also used reliability indices to assess the composite scales that measure the magnitude of these properties and Pearson correlations to understand how the different variables relate between them.

Configurational flexibility dimension. A principal component analysis including all items showed that most items that were intended to measure the implicit-heedful dimension did not relate as expected to any of the extracted factors. However, by trying a number of item combinations we were able to identify a combination of items that produced a factor corresponding to the dimension of interest. With these items, we performed a principal component analysis, and used the second un-rotated principal component as a measure of configurational flexibility property. These items and their correlation with the principal component are shown in Table 4-14. Items with positive correlation are closer to the implicit end of the dimension, while items with negative correlations are related to the heedful end. Most items reflect the communication system mechanism that we proposed in the theoretical framework.

The magnitude of configurational flexibility was measured by using three survey items. Because the items were, in fact, intended to capture the lack of

Table 4-14   Correlation Between Included Items and the Factor
Measuring Configurational Flexibility (Positive
Correlations–Implicit; Negative Correlations–Heedful)

Items used to extract the configurational flexibility factor	Correlation
A rich vocabulary had emerged to describe interdependencies between activity blocks	-0.123
The core team maintained strong internal capabilities for all the aspects of the project	-0.714
Work breakdown paralleled the preexisting boundaries between units and disciplines	0.222
Different sub-units had diverging interpretations of applicable terminology and norms	0.808

Table 4-15   Item and Scale Statistics for Configurational Flexibility Freedom

Items in the scale for configurational flexibility freedom (Alpha = 0.70)	Mean	Std. Dev.
Most conflicts were related to the interfaces or transfers between different subprojects	4.08	1.735
Problems, delays and changes in one part always had a major impact on all other parts	4.54	1.555
It was always hard to assemble or interoperate subsystems produced by distinct groups	3.56	1.511
Scale	**11.82**	**3.793**

configurational freedom, we used the following formula to compute the composite index for this measure:

Configurational Freedom = 24 − (Interface conflicts item + Impact on other parts item + Difficult interoperation item)

The descriptive statistics for the items and the scale are presented in Table 4-15. The scale has an acceptable alpha of 0.70.

Sequential flexibility dimension. A principal component extraction revealed that two items supposed to measure the proactive end of the sequential flexibility dimension did not correlate well with the extracted factor. However, the remaining items behaved as expected, including all items that intended to measure the agile end of this dimensions. Using them, we extracted a set of factors and selected the first un-rotated principal component to capture the sequential flexibility properties. The items that were retained and their correlations with the principal component that reflects this dimension are presented in Table 4-16.

We also computed a sequential flexibility freedom index, based on the sum of the three items included in the survey for this purpose. The resulting scale has an acceptable Cronbach's Alpha of 0.65. The items and descriptive statistics for them, and for the composite scale, are presented in Table 4-17.

Table 4-16   Correlation Between Included Items and the Factor Measuring Sequential Flexibility (Positive Correlations– Agile; Negative Correlations–Proactive)

Items used to extract the sequential flexibility factor	Correlation
Solutions were frozen only gradually, based on feedback from execution activities	-0.610
We prioritized the activities for which uncertainty was low and delayed the others	-0.487
Final decisions were delayed as much as possible to leave freedom for late changes	-0.760
Our team felt confident enough to acknowledge and address problems without delay	0.844
The project organization had clear areas of responsibility and decisional procedures	0.773
In case of difficulties, an issue was escalated to higher-level executives right away	0.389
Special task forces were set up immediately to deal with important emerging issues	0.568
The project organization quickly intensified communications when an issue emerged	0.624

Table 4-17   Item and Scale Statistics for Sequential Flexibility Freedom

Items in the scale for sequential flexibility freedom (Alpha = 0.65)	Mean	Std. Dev.
Even later on, nothing prevented the core team from adopting the best course of action	5.44	1.385
We never procrastinated but quickly converged on decisions using the latest evidence	4.95	1.407
Even after a decision was made, we could easily turn back and take a different route	3.93	1.470
Scale	**14.32**	**3.270**

Overall flexibility statistics. We also computed an overall scale for the overall flexibility freedom, by adding the three items (reversed) for the configurational flexibility freedom, as well as the three items for the sequential flexibility freedom. Item statistics have already been presented in Tables 4-15 and 4-17. The scale has an acceptable reliability, with a Cronbach's Alpha of 0.64, which can be increased to 0.69 by eliminating the item "Even after a decision was made, we could easily turn back and take a different route." We also computed the Pearson correlations between the various flexibility variables, which are presented in Table 4-18. The correlation between the configurational flexibility factor and the configurational flexibility freedom index has a negative sign, but this result is not statistically significant. Hence, we cannot say which of the ends of the configurational flexibility dimension, implicit or heedful, is more associated to the perceived configurational freedom. Second, the sequential flexibility factor is highly positively correlated to the sequential flexibility freedom ($r = 0.461$; $p < 0.01$), which suggests that the agile end of the sequential dimension, as defined by our measure, is more associated with the perceptions of flexibility freedom than the proactive end. Correlation results between the configurational freedom index and the sequential freedom index are positive but not statistically significant, which suggest that these may be aspects of organizational structure that are not necessarily related in the same project. Finally, the correlation between the sequential flexibility factor and the configurational flexibility factor is negative and highly significant. This means that properties, which our measures defined as belonging to agile sequential flexibility and to heedful configurational flexibility are often found in the same project, while signs of proactive sequential flexibility and implicit configurational flexibility are

Table 4-18   Correlations Between Various Flexibility Dimensions and Indicators

Configurational flexibility factor (implicit)	1			
Configurational flexibility freedom	-0.134 0.303	1		
Sequential flexibility factor (agile)	-0.604*** 0.000	0.261** 0.043	1	
Sequential flexibility freedom	-0.419*** 0.001	0.180 0.166	0.461*** 0.000	1
	Configurational Flexibility Factor (Implicit)	Configurational Flexibility Freedom	Sequential Flexibility Factor (Agile)	Sequential Flexibility Freedom

Note: ** $p < 0.05$; *** $p < 0.01$

Table 4-19   Correlation Between Included Items and the Factor Measuring Sustaining Resourcefulness (Positive Correlations–Absorptive; Negative Correlations–Cumulative)

Items used to extract the sustaining resourcefulness factor	Correlation
Rules let the core team retain all cost savings and reallocate them within the project	-0.331
Participants were greatly rewarded for being efficient and making cost-saving changes	-0.630
Project leaders cultivated links to entities that could become a source for more funding	0.747
The team developed the art of highlighting prospects and justifying resource requests	0.361

also found together. Given that the two freedom indices were not significantly correlated, this may suggest the existence of a certain tradeoff between configurational and sequential flexibility.

Resourcefulness

We used the same strategy as for cohesion and flexibility to validate the measures for the resourcefulness constructs and to understand the various relations and tradeoffs between them. Principal component analyses were the main tool for analyzing the sustaining and creating dimensions, while reliability analyses were used to assess the respective intensity scales.

Sustaining resourcefulness dimension. Like in the case of configurational flexibility, for this dimension, initial principal components analyses revealed that most loads did not yield a factor that would correlate as expected with the items intended to measure this dimension. By rethinking what items were in fact closer to the ends of the two dimensions, we selected four items. When we performed the principal component analysis again with these four items, the second extracted factor aligned with these items in ways that corresponded to our theoretical anticipations. We retained this factor, which explains 30 percent of the variance in these four items, as the measure of the sustaining resourcefulness dimension. The respective items and their correlations with the factor are presented in Table 4-19.

We also computed a composite index for cumulative resourcefulness abundance, which measures the extent to which the project organization made available to participants all the resources they needed in the case of unexpected events. The scale formed by the three items included in the survey to this effect did not form a scale with sufficient reliability (Cronbach's Alpha = 0.54). By dropping one of the items, the remaining two items formed a scale with an acceptable alpha of 0.66. The descriptive statistics for these items and for the scale are shown in Table 4-20.

Table 4-20   Item and Scale Statistics for Sustaining Resourcefulness Abundance

Items in the scale for sustaining resourcefulness abundance (Alpha = 0.66)	Mean	Std. Dev.
Whenever the project needed more resources, we obtained everything we requested	4.10	1.620
It was easy to expand the working hours, hire more personnel or accelerate the pace	4.08	1.605
Scale	8.18	2.784

Table 4-21   Correlation Between Included Items and the Factor Measuring Creating Resourcefulness (Positive Correlations– Innovative; Negative Correlations–Explorative)

Items used to extract the creating resourcefulness factor	Correlation
Team members had a variety of external contacts, enabling a broad solution search	-0.188
Any sub-team had easy access to advisory committees and a network of consultants	-0.508
Any sub-team could easily bring in specialists from the outside to help solve problems	-0.496
Project leaders stimulated the exchange of ideas between groups with different views	0.254
We used specific procedures that created a structure for the problem-solving process	0.459
Problem-solving processes valued the use of learning accumulated during this project	0.620

Creating resourcefulness dimension. Initial principal component analyses showed that two items on the explorative end of the creative resourcefulness dimension (external search for solutions) side, and two on the innovative end of this dimension (generating solutions internally) did not relate to any factors in ways that were meaningful in light of our theory. After eliminating these four items, we extracted again principal components. Item relations to the second extracted factor corresponded to theoretical expectations, and we selected this factor as a measure of the creating resourcefulness dimension. The retained items and their correlation with the selected factor are presented in Table 4-21.

We also created a composite measure for the creating resourcefulness abundance, which was formed with the three items included in the survey for this purpose. The resulting scale had an excellent reliability with a Cronbach's Alpha of 0.82. Descriptive statistics for the three items and for the scale are shown in Table 4-22.

Overall resourcefulness statistics. We also created an overall resourcefulness abundance index, which adds the two items from the two sustaining abundance index and the three items from the creating abundance index seen above. This measure has a Cronbach's Alpha of 0.69, which is quite acceptable for new scales. The correlations between the various measures of resourcefulness reveal only two significant relations, both across the two dimensions. First, creating abundance is negatively correlated to the sustaining factor. This can be interpreted as suggesting that a focus on absorptive abundance is detrimental to creating resourcefulness. Second, the creating abundance is correlated with the sustaining abundance, which has already been suggested by the relatively high Cronbach's Alpha of the overall

Table 4-22   Item and Scale Statistics for Creating Resourcefulness Abundance

Items in the scale for creating resourcefulness abundance (Alpha = 0.82)	Mean	Std. Dev.
We were able to find at least one solution for nearly all of the difficulties we faced	5.77	0.864
We were highly satisfied with the quality of ideas and solutions that we obtained	5.54	1.026
All participants agreed that our organization favored creativity and problem-solving	5.25	1.178
Scale	**16.56**	**2.649**

Table 4-23   Correlations Between Various Resourcefulness Dimensions and Indicators

Sustaining resourcefulness factor (absorptive)	1			
Sustaining resourcefulness abundance	-0.107 0.413	1		
Creating resourcefulness factor (innovative)	0.006 0.961	-0.127 0.328	1	
Creating resourcefulness abundance	-0.256** 0.047	0.275** 0.032	0.068 0.600	1
	Sustaining Resourcefulness Factor (Absorptive)	Sustaining Resourcefulness Abundance	Creating Resourcefulness Factor (Innovative)	Creating Resourcefulness Abundance

Note: ** p < 0.05; *** p < 0.01

abundance index discussed previously. This correlation justifies the discussion of these two aspects as the same aspect of the response capacity, but it is not high enough to raise concerns that the two dimensions may in fact be identical.

Response Capacity Discussion

The various analyses reported allowed us to understand the nature of the various response capacity properties. Most items that were included in the survey to capture these properties proved to be useful and behaved in ways that corresponded to our theoretical anticipations. Those aspects for which a larger number of items were excluded from the measures, such as configurational flexibility and sustaining resourcefulness, would warrant additional theorizing regarding their nature and the various dimensions that characterize them.

Another aspect that represents an important result is the relation between the various aspects of response capacity. We expected moderate correlations between the two dimensions that correspondent to each of the three main properties of response capacity. They are not distinct constructs but are not the same thing either. Such moderate correlation was obtained, for instance, in the case of resourcefulness dimensions. However, the very high correlation between the strengths of the two dimensions of cohesion, as well as between the heedful configurational and the agile sequential dimensions of flexibility, may suggest that respondents attribute to them a higher degree of commonalities than we expected. This may result perhaps from the fact that in the respondents' minds these aspects mirror certain new models of thinking about project execution promoted by the agile methods, Scrum, integrated project delivery, and other communities. However, they may also be more fundamentally related in the reality of projects.

To advance our understanding of the commonalities and tradeoffs of the response capacity, we also deemed it important to evaluate the tradeoffs that exist between various factors and scales across the three main response capacity properties. We began by calculating the correlations between the overall scales for each of the three properties, which all proved rather high and statistically significant. Hence, the correlation between the overall cohesion strength and the overall flexibility freedom was $r = 0.508$ ($p < 0.001$). The correlation between the overall cohesion strength and the overall resourcefulness abundance was $r = 0.512$ ($p < 0.001$). Finally, the correlation between the overall flexibility freedom and the overall resourcefulness abundance was $r = 0.416$ ($p = 0.001$). These quite high correlations suggest that indeed there is a property of project organizations that can be called response capacity. In fact, a scale formed with these three items has a good Cronbach's Alpha of 0.72. However, there is also a danger that such commonality between them may be the fruit of ex post attribution, halo effect, or other form of common method bias. Hence, results based on these commonalities should be interpreted very cautiously. The high correlation may also raise a problem of multicollinearity in regression analyses, in which these scales are used together as predictors. To deepen our investigation into the relations between different dimensions, we also calculated the correlations between various dimensions of the response capacity, which are reproduced in Tables 4-24a, 4-24b and 4-24c.

Results in Tables 4-24a, 4-24b, and 4-24c show significant correlations between almost all cohesion and flexibility variables, with a pattern that is almost identical for all cohesion variables, except that the adhesive cohesion factor has one nonsignificant and two marginally significant correlations with the flexibility variables. Regarding the correlations between cohesion and resourcefulness, results also show a number of highly significant correlations, but this number is lower than for the previous pair. The adhesive cohesion factor has only one marginally significant correlation with the resourcefulness variables, which suggests that this variable could be used as an independent predictor in regression and discriminant analyses. Finally, the correlations between flexibility and resourcefulness variables are also quite numerous. The configurational flexibility freedom and sustaining resourcefulness abundance have only marginally significant correlations with the other variables.

Given the large number of significant correlations, we performed a principal component analysis on all six response capacity factor variables to find out whether some meaningful underlying construct could explain the commonalities between them. This analysis yielded a neat and interesting alignment of these variables along two factors, which we termed, inspired by Burns and Stalker (1961), the organic factor and the mechanistic factor (see Table 4-25).

The mechanistic factor aligns with formal coercion, implicit configuration, proactive sequential flexibility, and absorptive sustaining resourcefulness. All these variables suggest relations that are more distant and self-centered. The organic factor aligns clearly with the embedded adhesion and innovative resource creation, and to some extent with governed coercion, agile sequential flexibility, and even with heedful configurational flexibility. All these variables suggest closer and more fluid interactions inside the project organization. These two factors suggest that there are two distinct aspects of managing, which may be combined to various degrees in projects. One is creating the working processes; the other is creating the human relations context.

Restructuring Processes and Unexpected Events

This section groups the measures of the more "dynamic" constructs that were included in the survey. The first group of constructs concerns restructuring processes that occur during and after planning, while the second concerns unexpected

Table 4-24   Correlations Between Variables Measuring Different Aspects of Response Capacity

a) Correlations between cohesion and flexibility variables

	Configurational Flexibility Factor (Implicit)	Configurational Flexibility Freedom	Sequential Flexibility Factor (Agile)	Sequential Flexibility Freedom
Adhesive cohesion factor (embedded)	-0.223* 0.084	0.206 0.112	0.374*** 0.003	0.273* 0.066
Adhesive cohesion strength	-0.457*** 0.000	0.247* 0.055	0.610*** 0.000	0.393*** 0.002
Coercive cohesion factor (governed)	-0.428*** 0.001	0.283** 0.027	0.539*** 0.000	0.341*** 0.007
Coercive cohesion strength	-0.616*** 0.000	0.283** 0.02	0.646*** 0.000	0.521*** 0.000

Note: *** $p < 0.01$; ** $p < 0.05$; * $p < 0.10$

b) Correlations between cohesion and resourcefulness variables

	Sustaining Resourcefulness Factor (Absorptive)	Sustaining Resourcefulness Abundance	Creating Resourcefulness Factor (Innovative)	Creating Resourcefulness Abundance
Adhesive cohesion factor (embedded)	0.077 0.553	0.065 0.619	0.203 0.116	0.217* 0.093
Adhesive cohesion strength	0.356*** 0.005	0.205 0.113	0.120 0.357	0.454*** 0.000
Coercive cohesion factor (governed)	-0.318** 0.012	0.246* 0.056	0.310** 0.015	0.253** 0.049
Coercive cohesion strength	-0.461*** 0.000	0.303** 0.018	0.161 0.216	0.530*** 0.000

Note: *** $p < 0.01$; ** $p < 0.05$; * $p < 0.10$

c) Correlations between resourcefulness and flexibility variables

	Configurational Flexibility Factor (Implicit)	Configurational Flexibility Freedom	Sequential Flexibility Factor (Agile)	Sequential Flexibility Freedom
Sustaining resourcefulness factor (absorptive)	0.404*** 0.001	0.220* 0.088	0.362*** 0.004	-0.299** 0.019
Sustaining resourcefulness abundance	-0.133 0.308	0.069 0.595	0.234* 0.070	0.215* 0.096
Creating resourcefulness factor (innovative)	-0.265** 0.039	0.075 0.565	0.416*** 0.001	0.216* 0.094
Creating resourcefulness abundance	-0.473*** 0.000	0.246* 0.027	0.448*** 0.000	0.537*** 0.000

Note: *** $p < 0.01$; ** $p < 0.05$; * $p < 0.10$

Table 4-25   Results of Principal Component Analysis of Response Capacity Factors

Response capacity factors	Meaning of factor extremes		Meta-factor	
	(+)	(–)	Mechanistic	Organic
Adhesive cohesion	Embedded	Pragmatic	0.010	**0.781**
Coercive cohesion	Governed	Formal	**-0.554**	0.533
Configurational flexibility	Implicit	Heedful	**0.741**	-0.314
Sequential flexibility	Agile	Proactive	**-0.655**	0.563
Sustaining resourcefulness	Absorptive	Cumulative	**0.865**	0.259
Creating resourcefulness	Innovative	Explorative	-0.127	**0.667**

events that occur during execution. These constructs can play an important mediator or moderator role in explaining the complex project outcomes.

Restructuring processes. We used 10 items drawn primarily from the qualitative research to develop a scale for the intensity of project and organizational restructuring, beginning with the late stages of the planning process. These items form a scale with a very good reliability (Cronbach's Alpha = 0.85). Descriptive statistics for the items and for the scale are presented in Table 4-26. Results show that, while the technical design and the execution sequence tend to change more often, major players, work processes, goals and requirements, and agreements do not change as often. The item with the highest variance referred to leader and managers change.

Event severity. Unexpected events intensity can be an important control variable for the role of response capacity factors in the success of complex projects. Therefore, we computed an event severity index, which relied on the three items included in the survey to this effect, in which each emphasized a different aspect, the potential consequences, the frequency, and the unexpected nature of these events.

Table 4-26   Item and Scale Statistics for the Restructuring Intensity Scale

Items in the scale for restructuring intensity (Alpha = 0.85)	Mean	Std. Dev.
The project leader and key managers changed several times during the project	3.45	2.121
Fresh insights on key issues led to shifts in organizational and contractual policies	3.97	1.771
The organizational chart was significantly restructured compared to the planned one	3.83	1.794
The project goals, scope or requirements changed significantly with respect to plans	3.12	1.705
Technical concepts, designs or operating procedures underwent several major changes	4.00	1.797
The planned execution sequence and milestones had to be repeatedly restructured	4.08	1.867
Shifting resource needs resulted in several major budget escalations or redistributions	3.76	1.969
Major participants such as owners, contractors and clients had to be replaced by others	2.41	1.488
Persisting conflicts forced the negotiation of new agreements between participants	3.12	1.759
Work processes proved inadequate and a lot of effort was spent to develop new ones	3.08	1.676
Scale	**34.82**	**11.801**

Table 4-27   Item and Scale Statistics for the Event Severity Scale

Items in the scale for event severity (Alpha = 0.76)	Mean	Std. Dev.
We had several events whose potential consequences could be qualified as severe	5.15	1.577
We experienced a flurry of major events that constantly put the project on the brink	3.60	1.713
Many events came as a total surprise for every member of the core project team	3.00	1.558
Scale	**11.74**	**3.987**

As can be seen from Table 4-27, average results show that events with a severe potential impact are a frequent occurrence in complex projects. However, many events are not a total surprise to managers but are somewhat anticipated by participants. The scale has a good reliability with a Cronbach's Alpha of 0.76.

Source of events. We also computed a factor that would qualify the main source of events as internal (errors, misjudgments, omissions) versus external (partners, stakeholders, economy, society, etc.). The measure is the second unrotated factor extracted using a principal component procedure based on the four items included in the survey to this effect. The items and their correlations with the factor are presented in Table 4-28. The event severity is not significantly correlated with the source of events; internal and external events can be equally severe.

Nature of event response. The survey also included a number of items that asked respondents about the dominant mode of response to unexpected events. Some of these were inspired by the response capacity dimensions. A principal component analysis showed that most of these events captured what can be understood as the difficulty of event response, for example, the extent to which it required radically restructuring the project organization. Therefore, we created a scale that measured the difficulty of event response. Item and scale statistics are presented in Table 4-29.

Effectiveness of event response. Another set of survey items was focusing on whether the ultimate response of the project organization was effective. No combination of these items formed a proper scale, as they were intended more like a semantic ladder, from most effective responses to total inability to respond. Therefore, these items were included individually in further analyses. Their descriptive statistics are included in Table 4-30.

Table 4-28   Correlation Between Included Items and the Factor
Measuring the Source of Events (Positive Correlations–
Internal; Negative Correlations–External)

Items used to extract the source of events factor	Correlation
Most events were somewhat anticipated but proved much more severe than expected	0.355
Most events came from errors, omissions and conflicts imputable to the project team	0.710
Most events resulted from autonomous actions of project partners and stakeholders	-0.280
Most events originated in the broader industrial, social and economic environment	-0.684

Table 4-29   Item and Scale Statistics for the Response Difficulty Scale

Items in the scale for response difficulty (Alpha = 0.66)	Mean	Std. Dev.
(Reversed) The event was solved without replacing any participants or modifying usual relations	3.34	1.824
Project shifted to crisis mode, with authoritarian decision making and close scrutiny	3.46	1.669
The response required fully redefining the project and restructuring its organization	2.85	1.631
Only the investment of considerable additional resources enabled a proper response	3.47	1.822
Preparing the response went through the elaboration of extremely innovative solutions	4.03	1.580
Scale	17.16	5.559

Performance

The survey included 12 items that measured project performance. We deemed it important to capture several aspects of project performance, because a project may be fully completed but not operate properly, etc. The diversity of aspects that compose project performance, led to the fact that for three of the four scales, reliability indicators were low, and even, in the case of completion performance, unacceptable. Therefore, we often used individual items in subsequent analyses. Descriptive statistics for the items, as well as scale alphas are reproduced in Table 4-31. We also produced an overall performance indicator, which is the sum of all 12 items, which is highly reliable, with a Cronbach's Alpha of 0.81.

4. Analyses of Influence Trajectories

The main goal of the analyses reported in this section is to help us understand the role of response capacity elements among the factors that influence the performance of complex projects. Our exploration of this issue was guided by the hypotheses developed in the theoretical section and refined during the qualitative stage of this research. Specifically, this section presents evidence that attempts to corroborate the influence trajectories obtained because of the qualitative study. In addition, we present other elements referring to factors that influence the project success, which were not addressed extensively in the qualitative chapter, such as initial conditions (complexity), restructuring processes, and unexpected events. The first such element, which is detailed in the following section, refers to the direct impact of complexity on the performance of the project.

Table 4-30   Descriptive Statistics for Response Effectiveness Items

Items for response effectiveness	Min.	Max.	Mean	Std. Dev.
The event was properly addressed and had no consequences for subsequent execution	1	7	4.47	1.686
Better responses were possible but constraints forced a response that was good enough	1	6	3.97	1.639
The response was not really optimal but it enabled us to eventually salvage the project	1	7	3.50	1.734
The event became a showstopper and the project had to be irrevocably abandoned	1	6	1.47	1.036

Table 4-31   Descriptive Statistics and Scales for the Items Measuring Project Performance

Items and scales used to measure project performance	Mean	Std. Dev.
Completion Performance (Alpha = 0.55)		
We put into service the entire planned scope of the project and some additional objects	5.58	1.306
The project went on line ahead of the planned launch date set when it was approved	4.10	1.946
The final project cost was below the budget that was approved at the go-ahead date	3.85	1.912
Technical Performance (Alpha = 0.73)		
All specified functional and performance goals were met and some even exceeded	5.82	1.103
Outstanding technical accomplishments made this project a worldwide reference	5.30	1.585
The project implemented technical innovations that were firsts in worldwide practice	4.56	1.803
Operational performance (Alpha = 0.68)		
Even when running at top regime, the project had no malfunctions, bugs or accidents	4.07	1.621
The operation and maintenance costs of this project are much lower than expected	3.97	1.211
No major new spending was needed in order to remedy problems with this project	4.48	1.822
Value creation performance (Alpha = 0.65)		
Sales and profits from this project are significantly better than expected at go-ahead	4.07	1.635
The users and stakeholders of this project are delighted with the value it provides them	5.48	1.269
The project greatly enhanced the reputation and strategic positioning of its owner	5.62	1.497

Impact of Complexity on Performance

Along with organizational routines and institutionalized models, the nature of the complexity can influence the approaches used for planning and managing complex projects. However, before understanding the more mediated trajectories, it is important to assess whether complexity affects performance directly. In other words, are projects that face, say, more difficult natural conditions more likely to have, say, a lower technical performance, or, perhaps, a higher one? To understand this, we performed a series of regressions, which tied various aspects of performance to various aspects of project complexity.

The first analysis investigated, using a multiple linear regression procedure, whether the composite measures of performance as a dependent variable were affected by the six principal components that measure complexity. However, this research did not produce significant results in terms of the adjusted R square. Among the significant coefficients, we mention the positive influence of Nature Complexity on the Completion and Overall outcomes. However, because of the nonsignificant results for the respective equations, we did not pursue these results.

Because some measures of performance aspects did not have a strong alpha, we decided to also perform regression analyses using individual items of performance. We applied a regression analysis for all performance items using all complexity items plus the project total cost. We used a stepwise enter procedure, in order to avoid multicollinearity problems that could have been caused by high correlations

Table 4-32   Regression of Scope Completion Performance Item on Complexity Conditions Items

Initial conditions items related to whether the entire intended scope was completed	Beta coefficients	
	Equation 0.05	Equation 0.10
The market we intended to serve was known for its severe swings in price and demand	–	0.257*
Adjusted R Square	–	**0.049***

Note: *** Significant at 0.01 and lower; ** Significant at 0.05 and lower; * Significant at 0.10 and lower

between certain complexity items. In each case, two sets of parameters for the stepwise regression were used. The first set, with the respective model denoted equation of 0.05, used a probability of F of 0.05 for entering a dependent variable in the equation and a probability of F or 0.10 for removing the variable from the model. The second set, with the respective set denoted equation 0.10 used 0.10 and 0.15, respectively. Results are presented in the following section.

For the completion performance item referring to whether the entire intended scope was completed, results are presented in Table 4-32. The only complexity item that appears to affect this performance aspect positively is whether the intended market is affected by severe swings in demand. This may happen, perhaps, because the scope is needed in order to reap a maximum of benefits before the next market downturn.

Results for the item referring to whether the project went on line ahead of the planned launch date set when it was approved are presented in Table 4-33. Similar to the analyses that used indices rather than individual variables, these results suggest that schedule performance is enhanced when projects initially face major issues related to natural conditions, and, perhaps, when projects are funded with public money. High performance in this aspect appears to be hampered by the fact that the project targets a market whose emergence is uncertain, and, perhaps, that it was much larger than all other projects that the owner had ever managed.

Table 4-33   Regression of Completion Schedule Performance Item on Complexity Conditions Items

Initial conditions items related to whether the project went on line ahead of the planned launch date set when it was approved	Beta coefficients	
	Equation 0.05	Equation 0.10
We faced major issues related to natural conditions (soil, water, weather etc.)	0.457***	0.479***
The project output targeted a market whose emergence and growth were still uncertain	-0.274**	-0.284**
The project was funded with public money or relied on government guarantees	–	0.313***
The project was much larger than all other projects the owner had ever managed	–	-0.271**
Adjusted R Square	**0.277***	**0.362***

Note: *** Significant at 0.01 and lower; ** Significant at 0.05 and lower; * Significant at 0.10 and lower

Table 4-34   Regression of the Completion Cost Performance Item on Complexity Conditions Items

Initial conditions items related to whether the final project cost was below the budget that was approved at the go-ahead date	Beta coefficients	
	Equation 0.05	Equation 0.10
Key applicable laws and regulations were ambiguous or untested in practice	-0.309**	-0.253*
Conditions forced us to rely on contractors or personnel from many different countries	–	-0.253*
Adjusted R Square	0.079**	0.125**

Note: *** Significant at 0.01 and lower; ** Significant at 0.05 and lower; * Significant at 0.10 and lower

Results for the completion cost performance are presented in Table 4-34. For this aspect of performance, the items that seem to have an influence, both of them negative, are untested or ambiguous laws and regulations, and, perhaps, the necessity to use contractors or personnel from many different countries.

Results for the technical performance item related to whether all specified functional and performance goals were met or exceeded are presented in Table 4-35. This item seems influenced by the fact that the project faced major issues related to natural conditions. Like in earlier cases, this kind of condition appears to have a positive influence on performance, which may be explained by the fact that it mobilizes participants, or, possibly, makes them more lenient in their subjective evaluation of performance.

The technical performance item that measures whether outstanding technical accomplishments made this project a worldwide reference appeared related to two conditions; namely, that the project was seen as an occasion for trying new financial or contractual methods and, perhaps, to the fact that the project was forced to rely on personnel from many different countries. These results are presented in Table 4-36.

Results for the item capturing whether the project implemented technical innovations that were firsts in worldwide practice are presented in Table 4-37. They suggest, quite logically, that this element of performance may be related to the fact that the project targeted emergent markets, faced major issues related to natural conditions, had bold goals, and, negatively, to the fact that the project was forced to minimize the disruption to ongoing operations and businesses. In addition, the total cost (size) of the project could perhaps increase the chances that some parts of it will include highly novel elements. As can be seen in Table 4-37, together, these

Table 4-35   Regression of the Functional Goals Performance Item on Complexity Conditions Items

Initial conditions items related to whether all specified functional and performance goals were met or exceeded	Beta coefficients	
	Equation 0.05	Equation 0.10
We faced major issues related to natural conditions (soil, water, weather etc.)	0.336**	0.335**
Adjusted R Square	0.087**	0.097**

Note: *** Significant at 0.01 and lower; ** Significant at 0.05 and lower; * Significant at 0.10 and lower

Table 4-36   Regression of the Outstanding Accomplishments Item on Complexity Conditions Items

Initial conditions items related to whether outstanding technical accomplishments made this project a worldwide reference	Beta coefficients	
	Equation 0.05	Equation 0.10
The project was seen as an occasion for trying new financial or contractual methods	0.334***	0.300**
Conditions forced us to rely on contractors or personnel from many different countries	–	0.218*
Adjusted R Square	**0.096***	**0.128***

Note: *** Significant at 0.01 and lower; ** Significant at 0.05 and lower; * Significant at 0.10 and lower

four or five factors could explain over one third of the variance of the item that was used as a dependent variable. Together, the above results suggest that technical performance items are often positively correlated with the technical complexity faced by the project.

Results related to the first item measuring operational performance, namely whether, even when running at top regime, the project had no malfunctions, bugs, or accidents, are presented in Table 4-38. This aspect of performance appears to be related positively with the fact that the project had to fit with preexisting technical systems or tight built surroundings, and negatively, perhaps, with the fact that project goals forced participants to adopt new or unique technical solutions.

Much like for the fact that functional and technical performance goals were met, the performance on the operation and maintenance costs appears to be positively related to the fact that the project faced major issues related to natural conditions. However, results presented in Table 4-39 suggest that this item of performance also appears perhaps to be influenced negatively by the fact that the project was the first to implement new project management processes and norms.

With respect to the performance aspect that no major new spending was needed to remedy problems with the project, the more stringent statistical constraints for the stepwise regression produced the outcome that no predictor was entered in the equations. However, the less stringent constraints resulted in a model with three

Table 4-37   Regression of the Innovation Firsts Item on Complexity Conditions Items

Initial conditions items related to whether the project implemented technical innovations that were firsts in worldwide practice	Beta coefficients	
	Equation 0.05	Equation 0.10
The project output targeted a market whose emergence and growth were still uncertain	0.327***	0.295***
We faced major issues related to natural conditions (soil, water, weather etc.)	0.367***	0.322***
Bold project goals forced us to use technical solutions that no one had tried before	0.314***	0.348**
The project had to minimize the disruption to ongoing operations and businesses	-0.244**	-0.258**
Total project cost (as a measure of size)	–	0.204*
Adjusted R Square	**0.359***	**0.388***

Note: *** Significant at 0.01 and lower; ** Significant at 0.05 and lower; * Significant at 0.10 and lower

Table 4-38   Regression of the "No Malfunctions" Item on Complexity Conditions Items

Initial conditions items related to whether, even when running at top regime, the project had no malfunctions, bugs or accidents	Beta coefficients	
	Equation 0.05	Equation 0.10
The project had to fit with preexisting technical systems or tight built surroundings	0.277**	0.290**
Bold project goals forced us to use technical solutions that no one had tried before	-	-0.223*
Adjusted R Square	**0.060****	**0.095****

Note: *** Significant at 0.01 and lower; ** Significant at 0.05 and lower; * Significant at 0.10 and lower

terms, which are summarized in the rightmost column of Table 4-40. The performance on this item was affected negatively by the initial challenge of maintaining full control over the artifacts that would be made, but was impacted positively by the initial recognition of the problem of ensuring coherent interoperation. Another condition that could be, perhaps, related negatively to this performance item is the fact that project implementation depended on decisions made by foreign governments. However, the significance level for this predictor is above 0.10.

With respect to value creation performance, the first item which referred to sales and profits produce only one result with marginal significance—namely that when timing is conditioned by urgent needs or limited windows of opportunity, the project has more chances to improve its sales and profits. This result is shown in Table 4-41.

Regarding the item measuring the user and stakeholder satisfaction with the value provided by the project, results provided in the Table 4-42 suggest that the only condition that the more stringent equation has shown to have a significant positive impact on performance was the presence of major issues related to natural conditions. However, the model produced by the less stringent conditions also includes positive influences from the initial problem of influencing natural processes affected by many invisible factors and by the fact that the project was funded with public money, as well as a negative influence from the fact that, during the project, the owner embarked on a major reorganization.

Finally, with regard to the performance aspect that the project enhanced the reputation and strategic positioning of its owner, results presented in Table 4-43 suggest that only the fact that key applicable laws were ambiguous and untested

Table 4-39   Regression of the Operation Costs Item on Complexity Conditions Items

Initial conditions items related to the outcome that the operation and maintenance cost of the project are much lower than expected	Beta coefficients	
	Equation 0.05	Equation 0.10
We faced major issues related to natural conditions (soil, water, weather etc.)	0.293**	0.302**
The project was the first to implement new project management processes and norms	-	0.229*
Adjusted R Square	**0.069****	**0.107****

Note: *** Significant at 0.01 and lower; ** Significant at 0.05 and lower; * Significant at 0.10 and lower

Table 4-40   Regression of the "No Major New Spending" Item on Complexity Conditions Items

Initial conditions items related to the outcome that no major new spending was needed in order to remedy problems with this project	Beta coefficients	
	Equation 0.05	Equation 0.10
Project implementation depended on decisions made by foreign government entities	-	-0.199
Our challenge was maintaining full control over the behavior of the artifacts we made	-	-0.438***
Our problem was ensuring coherent interoperation between scores of artifact functions	-	0.355**
Adjusted R Square	-	0.125**

Note: *** Significant at 0.01 and lower; ** Significant at 0.05 and lower; * Significant at 0.10 and lower

Table 4-41   Regression of the Sales and Profits Item on Complexity Conditions Items

Initial conditions items related to the fact that sales and profits from the project are significantly better than expected at go-ahead	Beta coefficients	
	Equation 0.05	Equation 0.10
Project timing was conditioned by urgent needs or limited windows of opportunity	-	0.227*
Adjusted R Square	-	0.034*

Note: *** Significant at 0.01 and lower; ** Significant at 0.05 and lower; * Significant at 0.10 and lower

Table 4-42   Regression of the User Delight Item on Complexity Conditions Items

Initial conditions items related to the outcome that users and stakeholders of the project are delighted with the value it provides them	Beta coefficients	
	Equation 0.05	Equation 0.10
We faced major issues related to natural conditions (soil, water, weather etc.)	0.335**	0.257**
We strived to gain influence over natural processes affected by many invisible factors	-	0.294**
The project was funded with public money or relied on government guarantees	-	0.317**
During this project, the owner organization embarked on a major restructuring	-	-0.290**
Adjusted R Square	0.096**	0.237***

Note: *** Significant at 0.01 and lower; ** Significant at 0.05 and lower; * Significant at 0.10 and lower

Table 4-43   Regression of the Strategic Reputation Item on Complexity Conditions Items

Initial conditions items related to whether the project greatly enhanced the reputation and strategic positioning of its owner	Beta coefficients	
	Equation 0.05	Equation 0.10
Key applicable laws and regulations were ambiguous or untested in practice	-	0.253*
Adjusted R Square	-	0.047*

Note: *** Significant at 0.01 and lower; ** Significant at 0.05 and lower; * Significant at 0.10 and lower

in practice appeared to have a positive influence. This may be indeed logical if the project succeeded in passing through the legal and political obstacles these conditions may have created.

Results regarding direct context influences on performance reveal few influences if composite indexes and factors are used to assess the influence. However, a finer, item-level analysis reveals many possible relations. While most of these influences seem logical, they should be considered cautiously because of the method used to obtain them as well as of the large number of predictor variables entered in the stepwise equation initially. The principal way in which the identified predictors were used in other analyses is as control variables.

Contextual Factors That Influence the Planning Approach

While the context-to-performance analyses span the entire length of the influence trajectory we are striving to understand, the first step in this trajectory is the possible influence of context on the planning approach used by the project. To assess these influences, we resorted again to regression equations involving, successively, the four planning factors as dependent variables, and the six complexity factors as the predictor variables. If many significant relations were obtained, we would be in the presence of a "contingency" (Thompson, 1967) mechanism, in which planning approaches would be adjusted to the realities of the context. If few relations are observed, it can perhaps be argued that a "neoinstitutional" mechanism would be at works (Meyer & Rowan, 1977), in which the selection would result from the rational models circulated by the project management practitioner communities, by the regulatory instance, etc.

Of course, the possibility exists that the factors that determine the planning approaches have not been captured by the contextual variables we included in our research. The main factor that our case studies have shown to influence planning was the project novelty for those that carried it out, and the influence went in the sense of encouraging approaches that are more experimental. The statistical analyses based on our survey results show that indeed the measures that can be linked conceptually to different kinds of novelty—namely the change factor, the innovation factor, and the emergence factor, have a certain relation to planning approaches. However, only on the knowledge approach this influence is statistically significant, as the change factor seems to be negatively and significantly related to a conceptual knowledge approach, and hence positively related to an experimental knowledge approach. In addition, an experimental approach also seems to be favored in an emerging context, but the relation is marginally significant. The entire equation that relates the project context to knowledge is marginally significant. The equations relating other planning factors to the context variables are not significant. The only other individual predictor relation to a planning approach is the negative, marginally significant influence of the emergence complexity factor on planning centralization, but this influence is part of a model that is statistically not significant (Table 4-44).

We also performed finer item-level analyses, by including all complexity items as predictors in a stepwise procedure using the less stringent conditions explained above ($p < 0.10$ for inclusion and $p < 0.15$ for exclusion). Table 4-45 presents the results for the four planning factors as outcome variables. One interesting aspect

Table 4-44   Regression of the Planning Factors on the Complexity Conditions Factors

Complexity predictor variables	Planning factors			
	Knowledge (conceptual)	Participation (centralized)	Argument (decisional)	Risk (integrative)
Change complexity factor	-0.296**	-0.129	-0.052	0.113
Innovation complexity factor	-0.188	-0.177	-0.076	0.118
Emergence complexity factor	-0.206*	-0.243*	-0.113	0.129
Nature complexity factor	0.109	0.111	0.179	-0.169
Constraints complexity factor	-0.052	0.031	0.020	-0.073
International complexity factor	0.047	-0.067	-0.163	-0.176
Adjusted R Square	**0.121***	**0.027**	**-0.022**	**0.003**

Note: *** Significant at 0.01 and lower; ** Significant at 0.05 and lower; * Significant at 0.10 and lower

is the prevalence of the four innovation complexity items as predictors, despite the fact that together they did not yield any significant relation in Table 4-44. Another interesting aspect is the fact that the implementation of new project management norms and processes reduces the likelihood of the use of conceptual knowledge and centralized planning. We used the items that came out as significant as control variables in various analyses involving the planning factors. We can assume that most other influences on planning follow from organizational policies or routines and from industry recipes or professional community recommendations, and are followed with little regard to the contextual conditions.

Table 4-45   Regression of the Planning Factors on Complexity Conditions Items

Complexity predictor items	Planning factors			
	Knowledge (conceptual)	Participation (centralized)	Argument (decisional)	Risk (integrative)
The project interfered with a sensitive natural area (wildlife, ecosystem, scenery)			0.325**	
Bold project goals forced us to use technical solutions that no one had tried before	-0.466***			
We strived to gain influence over natural processes affected by many invisible factors				-0.321**
Our problem was ensuring interoperation between scores of artifact functions				0.402***
We strived to maintain full control over the behavior of the artifacts we made		-0.287**		
The project was the first to implement new project management processes and norms	-0.274**	-0.252*		
The project was likely to become a battleground for political interests and militants			-0.261**	
Conditions forced us to rely on contractors or personnel from many different countries		-0.234*		
Adjusted R Square	**0.264***	**0.139***	**0.112**	**0.106**

Note: *** Significant at 0.01 and lower; ** Significant at 0.05 and lower; * Significant at 0.10 and lower

Unmediated Influence of Planning Variables on Performance

We used linear regression analysis to identify whether planning variables have a direct influence on the overall project performance index. We used two models, one including only the four planning factors as predictors and the second including project size as well. Results shown in Table 4-46 for model 1 (full sample) and model 2 suggest that three variables have an influence on performance that is at least marginally significant. Results confirm the finding from qualitative research that the prevalent influence of centralized planning and decisional plans is positive. However, results appear to reverse the finding that an integrative risk approach has a positive influence on performance. Instead, both models suggest that the integrative risk approach has a (significant if size is included and marginally significant otherwise) negative influence on the overall performance. Planning knowledge does not seem to have a significant influence, but coefficients are negative, implying that experimental rather than conceptual knowledge may favor performance. We also run model 1 on a subsample of the 30 largest projects to see whether these results hold. This appears to have resulted in the positive coefficient for the planning participation, and the negative one for the integrative factor, to become even larger. However, the coefficient for the decisional factor becomes almost zero. Instead, the coefficient for the conceptual knowledge becomes even more pronounced on the negative side, suggesting that experimental knowledge is better for large projects. However, these conclusions are speculative, because all coefficients and the equation itself are nonsignificant for the large projects sample.

We also attempted to corroborate the qualitative findings about different aspects of project performance. For each dependent variable, we performed two analyses, one with only planning factors as independent (explanatory) variables, and one with complexity factors added in the same equation as independent (control) variables. Results are presented in Table 4-47.

Completion performance. As can be seen from Table 3-3, and from the overall results of qualitative research, completion performance appears to be influenced by all planning variables. Particularly, planning knowledge, more precisely a reliance on experimental knowledge, appears to influence positively the completion performance. Planning participation has a mixed influence on completion performance. The plan argument, more specifically a decisional plan, has a positive influence on

Table 4-46   Regression of the Overall Project Performance on Planning Factors

	Model 1 (full sample)		Model 2		Model 1 (large projects)	
	Beta	Probability	Beta	Probability	Beta	Probability
Planning knowledge conceptual factor	-0.065	0.662	-0.137	0.355	-0.282	0.326
Planning participation centralized factor	0.255	0.063	**0.288**	0.033	0.452	0.116
Planning argument decisional factor	0.206	0.115	0.237	0.065	-0.050	0.827
Planning risk integrative factor	-0.258	0.066	**-0.319**	0.024	-0.401	0.142
Total cost (as a measure of project size)			**0.258**	0.047		
Adjusted R Square	**0.127**	0.025	**0.176**	0.010	-0.023	0.497

Note: Bold characters – Significant at 0.05 and lower, Underscored characters – Significant at 0.10 and lower

Table 4-47   Regression of Performance Variables on Planning and Complexity Factors

Independent variables	Dependent performance variables							
	Completion index		Technical index		Operational index		Value index	
	Eq. 1	Eq. 2	Eq. 1	Eq. 2	Eq. 1	Eq. 2	Eq. 1	Eq. 2
Planning knowledge factor (conceptual)	-0.023	-0.029	-0.071	-0.001	0.063	0.086	-0.132	-0.045
Planning participation factor (centralized)	0.364***	0.261*	0.008	0.074	0.167	0.188	0.221	0.214
Plan argument factor (decisional)	0.256**	0.220	0.038	0.146	0.072	0.079	0.227*	0.272*
Plan risk approach factor (integrative)	-0.182	-0.167	-0.125	-0.160	-0.277**	-0.348**	-0.156	-0.155
Total cost item		-0.024		0.289*		0.222		0.075
Change complexity factor		-0.036		0.126		-0.084		0.093
Innovation complexity factor		-0.077		0.156		0.158		0.138
Emergence complexity factor		-0.053		0.271*		0.214		0.101
Nature complexity factor		0.188		0.078		0.011		0.096
Constraints complexity factor		0.111		-0.122		0.041		-0.083
International complexity factor		-0.102		0.189		-0.198		0.098
Adjusted R Square	**0.215*****	**0.139***	**-0.056**	**0.102**	**0.089***	**0.071**	**0.061**	**-0.006**

Note: *** Significant at 0.01 and lower; ** Significant at 0.05 and lower; * Significant at 0.10 and lower

completion performance. Finally, the plan risk approach also has a mixed influence on completion performance. The multiple regression analysis of the completion performance index on planning variables confirms that a decisional plan has a positive influence on completion performance and suggests that centralized planning also had a positive impact. However, results do not seem to confirm the impact of knowledge. The addition of complexity variables reduces the significance of the impact of participation and argument variables.

Technical performance. With respect to this aspect, qualitative research suggested no influence from the planning knowledge but a strong positive influence from a centralized planning. In addition, there was no influence from the plan argument, but there was a weak influence from the plan risk approach, namely a weak positive influence from an integrative approach. Regression analyses using the technical performance index as a dependent variable show no interesting patterns, except perhaps the marginally significant positive influence of the total cost item and of the emergence complexity factor in equation 2. This prompted us to investigate technical performance at the level of individual items as dependent variables, which produced interesting results presented in Table 4-48. First, regression on the item measuring whether all technical goals were achieved confirms that centralized planning has a positive impact. Moreover, an allocative (not integrative as qualitative research suggested) risk approach also has a positive impact on this aspect of technical performance. However, these planning variables have no impact on other technical performance items. Concerning the worldwide reference performance item, no planning or complexity item appeared to have an impact. Finally, results concerning the "firsts in worldwide practice" performance item suggest that this aspect of performance is influenced heavily by the complexity conditions rather than by planning approaches. This contrasts with the situation for "all functional goals" and may explain why no direct influence from the planning variables on the technical performance index was detected.

Table 4-48   Regression of Technical Performance Items on Planning and Complexity Factors

Independent variables	Dependent technical performance items					
	All functional goals		Worldwide reference		Firsts in worldwide practice	
	Eq. 1	Eq. 2	Eq. 1	Eq. 2	Eq. 1	Eq. 2
Planning knowledge factor (conceptual)	-0.018	-0.003	0.075	0.142	-0.201	-0.127
Planning participation factor (centralized)	0.268**	0.291**	-0.089	-0.050	-0.104	0.017
Plan argument factor (decisional)	-0.014	0.018	0.055	0.138	0.037	0.168
Plan risk approach factor (integrative)	-0.328**	-0.365**	-0.101	-0.137	0.037	0.018
Change complexity factor		0.039		0.226		0.033
Innovation complexity factor		0.053		0.070		0.229*
Emergence complexity factor		0.265*		0.099		0.309**
Nature complexity factor		0.155		0.071		0.003
Constraints complexity factor		-0.019		-0.144		-0.112
International complexity factor		-0.027		0.149		0.277**
Total cost item		0.197		0.212		0.289*
Adjusted R Square	**0.122****	**0.130***	**-0.044**	**0.044**	**0.002**	**0.189****

Note: *** Significant at 0.01 and lower; ** Significant at 0.05 and lower; * Significant at 0.10 and lower

Operational performance. Qualitative research suggests for this aspect that centralized planning as well as an integrative plan risk approach both have a positive impact. The planning knowledge and the plan argument appeared to have no discernible impact on this dimension of performance. To corroborate these relations, we used a similar approach as for the previous two performance dimensions. Results presented in Table 4-47 show that a centralized planning approach has a positive coefficient, however, this result is not statistically significant. Regression results also suggest that an allocative risk approach, not an integrative one, as suggested by the qualitative results, is associated with higher operational performance.

Value creation performance. Qualitative results appeared to suggest a mixed impact of planning knowledge and of plan argument, no impact of participation, and a positive impact of an integrative plan risk approach on performance. We attempted to corroborate these results using the regression analyses reported in the last two columns of Table 4-47. Results suggest that a decisional plan is associated with higher value creation performance, but the association has marginal statistical significance.

Factors That Influence Organizational Restructuring

Organizational restructuring is negatively correlated with overall project performance ($r = -0.391$; $p = 0.002$), as well as with various aspects of project performance, particularly with completion performance ($r = -0,526$; $p = 0.000$), as well as with operational performance ($r = -0.293$; $p = 0.022$), and value creation performance ($r = -0.252$; $p = 0.052$). Only technical performance appears uncorrelated with organizational restructuring. Therefore, we considered it important to investigate whether initial conditions, as measured by the six complexity factors, or planning approaches, have an impact on the intensity of organizational restructuring. Therefore, we prepared four regression models that had the restructuring scale (see Table 4-26) as an outcome variable. The results obtained with the help of these models can be glanced from Table 4-49. We first assessed the impact of two "demographic" variables, namely duration (in months) and the percent of budget spent outside the country of the owner organization. Duration is highly correlated with total project cost and we consider it here as a measure of project size. However, we also considered that it simply increases the chances that the project organization would have to be restructured, as people leave, participants go bankrupt, etc. The budget spent outside owner's country induces the possibility of cultural and other conflicts that can also lead to restructuring.

Results presented in Table 4-49 show that both variables appear related positively with the intensity of restructuring, but only the percent spent outside the home country has a statistically significant coefficient (the model formed by the two items is marginally significant). The second model used all complexity factors as predictors. The entire equation is highly significant statistically, and it predicts almost one third of the variance of the restructuring index. Two areas of the initial context are significantly related to the outcome, namely emergence complexity, which increases the chances of restructuring, and nature complexity, which reduces the chances of restructuring. The third model uses the four planning factors and predictors of restructuring. The model has a high statistical significance and explains over one-third of the variance in the restructuring index. Conceptual knowledge, centralized planning and, especially, a decisional argument, are all negatively correlated with restructuring (the three coefficients are statistically significant). The fourth model includes together in the same equation the predictors

Table 4-49   Regression of Restructuring Index on Planning and Context Variables

Independent variables	Dependent variable restructuring			
	Model 1	Model 2	Model 3	Model 4
Duration in months (highly correlated with size)	0.194			0.086
Percent of budget spent outside owner country	0.274**			0.007
Change complexity factor		0.137		0.042
Innovation complexity factor		0.129		0.097
Emergence complexity factor		0.466***		0.366***
Nature complexity factor		-0.235**		-0.115
Constraints complexity factor		0.136		0.139
International complexity factor		0.168		0.081
Planning knowledge factor (conceptual)			-0.225**	-0.028
Planning participation factor (centralized)			-0.234**	-0.116
Plan argument factor (decisional)			-0.439***	-0.375***
Plan risk approach factor (integrative)			0.093	0.159
Adjusted R Square	**0.067***	**0.282***	**0.369***	**0.465***

Note: *** Significant at 0.01 and lower; ** Significant at 0.05 and lower; * Significant at 0.10 and lower

included in the first three models. This highly significant model explains almost one half of the variance of the restructuring index. However, only two predictors have statistically significant coefficients, namely the emergence complexity factor, which increases restructuring intensity, and the plan argument, which decreases it. The reason why other coefficients, which were significant in separate models, become non significant in the joint model could be that planning variables mediate the relations between complexity and restructuring, given that certain context variables affect planning variables (see Table 4-44).

In summary, restructuring appears to be related, on the one hand, to the fact that the project context is fraught with major uncertainties related to emergent processes in its key external environments, such as market and regulatory (see Table 4-4 for the items that load on the emergent complexity factor). On the other hand, restructuring appears to result from promotional (rather than decisional) plans. Restructuring, in turn, has a negative impact on project performance, but, of course, it may be the only way in which the project may be able to continue and reach some degree of completion.

The Relation Between Planning and Response Capacity Properties

One key influence investigated in the qualitative part was that between planning approaches and response capacity properties. We studied the same relation using the regressions shown in Table 4-50, which have response capacity factors, both factors and intensities, as dependent variables, and planning variables, as well as total cost and restructuring, as predictors. Results demonstrate that planning variables have an important impact on both the nature and the intensity of the response capacity properties. Nine out of 12 models produce at least a marginal level of significance overall (for eight of them the significance is high or very high). In all nine, at least one planning variable has a significant coefficient, and, even in one model that is not significant overall, one planning predictor has a significant coefficient. The most important impact seems to be produced by planning participation, with centralized planning having a significant positive impact on adhesive and coercive cohesion strength, on configurational and sequential freedom, as well as on sustaining (in nonsignificant model) and creating resource abundance.

Planning centralization is also associated with project organizations that rely on governed (as opposed to formal) coercion, on heedful (as opposed to implicit) configurational flexibility, on agile (as opposed to proactive) sequential flexibility, and on cumulative (as opposed to absorptive) sustaining resourcefulness. The second planning variable in terms of explaining response capacity properties is knowledge; namely, conceptual knowledge seems to be associated with less sequential freedom and less creative abundance. Reliance on conceptual knowledge also seems to be associated with formal, as opposed to governed, coercive cohesion. The third planning variable, plan argument, has only two associations with response capacity properties, one of which is marginally significant; namely, a decisional plan favors governed, as opposed to formal, coercive cohesion, and it has a marginally significant relation with the strength of adhesive cohesion. Finally, an integrative plan risk approach has a significant negative relation with the abundance of creating resourcefulness.

Table 4-50   Regression of Response Capacity Properties on Planning Variables and Intensity of Restructuring

| | Cohesion | | | | Flexibility | | | | Resourcefulness | | | |
| | Adhesive | | Coercive | | Configurational | | Sequential | | Sustaining | | Creating | |
	Embedded	Strength	Governed	Strength	Implicit	Freedom	Agile	Freedom	Absorptive	Abundance	Innovative	Abundance
Planning knowledge (conceptual)	0.209	-0.110	-0.283**	-0.202	0.126	-0.038	-0.136	-0.330***	0.141	-0.135	0.155	-0.339**
Planning participation (centralized)	0.101	0.265*	0.281**	0.433***	-0.313**	0.242*	0.372***	0.293**	-0.258*	0.337***	0.165	0.349***
Plan argument (decisional)	0.120	0.237*	0.342**	0.103	0.072	0.011	0.140	0.168	0.086	0.127	0.150	0.152
Plan risk approach (integrative)	0.048	-0.030	-0.187	-0.186	0.016	0.064	-0.179	-0.055	0.105	-0.125	0.200	-0.330**
Restructuring intensity	0.007	-0.184	0.030	-0.232	0.286*	-0.258	-0.207	-0.125	0.338**	0.233	0.039	-0.184
Total cost (project size)	0.032	0.140	0.247*	0.149	-0.210	0.180	0.357***	0.074	0.018	-0.027	0.057	0.199*
Adjusted R Square	**-0.018**	**0.152****	**0.150****	**0.275*****	**0.127****	**0.085***	**0.304*****	**0.089***	**0.116****	**0.006**	**-0.001**	**0.249*****

Note: *** Significant at 0.01 and lower; ** Significant at 0.05 and lower; * Significant at 0.10 and lower

Overall, these results confirm the significant relation between planning approaches and response capacity properties. However, they are somewhat disappointing concerning specific variables. For example, specific models do not seem to explain the adhesive cohesion properties. Among others, they do not confirm the positive relation between an integrative plan risk approach and embedded adhesive cohesion that we expected theoretically and as a result of the qualitative research. In addition, the respective model is unable to explain the prevalence of innovative versus exploratory creating resourcefulness.

We were also surprised by the limited explanatory power of the plan risk approach variable, which emerged as the most important predictor from our qualitative study. We even re-ran all models without the planning knowledge variable, which is correlated with the plan risk variable ($r = 0.29$; $p < 0.05$) and may have eroded some of its explanatory power, but results were the same as those obtained using the equation including all four planning predictors. A check whether the relation is quadratic (U-shaped) also did not reveal any significant relation. Finally, we analyzed item-level correlations between the items included in both measures to understand why there is no relation between them. Results presented in Table 4-51 show that, overall there are few significant correlations between these groups of variables, which may explain the result. Furthermore, the two significant correlations that were uncovered seemed to work in opposite directions—namely, two items associated with the same end of the adhesive cohesion dimension, appear correlated with different ends of the plan risk approach dimensions. This may suggest that certain response capacity factors are either not related to planning or related to very specific aspects of it, such as the fact of constantly evaluating gains and losses being related to the cost-plus, alliances and joint venture types of contracts. If, say, cohesion properties are not related to planning, then they are interesting in their own right, and our research can help reveal the properties related to performance. In practice, these properties can then perhaps be cultivated in their own right, through special efforts and careful monitoring during execution.

Finally, we also performed a regression of the two response capacity meta-factors, "mechanistic" and "organic," to identify their relation with the planning

Table 4-51   Correlations Between Items Included in Plan Risk and Adhesive Cohesion Measures

Items used to extract the adhesive cohesion factor	Items used to extract the plan risk approach factor			
	Fixed price and schedule contracts	Warranties and performance bonds	Owner assumed all risks	Cost plus contracts and alliances
Owners constantly adjusted incentives	0.129	-0.107	0.106	-0.059
Project advanced only if participants see gain	0.399***	-0.005	-0.134	0.045
Owners made clear what others get in return	0.203	0.112	0.121	0.113
Constantly reevaluating potential gains/losses	0.088	-0.046	0.097	0.258**
Team-building and partnering sessions	0.042	0.071	0.098	0.186
Participants occupied collocated offices	-0.121	0.040	0.019	-0.163
Consultants/contractor fully integrated in team	0.156	0.069	-0.089	-0.020
Efforts and liaisons to integrate newcomers	0.184	0.004	0.106	0.165

Note: *** Significant at 0.01 and lower; ** Significant at 0.05 and lower; * Significant at 0.10 and lower

Table 4-52   Regression of Response Capacity Meta-Factors on Planning Factors

Planning and context predictor variables	Response capacity dependent variables	
	Mechanistic meta-factor	Organic meta-factor
Planning knowledge conceptual factor	0.264*	0.130
Planning participation centralized factor	-0.368***	0.165
Plan argument decisional factor	0.011	0.250
Plan risk integrative factor	0.166	0.065
Total cost (as a measure of project size)	-0.190	0.174
Restructuring	0.348**	0.101
Adjusted R Square	**0.245*****	**0.024**

Note: *** Significant at 0.01 and lower; ** Significant at 0.05 and lower; * Significant at 0.10 and lower

variables, and use them in subsequent analyses regarding project performance. Results presented in Table 4-52 suggest a very interesting pattern; namely, planning variables explain almost a quarter of the variance in the mechanistic meta-factor and the model has two significant coefficients, while they do not explain almost any variance of the organic meta-factor and have no significant coefficient. The interpretation that we can give to this finding is that what we called the mechanistic meta-factor, which, as can be seen from Table 4-52, is associated with implicit configurational flexibility and absorptive sustaining resourcefulness as well as with formal cohesion and proactive sequential flexibility, may reflect aspects that can, to some extent, be programmed, starting with the planning phase. On the other hand, the organic meta-factor, which we saw as more related with human processes, reflected in embedded adhesive cohesion and innovative creating resourcefulness, as well as in governed coercive cohesion and agile sequential flexibility, may capture the outcome of structuring processes that are less amenable to programming from the planning stage. These processes could be, perhaps, steered through sustained efforts during the execution phase. Of course, these interpretations should

Table 4-53   Response Capacity Factors as Predictors of Response Difficulty

Response capacity factors	Overall response difficulty	Individual response difficulty items					
		Responded without modifying	Shifted in crisis mode	Partial changes only	Fully redefining project	Considerable additional resources	Extremely innovative solutions
Adhesive cohesion (embedded)	-0.270**	0.069	-0.208	-0.031	-0.051	-0.308**	-0.248*
Coercive cohesion (governed)	-0.101	0.208	-0.087	-0.142	-0.129	0.075	-0.011
Configurational flexibility (implicit)	-0.134	-0.222	-0.120	-0.439***	-0.068	-0.140	-0.391**
Sequential flexibility (agile)	-0.041	-0.231	-0.128	-0.287	-0.117	-0.032	-0.121
Sustaining resources (absorptive)	0.391***	-0.314**	0.395**	0.144	0.229	0.179	0.194
Creating resources (innovative)	-0.275**	0.224*	-0.088	0.143	-0.080	-0.378***	-0.094
Adjusted R Square	**0.268*****	**0.210*****	**0.194*****	**0.062**	**0.041**	**0.162****	**0.052**

Note: *** Significant at 0.01 and lower; ** Significant at 0.05 and lower; * Significant at 0.10 and lower

be considered carefully and further validated in both quantitative and qualitative research.

The Role of Response Capacity Properties in Project Performance

Results in the previous subsection suggest that response capacity properties could play a mediating as well as an autonomous role in explaining project performance. Before deciding which one of these roles corresponds to the various response capacity properties, we sought to investigate the links between these properties and project performance.

The nature of responses to events. A proximate outcome of the response capacity properties is the ability to respond to events in ways that are more effective. Therefore, we sought to identify whether response capacity properties are more associated with certain kinds of response than others. We used the individual items capturing response possibilities, as well as the overall response difficulty index, as dependent variables in regression analyses with response capacity factors as predictors. Results are presented in Table 4-54. The reader should note that the first individual item we considered, "responded without modifying," is the only one that was reversed as part of the overall difficulty index. In other words, high values on that variable are considered a sign of relatively easy response. It appears that the reliance on internal resources and innovative capabilities favors high values on this variable.

Results show that embedded adhesive cohesion favors easier responses, particularly those that do not require significant additional resources and extremely creative solutions, while coercive cohesion has no discernible effect. As expected theoretically, implicit configurational flexibility does not allow responses that involve only partial changes. It is indeed heedful configurational flexibility that enables such responses. The latter kind of flexibility is also associated with the use of extremely innovative solutions. Agile sequential flexibility does not appear to favor any particular type of response. In addition to being negatively related with "no modifying" responses, as was mentioned earlier, an emphasis on absorptive

Table 4-54   Regressions of Project Performance on the Response Capacity Factors

Response capacity factors	Overall performance	Performance dimensions			
		Completion	Technical	Operational	Value
Adhesive cohesion (embedded)	-0.020	0.109	-0.301**	0.335**	-0.226
Coercive cohesion (governed)	-0.132	-0.097	0.051	-0.231*	-0.172
Configurational flexibility (implicit)	-0.135	-0.022	-0.274*	-0.005	-0.053
Sequential flexibility (agile)	0.507***	0.402**	0.354*	0.325*	0.396**
Sustaining resourcefulness (absorptive)	-0.093	-0.212	0.270*	-0.275**	-0.092
Creating resourcefulness (innovative)	-0.051	-0.079	-0.178	0.075	0.130
Adjusted R Square	**0.228*****	**0.161****	**0.149****	**0.253*****	**0.126****
Mechanistic meta-factor	-0.428***	-0.392***	-0.209*	-0.333***	-0.307**
Organic meta-factor	0.187	0.160	0.029	0.302**	0.038
Adjusted R Square	**0.188*****	**0.150*****	**0.012**	**0.164*****	**0.064***

Note: *** Significant at 0.01 and lower; ** Significant at 0.05 and lower; * Significant at 0.10 and lower

sustaining resourcefulness also seems to favor the shift of project organizations into a crisis mode. An emphasis on innovative creating resources seems to favor solutions that do not require significant additional resources, as well as, marginally, solutions that do not require major modifications. Overall, pragmatic adhesive cohesion, absorptive sustaining resourcefulness, and explorative creating resourcefulness appear to be associated with responses having a higher degree of difficulty.

Impact of Response Capacity Variables on Performance Dimensions

Of course, the main interest of the response capacity variables was in assessing their contribution to explaining the performance of complex projects. To make this evaluation we used regression analyses, in which overall project performance and different performance dimensions were the dependent variables, and response capacity variables were the predictor variables. We used the response capacity factors as dependent variables. Corroborating results based on these variables appeared particularly important to us, because any significant relation was less likely to be the result of an ex-post attribution bias, in which, for example, the respondent of a successful project would also attribute higher scores to some properties that may sound as socially desirable. While the response capacity intensity indices may sound socially desirable, the response capacity factors are less likely to do so. If the reader recalls, they are one dimension with two ends, and each end sounds equally desirable. Using the example of sequential flexibility, being proactive is as desirable as being agile, and items reflecting each end of this dimension appear socially desirable. Some factors were the second principal component extracted from the respective items, which may mean that socially desirable aspects were captured by the first factor. Results based on these factors are presented in Table 4-54. In the upper part, results concern the six factors, while the lower part presents the results of another set of regressions, which used as predictors the two response capacity meta-factors, mechanistic and organic.

Results presented in Table 4-54 provide a strong corroboration for the importance of response capacity variables in explaining the performance of complex projects. Response capacity variables explain more than 20 percent of the variance in the overall performance variable. They are particularly good at explaining the operational performance of projects, for which they explain more than a quarter of the variance. For the three other performance variables, response capacity factors explain between 12 percent and 16 percent of the variance, and all models are statistically significant. Individual response capacity variables also have significant relations with the performance outcomes.

Adhesive cohesion has the most interesting impact. The embedded end of this dimension seems to favor very strongly the operational performance, a result that was also forcefully suggested by the qualitative research. However, its pragmatic end appears to favor as strongly the technical performance, which is the reverse of what qualitative research suggested. Perhaps, the pragmatic end may even have a positive influence on the value performance ($p = 0.112$ for value, this influence was not observed in qualitative research). The sign of the impact of embedded adhesive cohesion on the completion performance is positive, as was suggested by qualitative research, but the beta coefficient is far from being significant. The contradictory influences from adhesive cohesion that can be observed in Table 4-54 cancel each other out, and the result is a non significant influence of adhesive cohesion on overall performance.

The governed coercive cohesion, with its innovative end, has a marginally significant negative impact on operational performance, but no impact on the overall performance. In other words, it seems that it is better for the operating cost and reliability of the project to rely on arm's length relations with contractors. This result was not observed in the quantitative research. The latter indicated, however, that the governed coercive cohesion has a negative impact on completion performance. The sign of the coefficient presented in Table 4-54 is negative as well, but far from acceptable significance levels.

Configurational flexibility, with its implicit end, has a marginally significant negative impact on technical performance. In other words, developing a heedful configurational flexibility capability tends to increase the technical performance of the project. However, the impact of configurational flexibility is not significant at the level of overall performance. It is interesting to note that in qualitative research configurational flexibility was "avoided" by all trajectories, so these quantitative results are the first evidence of an impact of this variable on performance.

Sequential flexibility, with its agile extreme, has a particularly strong influence on the overall performance, as the standardized beta coefficient is over 0.5. This can be explained by the fact that this factor has a consistently positive and significant (in two of the cases significance is $p < 0.05$) influence on all aspects of performance. In qualitative research, only the impact on value was detected, and it had the reverse sign.

Sustaining resourcefulness, with its absorptive end, has a marginally significant positive influence on technical performance, but a significant negative influence on operational performance. In other words, being able to obtain additional funds and other resources from the outside network allows participants to build more technically advanced and innovative projects, but, being able to save, accumulate, and redistribute resources internally seems to lead to projects with better reliability and lower operational cost. The fact that these effects cancel each other may explain the fact that sustaining resourcefulness does not appear to have a significant impact on the additive overall performance index. In qualitative research, the only influence of sustaining resourcefulness was on value performance, with a positive impact of absorptive end. This influence was not corroborated (coefficient nonsignificant).

Finally, creating resourcefulness has no significant impact on any dimension of project performance. The largest coefficient would signal a negative impact of the innovative end on technical performance, which was also suggested by the qualitative research (the other predictions of that stage are not corroborated).

It is interesting to look at these results, in light of the hypotheses advanced in the theoretical chapter with regard to what aspects of the response capacity would enable the best response to unexpected events, and hence of performance. The theoretical chapter has predicted that embedded adhesion would ensure the highest level of cohesion in the face of events and hence of performance. While qualitative research seemed to corroborate this fact, the evidence from the survey is mixed because embeddedness seems to favor certain aspects of performance but not others. We also predicted that governed coercion would ensure the highest cohesion. This seems to be contradicted by both qualitative and quantitative results of this research.

We also argued theoretically that heedful configurational flexibility will ensure a higher degree of freedom in responding to events. This seems to be corroborated by the survey research (no indication from qualitative research). For the sequential flexibility, we argued that the agile end would provide a higher degree of freedom. This prediction was partially disconfirmed by the qualitative research, but it received a very strong corroboration in quantitative research. We argued as well that the absorptive sustaining resourcefulness would have more chances to ensure that the often sizable additional resources needed to respond to unexpected events will be available. This was corroborated to some extent by the qualitative research, but the evidence obtained from quantitative research is somewhat mixed. Finally, we argued that innovative creating resourcefulness would have higher chances to provide the needed ideas and solutions. This was disconfirmed in part by the qualitative research, which had prompted us to change our prediction, but the quantitative research has provided no additional evidence in this respect.

Trajectory Identification

This section presents the results of our search for evidence on whether response capacity variables mediate between the planning factors and project performance. In other words, we would like to know whether certain planning variables have an impact on performance mainly via their influence on response capacity variables that, in their turn, affect performance. We began this search by considering the overall performance index as a dependent variable. In Table 4-46, we can see that three strategic factors have a significant relation with the overall performance variable. Thus, when controlling for total project cost (size), planning participation (centralized) and plan argument (decisional) variables have a positive relation with overall performance, while plan risk approach (integrative) has a negative relation with overall performance. By looking then at Table 4-50, we can see that some of these three planning variables also influence some response capacity factors, which we, again, favor over intensity measures because of their lower chances of being affected by respondent biases. Thus, centralized planning affects positively the governed coercive cohesion and agile sequential flexibility, as well as, negatively, the implicit configurational flexibility. Decisional plan argument also affects positively the governed coercive cohesion. Integrative plan risk approach does not affect any response capacity factor. Now, by looking at Table 4-54, we can assess whether the affected response capacity factors affect, in turn, overall project performance, and form this way a mediating trajectory. The choice is relatively simple, because the only response capacity variable that significantly influences performance is sequential flexibility (agile), which is influenced by centralized planning. These three elements, centralized planning, sequential flexibility (agile) and overall performance form the only potential mediation trajectory, which is illustrated in Figure 4-4. We should note that this trajectory had no equivalent in the qualitative research stage, because in that stage we did not assess overall project performance. In addition, with a much lower number of cases, it was not possible to apply the test of mediation that will be described in the following paragraph.

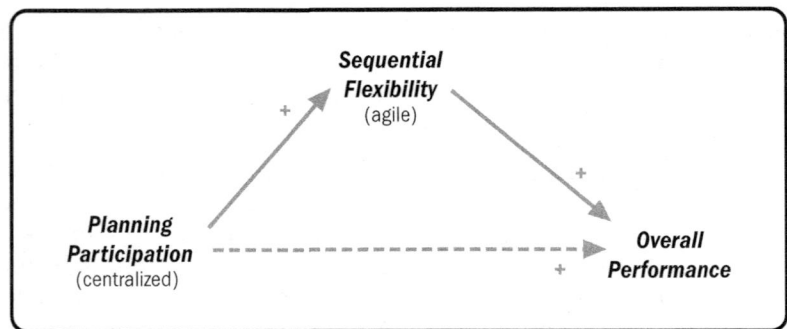

Figure 4-4   Sequential Flexibility Mediation Between
Centralized Planning and Overall Performance

If mediation exists, then, when introducing sequential flexibility in the model that shows a significant relation between planning participation and dependent variable overall performance, the coefficient for planning participation should become non significant. Indeed, this result was obtained, as can be seen from Table 4-55. In model 1, the planning participation factor is a significant predictor of overall project performance. Please note that in this table, the significance level p is noted in parentheses near the coefficient; all significant coefficients ($p < 0.10$) are also noted in bold characters. In model 2, we also add sequential flexibility as a predictor. The coefficient of planning participation becomes nonsignificant as a predictor. To check whether this is indeed a specific trajectory and not a more general effect of the sequential flexibility on all planning variables, including the others, with which it has no common mediation trajectory that ends in overall performance, we reproduced model 2 from Table 4-46, as model 3 in Table 4-55. In this model,

Table 4-55   Mediating Role of Sequential Flexibility Between Planning
Participation and Overall Performance

Independent variables	Dependent variable overall performance			
	Model 1	Model 2	Model 3	Model 4
Planning knowledge factor (conceptual)			-0.137 (0.355)	-0.188 (0.235)
Planning participation factor (centralized)	0.310 (0.018)	0.059 (0.661)	0.288 (0.033)	0.108 (0.452)
Plan argument factor (decisional)			0.237 (0.065)	0.239 (0.072)
Plan risk approach factor (integrative)			-0.319 (0.024)	-0,289 (0.049)
Total cost (project size)	0.176 (0.172)	0.037 (0.768)	0.258 (0.047)	0.177 (0.210)
Adhesive cohesion factor (embedded)				0.055 (0.706)
Coercive cohesion factor (governed)				-0.254 (0.118)
Configurational flexibility factor (implicit)				-0.177 (0.249)
Sequential flexibility factor (agile)		0.478 (0.001)		0.321 (0.098)
Sustaining resourceful's factor (absorptive)				-0.105 (0,472)
Creating resourcefulness factor (innovative)				0.025 (0.868)
Adjusted R Square	**0.080 (0.037)**	**0.226 (0.001)**	**0.176 (0.010)**	**0.255 (0.008)**

Table 4-56   Mediating Role of Sequential Flexibility Between Planning Participation and Completion Performance

Independent variables	Dependent variable completion performance			
	Model 1	Model 2	Model 3	Model 4
Planning knowledge factor (conceptual)			-0.040 (0.775)	-0.054 (0.735)
Planning participation factor (centralized)	0.383 (0.003)	0.216 (0.111)	0.373 (0.005)	0.242 (0.106)
Plan argument factor (decisional)			0.263 (0.035)	0.242 (0.076)
Plan risk approach factor (integrative)			-0.197 (0.144)	-0.135 (0.362)
Total cost (project size)	0.015 (0.906)	-0.088 (0.481)	0.067 (0.590)	0.007 (0.963)
Adhesive cohesion factor (embedded)				0.104 (0.486)
Coercive cohesion factor (governed)				-0.149 (0.374)
Configurational flexibility factor (implicit)				-0.033 (0.835)
Sequential flexibility factor (agile)		0.364 (0.010)		0.272 (0.175)
Sustaining resourceful's factor (absorptive)				-0.141 (0.348)
Creating resourcefulness factor (innovative)				-0.073 (0.628)
Adjusted R Square	**0.080 (0.037)**	**0.116 (0.012)**	**0.204 (0.004)**	**0.201 (0.024)**

three planning variable have significant coefficients. In model 4 from Table 4-55, we add all response capacity factors, none of which forms a mediation trajectory with any planning variable that would end in overall trajectory, except, of course, sequential flexibility. In model 4, all planning variables maintain their level of significance as predictors of overall performance, except planning participation. Because its relation with overall performance is mediated by sequential flexibility, the planning participation coefficient turns nonsignificant.

Encouraged by this result we sought other interesting trajectories that end in other performance measures. The trajectory that ends in completion performance is very similar with that of overall performance, in the sense that the other members of the mediation triangle are centralized planning and agile (as can be seen from Tables 4-47, 4-50, and 4-54). Results of mediation analysis are presented in Table 4-56. They also seem to indicate that mediation exists, perhaps not as spectacularly as in the case of overall performance. Unfortunately, we were unable to identify any other trajectory involving the other three performance variables as dependent variables.

Discriminant Analysis

We completed our investigation with an analysis that attempted to also consider the outcomes as multivariate. Considering the sample size, the best technique appeared to be discriminant analysis, which attempts to establish a number of functions that would explain the differences between groups based on a number of predictor variables. The classification of our cases into groups was the way to consider jointly all performance variables. We used a K-Means procedure to classify the cases into three groups based on the four performance variables. Table 4-57 presents the average performance scores of the three groups. Based on these scores, we called

Table 4-57   Group Centers Based on the Four Performance Variables

	Group centers		
	Superior performance	Disastrous performance	Completion and operation snags
Completion performance index	15.53	8.22	12.25
Technical performance index	16.26	10.33	17.63
Operational performance index	15.26	8.11	9.25
Value performance index	16.53	10.89	14.50

these groups, respectively, "superior performance," "disastrous performance," and "completion and operation snags."

Discriminant analysis uses the information about the case classification into groups and their scores on the predictor variables to determine functions that best explain this classification. With three groups, the maximum number of functions that can be established is two. In terms of predictors, we used the four strategy factors and the two response capacity meta-factors. This way, we had more than 10 cases per function, a requirement for obtaining reliable results from this procedure (Brown & Wicker, 2000). The standardized coefficients of the two functions are presented in Table 4-58. The magnitude of these coefficients represents the weight of the contribution of each of the six predictor variables to discriminating between groups. Function 1 contributes the most to distinguish between groups. The highest weight on this function is that of the planning risk (integrative) factor, followed by the response capacity mechanistic meta-factor and organic meta-factor, respectively. On the second function, which is not as good at discriminating the cases, the highest score is for the planning argument (decisional) factor, followed by the planning risk approach (integrative) factor, and by the planning participation (centralized) factor. One conclusion we can draw from this analysis of function coefficients is that, despite its less important than expected role in the results of regression analyses, the planning risk approach seems to play an important discriminating role between various project performance groups.

Table 4-58   Standardized Canonical Discriminant Function Coefficients

	Function	
	1	2
Planning knowledge (conceptual) factor	0.140	0.157
Planning participation (centralized) factor	-0.308	0.533
Plan argument (decisional) factor	0.217	-0.684
Plan risk approach (integrative) factor	0.696	0.521
Response capacity mechanistic meta factor	0.551	0.035
Response capacity organic meta factor	-0.532	0.201

Table 4-59   Structure Matrix Representing the Pooled Within-Groups Correlations Between Discriminating Variables and Standardized Canonical Discriminant Functions

	Function	
	1	2
Response capacity mechanistic meta-factor	0.576	-0.021
Plan risk approach (integrative) factor	0.573	0.569
Response capacity organic meta-factor	-0.366	0.210
Planning knowledge (conceptual) factor	-0.293	0.025
Plan argument (decisional) factor	-0.081	-0.586
Planning participation (centralized) factor	-0.478	0.483

Another important output of this analysis is the structure matrix (see Table 4-59), which presents the correlations between discriminating (predictor) variables and the two discriminant functions. These correlations should be interpreted in conjunction with the group centers for discriminant functions, which are presented in Table 4-60.

The scores for function 1 presented in Table 4-60 suggest that this function has low performance at high values. Therefore, the variables from Table 4-59 that are negatively correlated with it, such as organic meta-factor and conceptual knowledge factor, can be thought to improve performance, while those correlated positively, such as mechanistic meta-factor and the planning risk (integrative) factor are thought to reduce performance. The sense for function 2 is not as clear but, at least it can be seen that negative values tend to correlated with higher technical and value performance, so plan argument (decisional) can improve these aspects of performance, while plan participation (centralized) can perhaps reduce it.

5.   Discussion and Conclusions

The analyses presented in this chapter allowed us to validate the main tenets of our research project. We found that response capacity properties have a significant influence on various dimensions of project performance, both autonomously and as a mediator between planning variables and project performance. Particularly interesting in this respect is the finding of a distinction between the mechanistic meta-factor, which appears more amenable to deliberate influences, and the organic

Table 4-60   Unstandardized Canonical Discriminant Functions Evaluated at Group Means

Group	Function	
	1	2
Superior performance	-0.523	0.044
Disastrous performance	1.004	0.622
Completion and operation snags	0.651	-0.432

meta-factor, which appears to depend more on the autonomous processes that take place in the project organization. In addition, we found evidence that some planning variables also have a direct effect on performance. We also advanced our understanding of a new aspect; namely, how the context of the project at its initiation influences the planning approaches as well as project performance.

The methods we used suggest that we can put a lot of confidence in our results. First, the sample is more than four times larger and more diversified than the one used for qualitative research. It enabled us to perform comparative analyses that relied on sophisticated statistical techniques. Second, respondents evaluated their project independently of the researchers, and hence results are less likely to be influenced by researchers' biases or by the salience that a particular case may have acquired for them. Third, the way the measures of the most important constructs were built—namely by providing respondents with dimensions that had "socially desirable" alternatives on both ends and sometimes by extracting and using the second principal component from the resulting data—enabled us to avoid, to a certain extent, the biases that result from the fact that respondents evaluate these variables after they know project results.

Hence, quantitative results provide an important complement to the qualitative study reported in Chapter 3. Together these two stages of our research are beginning to provide a substantial amount of evidence in favor of our theoretical framework and hypotheses. However, further research, particularly one relying on econometric approaches, can increase even more our confidence in the patterns of relations that were described so far.

5

Theoretical and Practical Implications

By developing the concept of response capacity, we aimed to enhance our understanding of how the planning stage can be used to increase the chances that a complex project will achieve success in spite of unexpected occurrences. Our central hypothesis challenged the received view that planning consists of creating organizational structures, which, like an iron cage, channel the activities of project participants toward the attainment of project goals. We argued instead that planning sows the seeds of latent organizational capabilities, which, as the project advances, take participants in directions that deviate from planners' wishes. However, some of these capabilities also provide the remedies that enable a project to cope with the apparent loss of control. These particular capabilities form the response capacity that is defined as the system of emergent organizational properties that enable the project to react to unexpected events. The various dimensions of the response capacity, the characteristics of planning activities that are likely to influence these dimensions and the joint impact of planning and response capacity on project performance were the key issues addressed in our theoretical framework and subsequent empirical research.

The keystone of this framework is an effort to theorize the social structuring processes that transform projects into temporary organizations, which, in turn, constrain and influence participants in unintended and unsuspected ways. Our approach differed from other attempts at such theorizing in the literature by its emphasis on social interactions distributed throughout the project organization, as a source of emergent structuring processes and deviations from the initial plan. The theory stressed how structural elements emerge and are reproduced via evolving social networks, interaction routines and language couplings. We relied on this approach to improve our ability to account for dynamic processes in complex projects, compared to the views that consider project organizations as rational implements of functional schemes and as docile instruments in the hands of omniscient leaders.

The qualitative study was of particular help in deepening our understanding of these processes. Among the key insights that it provided is an understanding that the response capacity of projects relies on a balance between the elements that are dismantled and those that continue to exert their influence on actors after an unexpected event. In this respect, the reaction of a project to events is conditioned by the elements of the existing structure that are likely to resist the corrosive force of these events and will continue to influence actors, perhaps in a disarticulated way.

Qualitative research enabled us to identify elements that are more likely to continue to do so after a major event, and to disentangle the characteristics that favor an effective reaction in the face of events, those that enable just any reaction, from those that inescapably carry the project into disaster.

While our framework and empirical research highlighted the situated, unexpected, and emergent character of social action in projects, we have also cautiously rewoven these distributed processes into properties of project organizations seen as a whole. Therefore, our perspective enabled us to account for, and, we hope, eventually predict, patterns of systemic behavior in complex projects. Beginning in the comparative case study stage of the qualitative research, and continuing in full force in the quantitative stage of the research we were able to document and corroborate a pattern of relationships between variables that characterize the project as a system. The resulting pattern is expressed in a simplified form in Figure 5-1.

Among the contributions that these combined approaches enabled, the most important is suggesting that the planning, execution and subsequent performance of projects are closely interrelated, but in ways that are different, more intricate than usually assumed. This enabled us to shed new light on the nature of planning and of project organizations, both recurring issues in the project management research and practice.

We also developed and corroborated a comprehensive conceptualization of the response capacity. While building on prior research, this conceptualization brings together for the first time a wider range of organizational aspects present in projects and suggests a more nuanced understanding of their nature and variation, and of the way they complement each other or, on the contrary, demonstrate incompatibility and require tradeoffs. The response capacity concept creates a bridge to ideas emerging in the project management field, such as the practice-inspired research on agile methods and integrated project delivery.

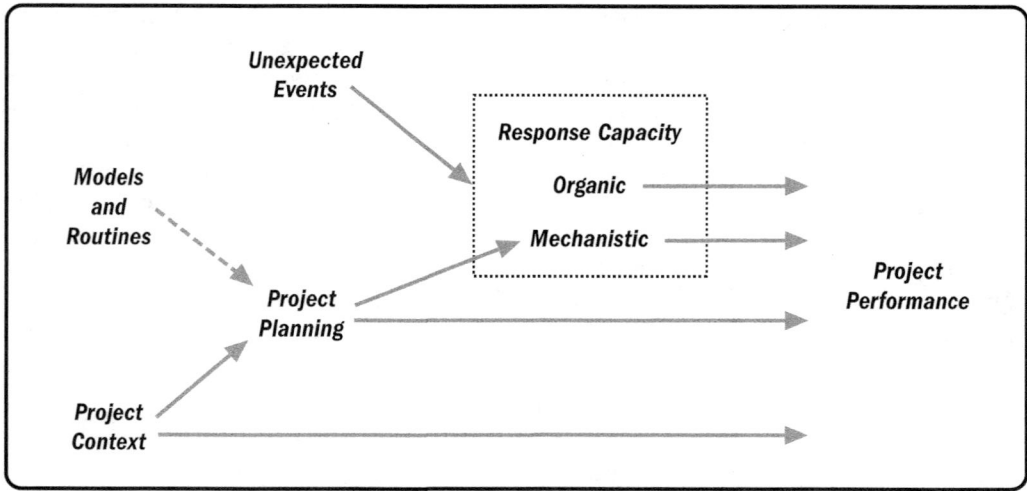

Figure 5-1   A Simplified Model of Influences Explaining the Performance of Complex Projects

The research reported here also enables a better conceptualization of planning activities by identifying the aspects that have the strongest potential impact on organizational structuring and the response capacity of complex projects. While prior research conflates different aspects of planning, by analyzing them jointly, through the lens of incompatible project archetypes, we propose dimensions that characterize planning in all projects, and attempt to disentangle the specific influence of each dimension on subsequent activities.

We also trace the entire longitudinal relation between project planning, organizational capabilities that emerge during execution, and realization and exploitation performance. We introduce the concept of influence trajectory to highlight the emergent pathways that occur because of choices made on each planning dimension. We also identify two kinds of aspects of the response capacity, which we call respectively mechanistic and organic. The latter is more amenable to influences from planning and is, therefore, more likely to intervene between planning and various project performance dimensions. The latter represents more autonomous processes that are closer to the depiction of emergence of organizational structures by researchers influenced by structuration theory. We argue that these aspects are both at work in the processes of any given project, and this is what allows us to argue that planning only plants the seeds rather than building the iron cage for the subsequent project organization.

By taking advantage of the unique opportunity afforded by the complex projects setting to disentangle the respective roles of deliberate and routine factors in organizational and strategic processes, these contributions can help to advance other management literature, such as that in business strategy. Like complex projects, business firms and other organizations, while being deliberately created and shaped, are also large, long term, and intricate enough to take on a pattern of their own and produce outcomes that are unintended, unexpected or even unsuspected by participants.

In terms of practical implications, the findings provided in this report would need additional corroboration before being translated into workable methods and recommendations. However, even now, we can argue that it revealed certain aspects to which managers and public authorities need to pay a closer attention. Some of the most prominent of these aspects appears to be the role of planning centralization. Results seem to indicate clearly that a more centralized planning leads to better outcomes, despite the benefits that the pluralistic planning can have by bringing a diversity of perspective to bear on planning decisions. Our qualitative and quantitative research seems to suggest that the benefits of centralization stem from the conditions it creates for the emergence of project organizations that are more agile, heedful, and resourceful. Another interesting conclusion that emerges from this research is the important role of the organic aspects of the response capacity. These do not seem to be as amenable to deliberate generation as the mechanistic aspects; however, they appear to have a role that is as important, if not more important, in explaining the success of projects. These organic elements emerge from collocation, communication, and joint work. Yet, the danger exists that, by trying too strongly to cultivate them, the result will be just another mechanistic approach, which can prove counterproductive for project performance. Finally, we also call attention to the role of the initiation context, which appears to influence the planning and the ultimate success of complex projects much more than we suspected. Aspects such as the transformational, innovative, and emergent nature of the context, along with the more commonly attended aspects, such as regulation, natural conditions and international stakeholders, should perhaps receive more attention in the project selection and planning process.

References

Amabile, T. M., Conti, R., Coon, H., Lazenby, J., & Herron, M. (1996). Assessing the work environment for creativity. *Academy of Management Journal, 39*(5), 1154–1184.

Ansoff, H. I. (1965). *Corporate strategy: An analytic approach to business policy for growth and expansion.* New York, NY: McGraw-Hill.

Aubry, M., Hobbs, B., & Thuillier, D. (2007). A new framework for understanding organisational project management through the PMO. *International Journal of Project Management, 25*(4), 328–336.

Baldwin, C. Y., & Clark, K. B. (2000). *Design rules: The power of modularity.* Cambridge, MA: MIT Press.

Barley, S. R. (1986). Technology as an occasion for structuring: Evidence from observations of CT scanners and the social order of radiology departments. *Administrative Science Quarterly, 31*(1), 78–108.

Barney, J. B. (1991). Firm resources and sustainable competitive advantage. *Journal of Management, 17*(1): 99–120.

Beck, U., Bonss, W., & Lau, C. (2003). The theory of reflexive modernization: Problematic, hypotheses and research programme. *Theory, Culture & Society, 20*(2): 1–33.

Berger, P., & Luckmann, T. (1966). *The social construction of reality.* Garden City, NY: Doubleday.

Besner, C., & Hobbs, B. (2008). Project management practice, generic or contextual: A reality check. *Project Management Journal, 39*(1): 16–33.

Bettis, R. A., & Hitt, M. A. (1995). The new competitive landscape. *Strategic Management Journal, 16,* 7–19.

Billings, R. S., Milburn, T., & Schaalman, M. L. (1980). A model of crisis perception: A theoretical and empirical analysis. *Administrative Science Quarterly, 25*(2), 300–316.

Birkett, N. J. (1986). Selecting the number of response categories for a Likert-type scale. *Proceedings of the American Statistical Association,* pp. 488–492.

Boehm, B. (1988). A spiral model of software development and enhancement. *IEEE Computer, 21*(5), 61–72.

Boehm, B. W., & Papaccio, P. N. (1988). Understanding and controlling software costs. *IEEE Transactions on Software Engineering, 14*(10), 1462–1477.

Boston Consulting Group. (1968). *Perspectives on experience.* Boston, MA: Boston Consulting Group.

Bourdieu, P. (1977). *Outline of a theory of practice.* Cambridge, UK: Cambridge University Press.

Brown, J. S., & Duguid, P. (1991). Organizational learning and communities-of-practice: Toward a unified view of working, learning, and innovation. *Organization Science, 2*(1), 40–57.

Brown, M. T., & Wicker, L. R. (2000). Discriminant analysis. In H. E. A. Tinsley & S. D. Brown (Eds.), *Handbook of applied multivariate statistics and mathematical modeling* (pp. 209–235). San Diego, CA: Academic Press.

Brown, S. L., & Eisenhardt, K. M. (1997). The art of continuous change: Linking complexity theory and time-paced evolution in relentlessly shifting organizations. *Administrative Science Quarterly, 42*(1), 1–34.

Burns, T., & Stalker, G. M. (1961). *The management of innovation.* London, UK: Tavistock.

Burt, R. S. (1992). *Structural holes: The social structure of competition.* Cambridge, MA: Harvard University Press.

Callon, M. (1986). Some elements of a sociology of translation: Domestication of the scallops and the fishermen of St Brieuc Bay. In J. Law (Ed.), *Power, action and belief: A new sociology of knowledge?* (pp. 196–223). London, UK: Routledge.

Callon, M. (1991). Techno-economic networks and irreversibility. In J. Law (Ed.), *A sociology of monsters: Essays on power, technology and domination* (pp. 133–161). London, UK: Routledge.

Campbell, J. L. (2007). Why would corporations behave in socially responsible ways? An institutional theory of corporate social responsibility. *Academy of Management Review, 32*(3), 946–967.

Carlile, P. R. (2002). A pragmatic view of knowledge and boundaries: Boundary objects in new product development. *Organization Science, 13*(4), 442–455.

Chapman, C. B., & Ward, S. C. (1994). The efficient allocation of risk in contracts. *Omega, International Journal of Management Science, 22*(6), 537–552.

Chapman, C. B., & Ward, S. C. (1996). *Project risk management: Processes, techniques and insights.* Chichester, UK: Wiley.

Christensen, C. (1997). *The innovator's dilemma.* New York, NY: Harper Business.

Clegg, S. R. (1990). *Modern organizations: Organization studies in the postmodern world.* Newbury Park, CA: Sage.

Cleland, D. I. (1986). Project stakeholder management. *Project Management Journal, 17*(4), 36–45.

Cockburn, I. M., & Henderson, R. M. (2000). Untangling the origins of competitive advantage. *Strategic Management Journal, 21*(10/11), 1123–1148.

Cohen, W. M., & Levinthal, D. (1990). Absorptive capacity: A new perspective of learning and innovation. *Administrative Science Quarterly, 35*(1), 128–152.

Corbin, J., & Strauss, A. (1990). Grounded theory research: Procedures, canons, and evaluative criteria. *Qualitative Sociology, 13*(1), 3–21.

Davies, A., Dodgson, M., & Gann, D. (2009). From iconic design to lost luggage: Innovation at Heathrow Terminal 5. *DRUID Summer Conference,* Copenhagen, Denmark.

Davies, A., Gann, D., & Douglas, T. (2009). Innovation in megaprojects: Systems integration at London Heathrow Terminal 5. *California Management Review, 51*(2), 101–125.

Davis, G. F., & Marquis, C. (2005). Prospects for organization theory in the early twenty-first century: Institutional fields and mechanisms. *Organization Science, 16*(4), 332–343.

Denis, J.-L., Lamothe, L., & Langley, A. (2001). The dynamics of collective leadership and strategic change in pluralistic organizations. *Academy of Management Journal, 44*(4), 809–837.

Dillman, D. A., Smyth, J. D., & Christian, L. M. (2009). *Internet, mail and mixed-mode surveys: The tailored design method* (3rd ed.). Hoboken, NJ: John Wiley & Sons.

Donaldson, T., & Preston, L. E. (1995). The stakeholder theory of the corporation: Concepts, evidence, and implications. *Academy of Management Review, 20*(1), 65–91.

Dougherty, D. (1992). Interpretive barriers to successful product innovation in large firms. *Organization Science, 3*(2), 179–202.

Dougherty, D. (2001). Reimagining the differentiation and integration of work for sustained product innovation. *Organization Science, 12*(5), 612–631.

Einhorn, H. J., & Hogarth, R. M. (1981). Behavioral decision theory: Processes of judgment and choice. *Annual Review of Psychology, 32*, 53–88.

Eisenhardt, K. M. (1989a). Building theories from case study research. *Academy of Management Review, 14*(4), 532–550.

Eisenhardt, K. M. (1989b). Making fast strategic decisions in high-velocity environments. *Academy of Management Journal, 32*(3), 543–576.

Eisenhardt, K. M. (2000). Paradox, spirals, ambivalence: The new language of change and pluralism. *Academy of Management Review, 25*(4): 703–705.

Eisenhardt, K. M., & Martin, J. (2000). Dynamic capabilities: What are they? *Strategic Management Journal, 21*, 1105–1121.

Emery, F. E., & Trist, E. L. (1965). The causal texture of organizational environments. *Human Relations, 18*, 21–32.

Emirbayer, M., & Mische, A. (1998). What is agency? *American Journal of Sociology, 103*(4), 962–1023.

Engwall, M. (2003). No project is an island: Linking projects to history and context. *Research Policy, 32*(5), 789–808.

Eppinger, S. D., Whitney, D. E., Smith, R. P., & Gebala, D. A. (1994). A model-based method for organizing tasks in product development. *Research in Engineering Design, 6*(1), 1–13.

Ewenstein, B., & Whyte, J. (2009). Knowledge practices in design: The role of visual representations as 'Epistemic Objects.' *Organization Studies, 30*(1), 7–30.

Fleck, L. (1979). *Genesis and development of a scientific fact.* Chicago, IL: University of Chicago Press.

Fleming, L., & Sorenson, O. (2004). Science as a map in technological search. *Strategic Management Journal, 25*(8–9), 909–925.

Floricel, S., & Dougherty, D. (2007). Where do games of innovation come from? Explaining the persistence of dynamic innovation patterns. *International Journal of Innovation Management, 11*(1), 65–92.

Floricel, S., & Miller, R. (2001). Strategizing for anticipated risks and turbulence in large-scale engineering projects. *International Journal of Project Management, 19*(8), 445–455.

Flyvbjerg, B., Holm, M. K. S., & Buhl, S. L. (2002). Underestimating costs in public works projects: Error or lie? *Journal of the American Planning Association, 68*(3), 279–296.

Flyvbjerg, B., Holm, M. K. S., & Buhl, S. L. (2006). Inaccuracy in traffic forecasts. *Transport Reviews, 26*(1), 1–24.

Galunic, D. C., & Eisenhardt, K. 2001. Architectural innovation and modular corporate forms. *Academy of Management Journal, 44*(6), 1229–1249.

Garfinkel, H. (1967). *Studies in ethnomethodology.* Englewood Cliffs, NJ: Prentice-Hall.

Gavetti, G., & Levinthal, D. (2000). Looking forward and looking backward: Cognitive and experiential search. *Administrative Science Quarterly, 45*(1), 113–137.

Giddens, A. (1984). *The constitution of society. Outline of the theory of structuration.* Berkeley and Los Angeles, CA: University of California Press.

Glaser, B., & Strauss, A. (1967). *The discovery of grounded theory.* Chicago, IL: Aldine.

Goffman, E. (1958). *The presentation of self in everyday life.* New York, NY: Doubleday.

Granovetter, M. (1985). Economic action and social structure: The problem of embeddedness. *American Journal of Sociology, 91,* 481–510.

Gulati, R. (1995). Social structure and alliance formation patterns: A longitudinal analysis. *Administrative Science Quarterly, 40,* 619–652.

Hällgren, M. (2007). *Avvikelsens Mekanismer* [Doctoral dissertation, Umeå University, Umeå, Sweden].

Hällgren, M., & Wilson, T. L. (2008). The nature and management of crises in construction projects: Projects-as-practice observations. *International Journal of Project Management, 26*(8), 830–838.

Hansen, M. T. (1999). The search-transfer problem: The role of weak ties in sharing knowledge across organization subunits. *Administrative Science Quarterly, 44,* 82–111.

Hargadon, A., & Sutton, R. (1997). Technology brokering and innovation in a product development firm. *Administrative Science Quarterly, 42,* 716–749.

Hart, O. E. (1988). Incomplete contracts and the theory of the firm. *Journal of Law, Economics, and Organization, 4*(1), 119–139.

Hayek, F. A. (1945). The use of knowledge in society. *American Economic Review, 35*(4), 519–530.

Hedström, P., & Swedberg, R. (1996). Social mechanisms. *Acta Sociologica, 39*(3), 281–308.

Henderson, R. M., & Clark, K. B. (1990). Architectural innovation: The reconfiguration of existing product technologies and the failure of established firms. *Administrative Science Quarterly, 35,* 9–30.

Hendry, J., & Seidl, D. (2003). The structure and significance of strategic episodes: Social systems theory and the routine practices of strategic change. *Journal of Management Studies, 40*(1), 175–196.

Hirsh, R. F. (1989). *Technology and transformation in the American electric utility industry.* Cambridge, UK: Cambridge University Press.

Hirschmann, A. O. (1970). *Exit, voice, and loyalty: Responses to decline in firms, organizations, and states.* Cambridge, MA: Harvard University Press.

Hobbs, B., & Andersen, B. (2001). Different alliance relationships for project design and execution. *International Journal of Project Management, 19*(8), 465–469.

Hodgson, D. E. (2004). Project work: The legacy of bureaucratic control in the post-bureaucratic organization. *Organization, 11*(1), 81–101.

Holmstrom, B. (1979). Moral hazard and observability. *Bell Journal of Economics, 10*(1), 74–91.

Hughes, T. (1983). *Networks of power.* Baltimore, MD: John Hopkins University Press.

Hume, D. (1748). *An enquiry concerning human understanding.* London, UK: T. Cadell.

Hwang, P., & Lichtenthal, J. D. (2000). Anatomy of organizational crises. *Journal of Contingencies and Crisis Management, 8*(3), 129–140.

Jarzabkowski, P., & Seidl, D. (2008). The role of meetings in the social practice of strategy. *Organization Studies, 29*(11), 1391–1426.

Jelinek, M., & Schoonhoven, C. B. (1990). *The innovation marathon: Lessons from high technology firms.* Cambridge, MA: Basil Blackwell.

Keeney, R. L. (1994). Creativity in decision making with value-focused thinking. *Sloan Management Review, 35*(4), 33–42.

Kerzner, H. (2009). *Project management: A systems approach to planning, scheduling, and controlling.* Hoboken, NJ: Wiley.

Kontopoulos, K. M. (1993). *The logics of social structure.* Cambridge, UK: Cambridge University Press.

Knorr-Cetina, K. (1997). Sociality with objects: Social relations in postsocial knowledge societies. *Theory Culture Society, 14*(1), 1–30.

Krieg. E. F., Jr. (1999). Biases induced by coarse measurement scales. *Educational and Psychological Measurement, 59*(5), 749–766.

Krishnan, V., Eppinger, S. D., & Whitney, D. E. (1997). A model based framework to overlap product development activities. *Management Science, 43*(4), 437–451.

Lampel, J. (2001). The core competencies of effective project execution: The challenge of diversity. *International Journal of Project Management, 19*(8), 471–483.

Langley, A. (1989). In search of rationality: The purposes behind the use of formal analysis in organizations. *Administrative Science Quarterly, 34*, 598–631.

Langley, A. (1999). Strategies for theorizing from process data. *Academy of Management Review, 24*(4), 691–710.

Latour, B. (1987). *Science in action.* Cambridge, MA: Harvard University Press.

Latour, B. (1991). *Nous n'avons jamais été modernes: Essai d'anthropologie symétrique.* Paris, France: La découverte.

Law, J. (2004). *After method: Mess in social science research.* London, UK: Routledge.

Lawrence, T. B., & Phillips, N. (2004). From Moby Dick to Free Willy: Macro-cultural discourse and institutional entrepreneurship in emerging institutional fields. *Organization, 11*(5), 689–711.

Lopes, L. (1987). Between hope and fear: The psychology of risk. *Advances in Experimental Social Psychology, 20*, 255–295.

Luhmann, N. (1993). *Risk: A sociological theory.* New York, NY: Aldine De Gruyter.

Luhmann, N. (1995). *Social systems.* Stanford, CA: Stanford University Press.

Lundin, R. A., & Söderholm, A. (1995). A theory of the temporary organization. *Scandinavian Journal of Management, 11*(4), 437–455.

MacCormack, A., Verganti, R., & Iansiti, M. (2001). Developing products on "Internet Time": The anatomy of a flexible development process. *Management Science, 47*(1), 133–150.

Macneil, I. R. (1978). Contracts: Adjustment of long-term economic relations under classical, neoclassical, and relational contract law. *Northwestern Law Review, 72*(6), 854–905.

March, J. G., & Shapira, Z. (1992). Variable risk preferences and the focus of attention. *Psychological Review, 99*(1), 172–183.

McGrath, R. G. (1997). A real options logic for initiating technology positioning investments. *Academy of Management Review, 22*(4), 974–996.

Merrow, E. W. (1988). *Understanding the outcomes of megaprojects.* Santa Monica, CA: Rand Corporation.

Meyer, A. D. (1982). Adapting to environmental jolts. *Administrative Science Quarterly, 27,* 515–537.

Meyer, J. W., & Rowan, B. (1977). Institutionalized organizations: Formal structure as myth and ceremony. *American Journal of Sociology, 83*(2), 340–363.

Meyers, L. S., Gamst, G., & Guarino, A. J. (2005). *Applied multivariate research: Design and interpretation.* Thousand Oaks, CA: Sage.

Miles, M. B., & Huberman, A. M. (1994). *Qualitative data analysis* (2nd ed.). Thousand Oaks, CA: Sage.

Miller, J. B. (2000). *Principles of public and private infrastructure delivery.* Boston, MA: Kluwer.

Miller, R. E., & Lessard, D. (2001). *The strategic management of large engineering projects.* Cambridge, MA: MIT Press.

Miller, R., & Floricel, S. (2001). Transformations in arrangements for shaping and delivering engineering projects. In R. E. Miller & D. Lessard (Eds.), *The strategic management of large engineering projects* (pp. 51–74). Cambridge, MA: MIT Press.

Miliken, F. J., & Martins, L. (1996). Searching for common threads: Understanding the multiple effects of diversity in organizational groups. *Academy of Management Review, 21*(2), 402–433.

Mintzberg, H. (1994). *The rise and fall of strategic planning.* New York, NY: Free Press.

Meyers, L. S., Gamst, G., & Guarino, A. J. (2005). *Applied multivariate research: Design and interpretation.* Thousand Oaks, CA: Sage.

Naoum, S. (2003). An overview into the concept of partnering. *International Journal of Project Management, 21*(1), 71–76.

Nelson, R. R., & Winter, S. G. (1982). *An evolutionary theory of economic change.* Cambridge, MA: Belknap.

Nightingale, P. (1998). A cognitive model of innovation. *Research Policy, 27*(7), 689–709.

Nunnally, J. C. (1976). *Psychometric theory.* New York, NY: McGraw-Hill.

Oliver, C. (1991). Strategic responses to institutional processes. *Academy of Management Review, 16*(1), 145–179.

Orton, J. D., & Weick, K. (1990). Loosely coupled systems: A reconceptualization. *Academy of Management Review, 15*(2), 203–223.

Orlikowski, W. (1992). The duality of technology: Rethinking the concept of technology in organizations. *Organization Science, 3*(3), 398–427.

O'Sullivan, A. (2003). Dispersed collaboration in a multi-firm, multi-team product-development project. *Journal of Engineering and Technology Management, 20*(1–2), 93–116.

Packendorff, J. (1995). Inquiring into the temporary organization: New directions for project management research. *Scandinavian Journal of Management, 11*(4), 319–333.

Papadimitriou, K., & Pellegrin, C. (2007). Dynamics of a project through Intermediary Objects of Design (IODs): A sensemaking perspective. *International Journal of Project Management, 25*(5), 437–445.

Patton, M. Q. (1990). *Qualitative evaluation and research methods* (2nd ed.). Thousand Oaks, CA: Sage.

Pfeffer, J., & Salancik, G. (1978). *The external control of organizations.* New York, NY: Harper and Row.

Pinch, T. J., & Bijker, W. E. (1984). The social construction of facts and artefacts: Or how the sociology of science and the sociology of technology may benefit each other. *Social Studies of Science, 14*(3), 399–441.

Polanyi, M. (1966). *The tacit dimension.* Garden City, NY: Doubleday.

Poppo, L., & Zenger, T. (2002). Do formal contracts and relational governance function as substitutes or complements? *Strategic Management Journal, 23*(8), 707–725.

Prahalad, C. K., & Hamel, G. (1990). The core competence of the corporation. *Harvard Business Review, 68*(3), 79–90.

Reagans, R., & Zuckerman E. W. (2001). Networks, diversity, and productivity: The social capital of corporate R&D teams. *Organization Science, 12*(4), 502–517.

Reid, S. E., & de Brentani, U. (2004). The fuzzy front end of new product development for discontinuous innovations: A theoretical model. *Journal of Product Innovation Management, 21*(3), 170–184.

Rindova, V. P., & Kotha, S. (2001). Continuous 'morphing': Competing through dynamic capabilities, form and function. *Academy of Management Journal, 44*(6), 1263–1280.

Sanchez, R., & Mahoney, J. (1996). Modularity, flexibility, and knowledge management in product and organization design [Winter special issue]. *Strategic Management Journal, 17*, 63–76.

Sapolsky, H. M. (1972). *The polaris system development.* Cambridge, MA: Harvard University Press.

Sapsed, J., & Salter, A. (2004). Postcards from the edge: Local communities, global programs and boundary objects. *Organization Studies, 25*(9), 1515–1534.

Schilling, M. A. (2000). Towards a general modular systems theory and its application to interfirm product modularity. *Academy of Management Review, 25*(2), 312–334.

Schwab, D. P. (1980). Construct validity in organizational behavior. *Research in Organizational Behavior, 2*, 3–43.

Sergi, V. 2009 *La fabrication d'un projet technologique: Étude des pratiques collectives et de la capaciteé d'action des documents* [Doctoral dissertation: HEC Montreal, Montreal, Quebec].

Shenhar, A. J. (2001). One size does not fit all projects: Exploring classical contingency domains. *Management Science, 47*(3), 395–414.

Simon, H. A. (1978). Rationality as process and product of thought. *Journal of American Economic Association, 68*(2), 1–16.

Simon, H. A. (1981). *The sciences of the artificial* (3rd ed.). Cambridge, MA: MIT Press.

Simondon, G. (1989). *Du mode d'existence des objets techniques.* Paris : Aubier-Montaigne.

Simonin, B. L. (1999). Ambiguity and the process of knowledge transfer in strategic alliances. *Strategic Management Journal, 20*(7), 595–623.

Söderholm, A. (2008). Project management of unexpected events. *International Journal of Project Management, 26*(1), 80–86.

Stinchcombe, A. L. (1990). *Information and organizations.* Berkeley, CA: University of California Press.

Stinchcombe, A. L., & Heimer, C. (Eds.). (1985). *Organization theory and project management.* Bergen, Norway: Scandinavian University Press.

Star, S. L., & Griesemer, J. R. (1989). Institutional ecology, 'translations' and boundary objects: Amateurs and professionals in Berkeley's Museum of Vertebrate Zoology, 1907–39. *Social Studies of Science, 19*(3), 387–420.

Teece, D. J., Pisano, G., & Shuen, A. (1997). Dynamic capabilities and strategic management. *Strategic Management Journal, 18*, 509–533.

Thomas, L. G. (1996). The two faces of competition: Dynamic resourcefulness and the hypercompetitve shift. *Organization Science, 7*(3), 221–242.

Thomke, S., & Reinertsen, D. (1998). Agile product development: Managing development flexibility in uncertain environments. *California Management Review, 41*(1), 8–30.

Thompson, J. D. (1967). *Organizations in action.* New York, NY: McGraw-Hill.

Tucker, T. (2010). *Supply chain orientation: Refining a nascent construct* [Unpublished doctoral thesis]. Department of Management Sciences, University of Waterloo, Ontario, Canada.

Turner, J. R., & Müller, R. (2005). The project manager's leadership style as a success factor on projects: A literature review. *Project Management Journal, 36*(1), 49–61.

Uzzi, B. (1997). Social structure and competition in interfirm networks: The paradox of embeddedness. *Administrative Science Quarterly, 42*, 35–67.

Ulrich, K. (1995). The role of product architecture in the manufacturing firm. *Research Policy, 24*(3), 419–440.

Van de Ven, A. H., & Poole, M. S. (1995). Explaining development and change in organizations. *Academy of Management Review, 20*(3), 510–540.

Verganti, R. (1999). Planned flexibility: Linking anticipation and reaction in product development projects. *Journal of Product Innovation Management, 16*(4), 363–376.

Volberda, H. W. (1996). Toward the flexible form: How to remain vital in hypercompetitive environments. *Organization Science, 7*(4), 359–374.

Von Branconi, C., & Loch, C. (2004). Contracting for major projects: Eight business levers for top management. *International Journal of Project Management, 22*(2), 119–130.

Weber, M. (1968). *Economy and society.* New York, NY: Bedminister.

Weick, K. E. (1979). *The social psychology of organizing* (2nd ed.). Reading, MA: Addison-Wesley.

Weick, K. E., & Roberts, K. H. (1993). Collective mind: Heedful interrelations on flight decks. *Adminstrative Science Quarterly, 38*, 357–381.

Wernerfelt, B. (1984). A resource based view of the firm. *Strategic Management Journal, 5*(2), 171–180.

Whittington, R. (1996). Strategy as practice. *Long Range Planning, 29*(5), 731–735.

Williams, T., & Samset, K. (2010). Issues in front-end decision making on projects. *Project Management Journal, 41*(2), 38–49.

Williamson, O. E. (1981). The economics of organization: The transaction cost approach. *American Journal of Sociology, 87*(3), 548–577.

Winch, G. (2004). Rethinking project management: Project organisations as information processing systems. *PMI Research Proceedings Post-Conference Book.* Newtown Square, PA: Project Management Institute.

Winner, L. (1977). *Autonomous technology: Technics-out-of-control as a theme in political thought.* Cambridge, MA: MIT Press.

Winter, M., Smith, C., Morris, P., & Cicmil, S. (2006). Directions for future research in project management: The main findings of a UK government-funded research network. *International Journal of Project Management, 24*(8), 638–649.

Woodman, R. W., Sawyer, J. E., & Griffin, R. W. (1993). Toward a theory of organizational creativity. *Academy of Management Review, 18*(2), 293–321.

Zahra, S. A., & George, G. (2002). Absorptive capacity: A review, reconceptualization, and extension. *Academy of Management Review. 27*(2), 185–203.

Zollo, M., & Winter, S. G. (2002). Deliberate learning and the evolution of dynamic capabilities. *Organization Science, 13*(3), 339–351.

Appendix A: Questionnaire for Semi-Structured Interviews

A. Planning

1. Please briefly describe **the context and the intended output** (artifact, process, system, technology) of this project. Where did the project idea originate and how was it defined?
2. How the project was **initially structured** in terms of scope, team members, participants, schedule, budget, supervision, contracts etc.? How was this structure developed?
3. What were the **major uncertainties** that you deemed capable of affecting the success of the project? How did you plan to resolve these uncertainties?

B. Execution

4. Please describe the **activities realized** during the project in terms of major phases, participants, milestones, etc. How did the project scope evolve during these activities?
5. How did the project **organization grow and evolve** during these activities? Please discuss the difference between initial plans and the actual organization during the peak of activity.
6. Please describe the **patterns of collaboration** between project participants. How did they help each other? What were the contents, channels, and pace of their communications?
7. Please describe the typical **misunderstandings and conflicts** that occurred during these activities. What were their sources?

C. Flexibility

8. What were the major **unexpected events** (negative or positive) that affected this project? How did you learn about them?
9. What was the **initial reaction** of the project team to these events? How did these events impact the relations between various project participants?
10. What was the **eventual response** of the project to these events? How was this response developed? What encouraged or obstructed the creativity of the project team?
11. How did you obtain the **additional resources** needed to react to these events? What helped or hampered your efforts to obtain these resources?

12. What **changes** did you have to make to the organizational and contractual **structure** of the project in order to respond to these events? What precluded your intended changes?
13. What was the **ultimate impact** of these events on the project?

D. Outcomes

14. What did you **learn from this project** about preventing negative events and exploiting positive events? How did this learning influence your project management approach?
15. How would you characterize the **project performance** in terms of:
    a. budget and schedule?
    b. technical success?
    c. sales and financial return?
    d. strategic advances for your organization?

Appendix B:
The Pattern Identification Table
Completed for Each Case

	CASE NAME	
Project context		
	Industry Size ($, no of people, duration) Technical complexity – natural environment – brownfield – innovativeness Institutional complexity – regulation – politics – contractual and organizational novelty	
Planning		
Process – knowledge	Most likely (e.g., conceptual) Evidence for conceptual – – Evidence for experimental – –	
Process – participation	Clearly (e.g., pluralist) Evidence for pluralist – – Evidence for centralized – –	
Plan – argument	Most likely (e.g., decisional) Evidence for promotional – – Evidence for decisional – –	

	CASE NAME *(continued)*
Plan – risk approach	Clearly (e.g., allocative) Evidence for allocative – – Evidence for integrative – –
Structuring	
Structuring episodes	Intense/weak deviation – Conflicts – Leadership changes – Restructuring – New agreements
Emergent structure	
Cohesion – adhesive	Most likely (e.g., embedded) Evidence for embedded – – Evidence for pragmatic – –
Cohesion – coercive	Clearly (e.g., governed) Evidence for governed – Evidence for formal – –
Flexibility – configurational	Most likely (e.g., heedful) Evidence for heedful – – Evidence for implicit – –
Flexibility – sequential	Clearly (e.g., agile) Evidence for agile – Evidence for proactive – –
Resourcefulness – sustaining	Most likely (e.g., absorptive) Evidence for absorptive – – Evidence for cumulative – –

	CASE NAME (continued)
Resourcefulness – creating	Clearly (e.g., searching) Evidence for explorative – – Evidence for innovative – –
Main unexpected events	Severe/mild – worse than expected – internal unexpected (errors) – external unexpected
Response to events	Effective/ineffective – dictatorship – escalation to crisis mode – project redefinition – abandonment – –
Performance	
Technical	Rating (high, low) Evidence – percentage functions achieved – technical performance vs. specifications
Completion	Rating (high, low) Evidence – cost overrun – schedule overrun
Operational	Rating (high, low) Evidence – malfunctions – accidents
Value	Rating (high, low) Evidence – strategic advances – sales/profitability
Other observations	

Appendix C:
Final Quantitative Questionnaire

SURVEY ON THE RESPONSE CAPACITY OF COMPLEX PROJECTS

Prescriptions for the planning of complex projects focus on the identification of uncertainties and of measures that could mitigate the ensuing risks. However, many events and circumstances that affect a project over its lifecycle cannot be anticipated early on. This research aims to enhance our understanding of how the planning stage of a project can be used to increase the chances that a project will achieve its goals in spite of unexpected occurrences. Our main idea is that planning does not create an organizational structure that, like an iron cage, will invariably guide project participants toward attaining the planners' goals. Instead, planning plants the seeds of intricate organizational capabilities that eventually acquire a degree of autonomy with respect to the planners' wishes. Chief among these capabilities is the response capacity, a series of properties that enable projects to react to unexpected events. The nature of these capabilities and the way planning influences them are the main issues that we are trying to address with this study.

This research program has received financial support from the Social Sciences and Humanities Research Council of Canada (project title: Increasing the Response Capacity of Complex Projects: Preparing for the Unknown in the Planning Stage) and from Project Management Institute (project title: Increasing Project Flexibility: Preparing for the Unknown in the Concept Stage). It is also part of the activities of the Research Chair in Project Management at the Université du Québec à Montreal (UQÀM).

In order to help us answer our research questions, we kindly ask you to select a complex project recently completed by your organization and to answer the following questions in relation to this project. A complex project has a high degree of uniqueness or novelty, or has to address a large number of qualitatively distinct, but interrelated, aspects. Large projects (say with a budget over $100 million) are usually, although not necessarily, complex. If at least some of the answers you select in the first section of the questionnaire have high scores you can be sure the project you have chosen is complex. This study concerns projects of many kinds, so some survey items may not be applicable to the project for which you complete the survey. When this occurs, please answer "**strongly disagree**."

The answers you will provide will remain confidential and the results of the survey will only be published in an aggregate form, which will not allow the identification of specific firms or projects. For further inquiries, or to obtain the survey as a MS-Word document, please contact Professor Serghei Floricel, Principal Investigator, at floricel.serghei@uqam.ca or 1-514-987-3000 x 2356.

I. THE PROJECT AND ITS CONTEXT

1. Key project demographics

Project name or brief description _____

What is the main sector of activity for which the output of your project is intended (e.g., mining, transportation pharmaceutical, telecom)? _____

Start year (budget approval): _____ *Duration in months:* _____

How many individuals were members of the core team responsible for planning and managing the project?
- ☐ 1–5
- ☐ 5–20
- ☐ 20–50
- ☐ 50–100
- ☐ 100–500
- ☐ 500–1000
- ☐ 1000 and more

What was the total number of persons involved in the project at the peak of its activities?
- ☐ 1–50
- ☐ 50–200
- ☐ 200–1000
- ☐ 1000–5000
- ☐ 5000–10,000
- ☐ 10,000–50,000
- ☐ 50,000 and more

What was the total project cost (in million US dollars)?
- ☐ less than 20
- ☐ 20–200
- ☐ 200–500
- ☐ 500–1000
- ☐ 1000–5000
- ☐ 5000–10,000
- ☐ 10,000 and over

Percent of budget spent outside owner organization (contracts, etc.)? _____
... outside owner's country? _____

2. How well do the next statements describe the context in which the project was initiated?

a) Technical complexity	Strongly disagree		Neutral			Strongly agree	
We faced major issues related to natural conditions (soil, water, weather, etc.)	1	2	3	4	5	6	7
The project interfered with a sensitive natural area (wildlife, ecosystem, scenery)	1	2	3	4	5	6	7
The project had to fit with preexisting technical systems or tight built surroundings	1	2	3	4	5	6	7
The project had to minimize the disruption to ongoing operations and businesses	1	2	3	4	5	6	7
Bold project goals forced us to use technical solutions that no one had tried before	1	2	3	4	5	6	7
Our challenge was maintaining full control over the behavior of the artifacts we made	1	2	3	4	5	6	7
We strived to gain influence over natural processes affected by many invisible factors	1	2	3	4	5	6	7
Our problem was ensuring coherent interoperation between scores of artifact functions	1	2	3	4	5	6	7

b) **Organizational complexity**

	Strongly disagree		Neutral			Strongly agree	
The project was much larger than all other projects the owner had ever managed	1	2	3	4	5	6	7
Project timing was conditioned by urgent needs or limited windows of opportunity	1	2	3	4	5	6	7
During this project, the owner organization embarked on a major restructuring	1	2	3	4	5	6	7
The project was the first to implement new project management processes and norms	1	2	3	4	5	6	7
The project was seen as an occasion for trying new financial or contractual methods	1	2	3	4	5	6	7
Conditions forced us to rely on contractors or personnel from many different countries	1	2	3	4	5	6	7

c) **Institutional and market complexity**

	Strongly disagree		Neutral			Strongly agree	
Regulatory approval was a critical precondition for initiating or exploiting the project	1	2	3	4	5	6	7
Key applicable laws and regulations were ambiguous or untested in practice	1	2	3	4	5	6	7
The project was likely to become a battleground for political interests and militants	1	2	3	4	5	6	7
The project was funded with public money or relied on government guarantees	1	2	3	4	5	6	7
Project implementation depended on decisions made by foreign government entities	1	2	3	4	5	6	7
The project output targeted a market whose emergence and growth were still uncertain	1	2	3	4	5	6	7
The market we intended to serve was known for its severe swings in price and demand	1	2	3	4	5	6	7

II. PROJECT PLANNING

How well do the following statements describe the planning of your project?

a) **Use and production of knowledge for planning purposes**

	Strongly disagree		Neutral			Strongly agree	
We fully relied on templates, models and data already existing in our organization	1	2	3	4	5	6	7
Past learning captured in rules and information systems was more than enough for us	1	2	3	4	5	6	7
Planning decisions followed directly from regulatory norms or industry standards	1	2	3	4	5	6	7
We brought in all needed expertise by hiring experienced managers or consultants	1	2	3	4	5	6	7
We studied many similar projects in order to identify the critical success factors	1	2	3	4	5	6	7
We had to produce lots of new data and models before being able to shape this project	1	2	3	4	5	6	7
We used a pilot project or the early stages of this project in order to gain experience	1	2	3	4	5	6	7
We carefully validated all our decisions based on simulation or external feedback	1	2	3	4	5	6	7

	Strongly disagree		Neutral			Strongly agree	
The planning process went through several iterations that totally redefined the project	1	2	3	4	5	6	7
The planning was full of twists and turns as a result of our learning and discoveries	1	2	3	4	5	6	7
We expected to change plans for later phases based on learning from earlier phases	1	2	3	4	5	6	7

b) Participants in the planning and decision process

	Strongly disagree		Neutral			Strongly agree	
One organization maintained a complete control over the entire planning process	1	2	3	4	5	6	7
Inside the lead organization, a single unit retained all the decision power for planning	1	2	3	4	5	6	7
One team was responsible for carrying out the entire planning process for this project	1	2	3	4	5	6	7
The planning of this project was supervised by a committee of external experts	1	2	3	4	5	6	7
Planning was under strict formal supervision by an internal unit such as a project office	1	2	3	4	5	6	7
Numerous units within the lead organization had a strong say in the planning process	1	2	3	4	5	6	7
Planning decisions were negotiated between a few equally powerful organizations	1	2	3	4	5	6	7
Planning depended on input or sanction from key client, contractor or financial backer	1	2	3	4	5	6	7
Planning was a democratic process within a broad coalition of equal participants	1	2	3	4	5	6	7
Every decision was scrutinized by regulators, certification bodies or political groups	1	2	3	4	5	6	7

c) The nature of arguments included in the plan

	Strongly disagree		Neutral			Strongly agree	
The plan emphasized the values and the higher ends that the project would serve	1	2	3	4	5	6	7
The plan stressed the strategic benefits resulting from a swift project execution	1	2	3	4	5	6	7
The plan concentrated almost exclusively on the definition of project goals	1	2	3	4	5	6	7
Plan documents appealed to emotions in order to gain support for the project	1	2	3	4	5	6	7
The plan maintained a degree of ambiguity even with respect to important issues	1	2	3	4	5	6	7
The plan included detailed analyses based on multifaceted evidence for all issues	1	2	3	4	5	6	7
Plan documents spoke to the prudence and reason of those who approved the project	1	2	3	4	5	6	7
The plan included a thorough analysis and mitigation measures for all possible risks	1	2	3	4	5	6	7
The plan provided a realistic and comprehensive estimation of project costs	1	2	3	4	5	6	7
The plan provided decision makers with very detailed and comprehensive information	1	2	3	4	5	6	7

d) *The approach proposed in the plan for addressing project risk*

	Strongly disagree		Neutral			Strongly agree	
The plan imposed rigorous procedures for tracking cost, deliverables and schedule	1	2	3	4	5	6	7
The plan strictly delimited the responsibility area for every participant in the project	1	2	3	4	5	6	7
The plan pushed all risks to other participants with fixed price and schedule contracts	1	2	3	4	5	6	7
All contracts had to include clear and detailed specifications with substantial penalties	1	2	3	4	5	6	7
The project was broken into small work packages with clear milestones and deadlines	1	2	3	4	5	6	7
Suppliers and contractors had to provide significant warranties and performance bonds	1	2	3	4	5	6	7
Fostering collaboration between participants was seen as the only way to reduce risk	1	2	3	4	5	6	7
The owner assumed all risks in order to secure cooperation from other participants	1	2	3	4	5	6	7
Cost plus contracts, alliances or joint ventures were preferred as a way to build trust	1	2	3	4	5	6	7
The plan entrusted the parties to major contracts with jointly defining specifications	1	2	3	4	5	6	7
Quality and expertise, rather than price, were the main contractor selection criteria	1	2	3	4	5	6	7

III. RESTRUCTURING AFTER THE INITIAL PLANNING PERIOD

How well do the following statements describe what happened after the project received the go-ahead from its owners and financial backers?

	Strongly disagree		Neutral			Strongly agree	
The project leader and key managers changed several times during the project	1	2	3	4	5	6	7
Fresh insights on key issues led to shifts in organizational and contractual policies	1	2	3	4	5	6	7
The organizational chart was significantly restructured compared to the planned one	1	2	3	4	5	6	7
The project goals, scope or requirements changed significantly with respect to plans	1	2	3	4	5	6	7
Technical concepts, designs or operating procedures underwent several major changes	1	2	3	4	5	6	7
The planned execution sequence and milestones had to be repeatedly restructured	1	2	3	4	5	6	7
Shifting resource needs resulted in several major budget escalations or redistributions	1	2	3	4	5	6	7
Major participants such as owners, contractors and clients had to be replaced by others	1	2	3	4	5	6	7
Persisting conflicts forced the negotiation of new agreements between participants	1	2	3	4	5	6	7
Work processes proved inadequate and a lot of effort was spent to develop new ones	1	2	3	4	5	6	7

IV. THE RESPONSE CAPACITY OF THE PROJECT ORGANIZATION

How well do the next statements describe the project organization at the peak of execution?

a) Cohesion

	Strongly disagree		Neutral			Strongly agree	
Owners constantly adjusted the incentives in order to keep all participants motivated	1	2	3	4	5	6	7
Leaders regularly impressed upon participants the benefits of sticking with the project	1	2	3	4	5	6	7
We all believed that a project advances only if participants see a gain for themselves	1	2	3	4	5	6	7
When requesting more effort, owners always made clear what others will get in return	1	2	3	4	5	6	7
Everyone was constantly reevaluating the potential gains and losses from this project	1	2	3	4	5	6	7
Many team-building and partnering sessions were held throughout project execution	1	2	3	4	5	6	7
All major participants occupied collocated offices or met face to face every week	1	2	3	4	5	6	7
The core of the project team remained stable throughout the execution phase	1	2	3	4	5	6	7
Consultants and contractor representatives were fully integrated in the core team	1	2	3	4	5	6	7
Specific efforts and liaison positions helped integrate newcomers and remote teams	1	2	3	4	5	6	7
In case of problems, everyone focused on finding a solution rather than blaming others	1	2	3	4	5	6	7
When participants faced difficulties they obtained help from others without delay	1	2	3	4	5	6	7
Personal bonds and mutual trust kept participants united in the face of adversity	1	2	3	4	5	6	7
Clients constantly explained the intentions and expectations behind contractual terms	1	2	3	4	5	6	7
Parties to a contract held meetings routinely to discuss concerns and to air objections	1	2	3	4	5	6	7
Owners were open to reinterpreting and renegotiating contractual responsibilities	1	2	3	4	5	6	7
A practice of promptly addressing and solving contractual disputes had emerged	1	2	3	4	5	6	7
Changes and new commitments were carefully recorded and added to agreements	1	2	3	4	5	6	7
Owners never discussed contractual provisions to avoid diluting their legal power	1	2	3	4	5	6	7
Owners held contractors at arm's length by following initial agreements to the letter	1	2	3	4	5	6	7
Owners never hesitated to threaten using all contractual levers at their disposal	1	2	3	4	5	6	7
Mechanisms for strictly tracking contractual advances and cost had been developed	1	2	3	4	5	6	7
Formal criteria and procedures were strictly followed even when counterproductive	1	2	3	4	5	6	7
Relations between participants were adversarial even before major problems started	1	2	3	4	5	6	7

	Strongly disagree		Neutral			Strongly agree	
When problems appeared, leaders had a hard time imposing their decisions on others	1	2	3	4	5	6	7
The core team was often unable to maintain adequate ties between the various groups	1	2	3	4	5	6	7

b) *Flexibility*

	Strongly disagree		Neutral			Strongly agree	
Frequent meetings helped uncover how decisions in one subproject affected the others	1	2	3	4	5	6	7
A rich vocabulary had emerged to describe interdependencies between activity blocks	1	2	3	4	5	6	7
The core team maintained strong internal capabilities for all the aspects of the project	1	2	3	4	5	6	7
Specially designated experts worked to clarify the interfaces between subprojects	1	2	3	4	5	6	7
Tests and simulations were used to identify unforeseen interactions between parts	1	2	3	4	5	6	7
Work breakdown paralleled the preexisting boundaries between units and disciplines	1	2	3	4	5	6	7
Different subunits had diverging interpretations of applicable terminology and norms	1	2	3	4	5	6	7
Technical coordination between the opposite parties in a contract was always difficult	1	2	3	4	5	6	7
Information systems did not convey all needed information between project sub-teams	1	2	3	4	5	6	7
Decisions were rarely communicated in a timely manner to all affected participants	1	2	3	4	5	6	7
Most conflicts were related to the interfaces or transfers between different subprojects	1	2	3	4	5	6	7
Problems, delays and changes in one part always had a major impact on all other parts	1	2	3	4	5	6	7
It was always hard to assemble or interoperate subsystems produced by distinct groups	1	2	3	4	5	6	7
Solutions were frozen only gradually, based on feedback from execution activities	1	2	3	4	5	6	7
We prioritized the activities for which uncertainty was low and delayed the others	1	2	3	4	5	6	7
Final decisions were delayed as much as possible to leave freedom for late changes	1	2	3	4	5	6	7
We developed several concepts and solutions in parallel to keep our options open	1	2	3	4	5	6	7
We prepared ahead of time several action scenarios, as alternatives in case of trouble	1	2	3	4	5	6	7
Our team felt confident enough to acknowledge and address problems without delay	1	2	3	4	5	6	7
The project organization had clear areas of responsibility and decisional procedures	1	2	3	4	5	6	7
In case of difficulties, an issue was escalated to higher-level executives right away	1	2	3	4	5	6	7
Special task forces were set up immediately to deal with important emerging issues	1	2	3	4	5	6	7
The project organization quickly intensified communications when an issue emerged	1	2	3	4	5	6	7

	Strongly disagree		Neutral			Strongly agree	
Even later on, nothing prevented the core team from adopting the best course of action	1	2	3	4	5	6	7
We never procrastinated but quickly converged on decisions using the latest evidence	1	2	3	4	5	6	7
Even after a decision was made, we could easily turn back and take a different route	1	2	3	4	5	6	7

c) *Resourcefulness*

	Strongly disagree		Neutral			Strongly agree	
Contingencies included in the budget were spent stingily, only in critical situations	1	2	3	4	5	6	7
Rules let the core team retain all cost savings and reallocate them within the project	1	2	3	4	5	6	7
Participants were greatly rewarded for being efficient and making cost-saving changes	1	2	3	4	5	6	7
Most time and money reserves remained secret, to keep participants under pressure	1	2	3	4	5	6	7
Owners readily cut or delayed other activities to keep resources flowing to this project	1	2	3	4	5	6	7
Project leaders cultivated links to entities that could become a source for more funding	1	2	3	4	5	6	7
The team developed the art of highlighting prospects and justifying resource requests	1	2	3	4	5	6	7
Project routines helped us anticipate the activities likely to run into resource shortages	1	2	3	4	5	6	7
The team kept the project on the priority list of top executives and financial backers	1	2	3	4	5	6	7
Rules gave the team considerable freedom to contract or recruit costly extra resources	1	2	3	4	5	6	7
Initial funding and subsequent additions were more than enough to cover all our needs	1	2	3	4	5	6	7
Whenever the project needed more resources, we obtained everything we requested	1	2	3	4	5	6	7
It was easy to expand the working hours, hire more personnel or accelerate the pace	1	2	3	4	5	6	7
The team developed a strong capability to formulate problems and evaluate solutions	1	2	3	4	5	6	7
When facing a problem, we put all our faith in finding an expert who can help solve it	1	2	3	4	5	6	7
Team members had a variety of external contacts, enabling a broad solution search	1	2	3	4	5	6	7
Any sub-team had easy access to advisory committees and a network of consultants	1	2	3	4	5	6	7
Any sub-team could easily bring in specialists from the outside to help solve problems	1	2	3	4	5	6	7
We approached problems by trying our own solutions until we found one that worked	1	2	3	4	5	6	7
Project leaders encouraged participants to express any idea and attempt risky solutions	1	2	3	4	5	6	7
Project leaders stimulated the exchange of ideas between groups with different views	1	2	3	4	5	6	7
We used specific procedures that created a structure for the problem-solving process	1	2	3	4	5	6	7

	Strongly disagree		Neutral			Strongly agree	
Problem-solving processes valued the use of learning accumulated during this project	1	2	3	4	5	6	7
We were able to find at least one solution for nearly all of the difficulties we faced	1	2	3	4	5	6	7
We were highly satisfied with the quality of ideas and solutions that we obtained	1	2	3	4	5	6	7
All participants agreed that our organization favored creativity and problem-solving	1	2	3	4	5	6	7

V. UNEXPECTED EVENTS AND PROJECT REACTIONS

How well do the following statements describe the major events that happened during project execution and the subsequent reaction processes?

a) *The nature of events*	Strongly disagree		Neutral			Strongly agree	
We had several events whose potential consequences could be qualified as severe	1	2	3	4	5	6	7
We experienced a flurry of major events that constantly put the project on the brink	1	2	3	4	5	6	7
Many events came as a total surprise for every member of the core project team	1	2	3	4	5	6	7
Most events were somewhat anticipated but proved much more severe than expected	1	2	3	4	5	6	7
Most events came from errors, omissions and conflicts imputable to the project team	1	2	3	4	5	6	7
Most events resulted from autonomous actions of project partners and stakeholders	1	2	3	4	5	6	7
Most events originated in the broader industrial, social and economic environment	1	2	3	4	5	6	7

b) *The nature of the project reaction to the most critical event*	Strongly disagree		Neutral			Strongly agree	
The event was solved without replacing any participants or modifying usual relations	1	2	3	4	5	6	7
Project shifted to crisis mode, with authoritarian decision making and close scrutiny	1	2	3	4	5	6	7
The response led to changes in some parts of the project but left the rest unchanged	1	2	3	4	5	6	7
The response required fully redefining the project and restructuring its organization	1	2	3	4	5	6	7
Only the investment of considerable additional resources enabled a proper response	1	2	3	4	5	6	7
Preparing the response went through the elaboration of extremely innovative solutions	1	2	3	4	5	6	7

c) *The effectiveness of the project reaction to the most critical event*	Strongly disagree		Neutral			Strongly agree	
The event was properly addressed and had no consequences for subsequent execution	1	2	3	4	5	6	7
Better responses were possible but constraints forced a response that was good enough	1	2	3	4	5	6	7
The response was not really optimal but it enabled us to eventually salvage the project	1	2	3	4	5	6	7
The event became a showstopper and the project had to be irrevocably abandoned	1	2	3	4	5	6	7

VI. PROJECT PERFORMANCE

How well do the following statements describe the success of this project?

a) *Completion performance*

	Strongly disagree		Neutral			Strongly agree	
We put into service the entire planned scope of the project and some additional objects	1	2	3	4	5	6	7
The project went on line ahead of the planned launch date set when it was approved	1	2	3	4	5	6	7
The final project cost was below the budget that was approved at the go-ahead date	1	2	3	4	5	6	7

b) *Technical performance*

	Strongly disagree		Neutral			Strongly agree	
All specified functional and performance goals were met and some even exceeded	1	2	3	4	5	6	7
Outstanding technical accomplishments made this project a worldwide reference	1	2	3	4	5	6	7
The project implemented technical innovations that were firsts in worldwide practice	1	2	3	4	5	6	7

c) *Operational performance*

	Strongly disagree		Neutral			Strongly agree	
Even when running at top regime, the project had no malfunctions, bugs or accidents	1	2	3	4	5	6	7
The operation and maintenance costs of this project are much lower than expected	1	2	3	4	5	6	7
No major new spending was needed in order to remedy problems with this project	1	2	3	4	5	6	7

d) *Value creation performance*

	Strongly disagree		Neutral			Strongly agree	
Sales and profits from this project are significantly better than expected at go-ahead	1	2	3	4	5	6	7
The users and stakeholders of this project are delighted with the value it provides them	1	2	3	4	5	6	7
The project greatly enhanced the reputation and strategic positioning of its owner	1	2	3	4	5	6	7

Thank you very much for completing this questionnaire. Please enter your email to enable us to send you the results of the more advanced analyses we will perform on this survey

If you prefer not to enter the email here, please enter a six-digit number and then send an email to responsecapacity.survey@uqam.ca indicating the six-digit number and your coordinates in order to receive the forthcoming reports and publications detailing the results of this research

Appendix D: Model of Email Used to Solicit Respondents for the Quantitative Survey

Dear [Respondent Name],

Based on your recent presentation at [Conference Name and Date], I believe you could be a valuable source of information for a study I conduct concerning the response capacity of complex projects, such as [Project Name].

My name is Serghei Floricel and I am a professor of project management at the University of Quebec in Montreal (UQAM). This research is based on the assumption that the success of complex projects depends to a large extent on their capacity to respond to unexpected events that occur during execution. We want to understand how project managers could cultivate this kind of capacity from the planning stage.

I would like to invite you to participate in a survey that would take approximately 30 minutes of your time. It would involve answering some questions about the planning and execution of [Project Name] or of another recently completed complex project in which you were closely involved. In exchange, I will send you, well in advance of its publication, a research report that will detail the results of this research and their practical implications. But even before that, you will directly benefit from completing this survey by:

- learning about a number of factors that our prior case-study research identified as important for developing the response capacity of complex projects;
- taking advantage of our questions to reflect back on your experience with this project and to reconsider it from a fresh perspective;
- generating insights that would help improve your effectiveness in planning and managing complex projects.

This study has received financial support from Project Management Institute (http://www.pmi.org/Knowledge-Center/Research-Current-Research.aspx) and from the Social Sciences and Humanities Research Council of Canada (http://www.sshrc. ca), and is part of the activities of the Research Chair in Project Management at UQAM (http://www.chairegp.uqam.ca/en/research/axes/8-les-modes-de-gouvernance-en-gestion-de-projet.html). The research has been reviewed and received ethics clearance through the Institutional Committee for Research Ethics of UQAM. All answers and participants will remain confidential and results will only be presented in aggregate form. You can find more information about this research and our team on the following site:

http://www.gpi.uqam.ca/en/steering/68-response-capacity.html

If you are interested in participating, please reply to this email and I will provide you a link to the survey. I would welcome any ideas about other complex projects that could be included in this study and I encourage you to share my contact information with any colleagues that might be interested in participating.

Sincerely,
Serghei Floricel

Author Biographies

Serghei Floricel is an associate professor of project management at the University of Quebec in Montreal, Canada. His research focuses on the management of innovation projects and portfolios, and on the strategic management of complex projects, in particular on preparing for, and responding to, unexpected events. He also studies processes of innovation in industrial sectors, and strategic processes in firms. He holds a PhD in Administration, an MBA, and a bachelor's degree in Mechanical Engineering.

Sorin Piperca is a PhD candidate at the School of Management, at the University of Quebec in Montreal. His research focuses on structuring processes, project management and interorganizational collaborations. He holds a master's degree in quality management and a bachelor's degree in management in electrical engineering from "Politehnica" University of Bucharest, Romania. He also studied sociology at the University of Bucharest.

Marc Banik teaches innovation management at the Université du Québec à Montréal, specializing in biotechnology and pharmaceutical R&D. His research focuses on regulatory and intellectual property strategy and policy for R&D in public and private organizations. He obtained his Ph in Agricultural Economics and Business Management from the University of Illinois at Urbana-Champaign.